narrative and its nonevents

VICTORIAN LITERATURE AND CULTURE SERIES
Herbert F. Tucker, Editor
William R. McKelvy, Jill Rappoport, and Andrew M. Stauffer, Associate Editors

narrative and its nonevents

The Unwritten Plots That Shaped Victorian Realism

CARRA GLATT

UNIVERSITY OF VIRGINIA PRESS
Charlottesville and London

University of Virginia Press
© 2022 by the Rector and Visitors of the University of Virginia
All rights reserved
Printed in the United States of America on acid-free paper

First published 2022

9 8 7 6 5 4 3 2 1

Library of Congress Cataloging-in-Publication Data

Names: Glatt, Carra, author.
Title: Narrative and its nonevents : the unwritten plots that shaped Victorian realism / Carra Glatt.
Description: Charlottesville : University of Virginia Press, 2022. | Series: Victorian literature and culture series | Includes bibliographical references and index.
Identifiers: LCCN 2022038411 (print) | LCCN 2022038412 (ebook) | ISBN 9780813948706 (hardcover) | ISBN 9780813948867 (paperback) | ISBN 9780813948713 (ebook)
Subjects: LCSH: English fiction—19th century—History and criticism. | Realism in literature. | Narration (Rhetoric)
Classification: LCC PR878.R4 G56 2022 (print) | LCC PR878.R4 (ebook) | DDC 823/.809—dc23/eng/20221020
LC record available at https://lccn.loc.gov/2022038411
LC ebook record available at https://lccn.loc.gov/2022038412

Cover art: istock.com/Luda311

CONTENTS

Acknowledgments — vii

Introduction: The Nonexistent, the Counterfactual, and the Unwritten — 1

1. Seeing Shadows: The Romantic Underplots of Victorian Realism — 35

2. Raising the Veil: Horror by Proxy in the Sensation Novel — 77

3. "A Thing Quite Other than Itself": Henry James and the Proxy Narrative — 110

4. Fancying the Delight: Hypothetical Realism in *The Woodlanders* and *Mary Barton* — 137

Epilogue: Returning Dickens to the Map — 175

Notes — 187
Works Cited — 197
Index — 209

ACKNOWLEDGMENTS

This book has been the work of years and owes its existence to the advice and support of many teachers, friends, and colleagues. I am indebted, in the first place, to my doctoral advisers, Elaine Scarry, Philip Fisher, and Leah Price, for guiding me through the earliest drafts of what became this manuscript. *Narrative and Its Nonevents* is what it is in large part because of the time and effort each of them spent commenting on my work—and, beyond that, because of the care that they and many of my other teachers at Harvard and Princeton took to model the modes of reading and scholarship that I hope this book reflects.

I wish to thank as well Sue Lanser, who offered me invaluable advice at the book proposal stage, and Yael Shapira and William Kolbrener, my colleagues at Bar-Ilan, who gave me the benefit of their experiences as I moved through the editing and publication process. I am deeply grateful to Eric Brandt and the editors of University of Virginia Press's Victorian Literature and Culture Series for their ever-patient and generous assistance through multiple revisions, and to the several reviewers whose comments and criticisms helped me to an immeasurably richer and more polished final product.

Parts of chapter 1 were first published as "Genre and the Counterfactual in *The Old Curiosity Shop*" in *Dickens Quarterly* 31, no. 2 (2014). A large portion of chapter 3 previously appeared as "Proxy Narrative in *The Ambassadors*: Reconfiguring James's Ending," in *Narrative* 24, no. 1 (2016). I thank the late David Paroissien and Jim Phelan, respectively, for their helpful editorial feedback on these articles.

Finally, I need to thank my father, Howard Glatt, my first teacher and still my best. Many people have contributed to this book, but there is not a word in it that I don't owe to you.

narrative and its nonevents

INTRODUCTION

The Nonexistent, the Counterfactual, and the Unwritten

This book is about what does not happen in the Victorian novel. The description may sound absurd; the set of events that do not occur in the Victorian novel is infinite, comprising everything from the Second World War to the murder of Dorothea Brooke to the plots of every novel written before 1837 or after 1901. Yet consideration of alternatives to a given state of affairs is crucial to our understanding of a novel. "In the beginning," Paul Goodman writes in his 1954 *The Structure of Literature*, "anything is possible; in the middle things become probable; in the ending everything is necessary" (14). Plot emerges out of the gradual elimination of possibilities, from the revelation, on the first page of a work, that we are in nineteenth-century London and not sixteenth-century Paris to the final disclosure that the hero's comic sidekick has settled down with Betty the barmaid and not Susan the seamstress.

The vast majority of the possibilities generated in the course of this process are trivial. The dinner party a character attends on a Tuesday might just as well have occurred on Monday or Wednesday had the author not bothered to specify, something he or she may happen to do only well after introducing to our consciousness a party of then-indeterminate date. On the other end of the probability spectrum, most alternatives to an actual plot are too random or fanciful to be worth contemplating. One might suspend disbelief enough to *accept* that an Englishman named Jonathan Harker lives in a world populated by blood-sucking fiends, once informed of this fact, but only sufficiently ominous telegraphing by the text allows a reader of *Dracula* rationally to *expect* it. Similarly, while a reader might plausibly wonder whether Jane Eyre will wind up shunning romantic marriage for a life of religious vocation, it is probable that no reader, at least until the present moment, has imagined an alternative in which Jane becomes an acrobat in a traveling circus. Even superficially more reasonable possibilities will often be beyond the scope of consideration for any reader possessing the slightest familiarity with the conventions of narrative; we do not believe that there is any serious risk of Elizabeth Bennet either marrying Mr. Collins or remaining single, although both outcomes would be far more likely for a woman of her social position than marriage to one of the richest men in England.

Other unrealized possibilities, by contrast, are vital to the dynamics of a narrative. Sometimes, a text introduces such possibilities directly. As Angel Clare prepares to cast his wife out, the narrator of *Tess of the D'Urbervilles* expresses the space between reconciliation and tragedy in a brutal quirk of grammar: "If Tess had been artful, had she made a scene, fainted, wept hysterically . . . he would probably not have withstood her. But . . . the many effective chords which she could have stirred by an appeal were left untouched" (253). Only present-tense tears will do; the conditional can taunt us, but not influence Angel. Other potential outcomes may be embedded implicitly in the design of a narrative. The same readerly instincts that warn us away from considering the murder of Dorothea Brooke might mislead us into initially anticipating that our heroine will marry, not Ladislaw, but Lydgate. Structurally equivalent, Dorothea and Lydgate, the principal female and male protagonists of *Middlemarch*, are also more obviously suited to one another than Dorothea is to Ladislaw, whose vaunted reformist zeal is as liable as not to collapse into mere petulance or peter out into dilettantism. It is easy enough to imagine a version of *Middlemarch* in which Dorothea and Lydgate, saved from early romantic folly by the timely deaths of their unsuitable partners, find happiness in pursuing a shared but now wisely tempered concern for the public good.

But none of this, of course, happens. Lydgate dies in middle age after being forced to give up his ambitions toward medical reform at the joint urging of his wallet and his wife. Dorothea fares better in what appears to be a perfectly happy marriage to Will, whose wife's influence (and money) leads him finally to commit himself to a career as "an ardent public man" (792). Yet the inescapable force of what might have been shapes our response to the novel. Lydgate's belated discovery of a woman who could in fact have been the partner and helpmeet he so needs underscores the magnitude of his mistake. In Dorothea's case, the effect of the eliminated possibility is subtler but perhaps more striking. Dorothea's fate could be mistaken for the conventional happiness of the marriage plot as she settles down to marriage, motherhood, and a life of quiet usefulness. The novel's own awareness of alternatives to this life, however, complicates the final tableau. Most obvious in its portrayal of Dorothea as a thwarted Saint Theresa, the sense of compromise inherent in the narrowing of Dorothea's ambitions is underscored by her marriage to a man who, for all his merits, may not represent the best of all possible husbands. No less a reader than Henry James observed that "we are doubtless less content with Ladislaw on account of the . . . neighboring figure of Lydgate," whose late-novel interactions with Dorothea "suggest a wealth of dramatic possibility between them" (D. Carroll, *George Eliot* 356).[1] Deselected, but far from insubstantial, the rival plot thus lives on to inform and challenge its triumphant opponent.

This book argues for the central role of these non-actualized plots—hereafter called unwritten plots—in Victorian narrative construction. Not merely absent from a text, an unwritten plot is the rejected outgrowth of a possibility that has been systematically eliminated from a given narrative world. Rather than *not* written, it is *un*written, the casualty of a zero-sum game in which several plots may emerge out of the cloud of inchoate possibilities, but only one can endure into fully realized fictional life. Yet like so many erasures, the unwritten plot leaves its mark on what remains. It is the suggestive ellipsis left to finish out abandoned utterance, the faded ink on a palimpsest that must be read once, and then painstakingly again, to be understood. It is stubborn blood crying out under luminol; old initials, belonging to one no longer beloved, peeking out through the resourceful tattoo artist's attempt at transfiguration. We read the traces and understand more fully both what we have lost, and what, however painfully and imperceptibly, we have gained.

Part of that gain, this book suggests, is the realist novel itself. The realist novel is characterized by a proliferation of possibilities. Abandoning the allegorical mode, in which characters are bound by fixed identities to reach a predetermined conclusion, and turning away from classical and historical plots with outcomes already known to audiences, the realist novel is designed to simulate the openness and uncertainty of ordinary human experience. We are invested in the stories of a Crusoe or Pamela or Tom Jones in part because we can't be entirely sure how those stories will end; the virtuous Pamela could prove a ruined Clarissa up until the decisive moment in which she marries.

Yet even as it broadens some representative possibilities, realism is characterized by the suppression of others. Even the most expansive definitions of realism normally exclude works dealing in utter impossibilities; a principle of underlying fidelity to the conditions of ordinary life might bend to accommodate the *improbabilities* of coincidence and melodrama but would break under the weight of the fantastic. Realist novels, however, restrict as well events and outcomes that lie firmly within the realm of the possible: humans rarely realize all the most fantastic possibilities available to them, and neither, by and large, do characters in Victorian novels. The pleasure of its marriage plots notwithstanding, the nineteenth-century novel is the novel of compromise, more interested in the capacity of individuals to come to terms with invariably imperfect conditions than in their capacity to overcome them. For Franco Moretti, the English bildungsroman offered the socially accommodationist counterpart to its European cousin's aggressively destructive, tragic drive toward self-affirmation. For Lukács, the modern novel itself was a fundamentally fallen landscape, "the epic of a world that has been abandoned by God" (*The Theory of the Novel* 88). George Eliot, more gently, wrote of the "home epic" that remained when the grandeur of the classical one had been lost to us. Common to all these definitions is the sense of at least a certain variety of novel as a site of sharply and poignantly limited possibilities. Where we wind up, in such a novel, is less the chosen consummation of narrative desire than the half-elegiac, half-grateful cry of the lone survivor reaching shore.

The novels that this book studies are mainly the novels of the Victorian era proper, a period during which the meaning of realism itself narrowed, in effect if not yet in name. The broader realist tradition defined, most prominently, by Ian Watt, constituted a formal revolution in which heavily stereotyped depictions of exceptional or exemplary figures, often taken from the worlds of history and legend, gave way to focused, mimetic representation of the thoughts and experiences of ordinary people. This revolution did not reach its apotheosis until the nineteenth century, when free indirect discourse replaced the epistolary as the primary mechanism for conveying a character's inner life, and characterization itself progressed from depictions of the good, the bad, and the reforming to more stubbornly "mixed" character types.[2] Notionally, however, these developments, too, were anticipated by the eighteenth-century realist aesthetic of Defoe, Fielding, and Richardson, whose works, in Watt's account, advanced the claims of both intensive attention to individual consciousness and the elevation of particularized, non-allegorical character types. The effect of the contributions of these early mimetic realists was so great as to influence nearly all subsequent prose fiction; even works that might be definitionally excluded from the genre—fantasy, certain historical fictions, works dealing with notable personages and traditionally epic events—largely adopted the descriptive modes, plot structures, and affective strategies associated with realism. Certainly, this influence could be felt across the generic spectrum of the canonical and quasi-canonical nineteenth-century British novel, situated chronologically before the modernist revolt against traditional plotting and an ocean away from the revitalized allegorical mode of the American Renaissance.

The middle of that century, however, saw the rise of a Victorian realist tradition distinct from Watt's prevailing formal realism. I provide a fuller account of Victorian realism and its attributes later in the introduction. Yet, in brief, it is only in the Victorian novel, I would like to suggest, that the sense of compromise and limitation that I have already noted as characteristic of "realism" became dominant—or, in other words, that that concern with the *possible* became increasingly tempered with concern for the *probable*. This is not, of course, to say that Victorian novels confine themselves to representing especially likely events; even the least sensationalistic exemplars of the form often include, to varying degrees of prominence, hidden identities, long-buried family secrets, murder plots, and all manner of coincidences. But in their overall orientation—and, particularly, in their final dispositions—Victorian realist novels reflect an abiding commitment to the deflation of expectations, what Eliot called the "faintness of heart at the new real future which replaces the imaginary" (*Middlemarch* 184). This is not an invariably sad or despairing process; the realm of what is both technically possible and sufficiently probable, it turns out, can continue to accommodate a high level of both personal and narrative fulfillment. Yet in this newly foreshortened landscape, some, perhaps deeply desired things, as Dickens reminds his readers at the end of *Hard Times*, are not to be.

Among these things, this book argues, are the contents of what I am calling unwritten plots. What separates an unwritten plot from the infinite number of plots that are simply nonexistent is its narrative plausibility, and what gives a plot narrative plausibility is its resemblance to other, at least superficially similar plots. Consequently, the plots that read as most plausible, in a Victorian realist novel—indeed, sometimes as more plausible than the plot that actually develops—are plots associated with conventions that were then being challenged or displaced. Intimations of the supernatural give way to thoroughly rational explanations; the heady exuberance of the picaresque is transmuted into the more painful maturation of the bildungsroman. Thackeray's *Vanity Fair* alludes to Bunyan while betraying the moral clarity of allegory; disdaining either to reform or punish Becky, the novel gives her virtuous opposite Amelia only an equivocal, heavily ironized reward. Eliot and the Brontës flirt with but ultimately abandon the tropes of the conversion narrative: one disappointed reviewer of *Jane Eyre* complained that with the early death of Jane's saintly friend Helen Burns, the novel's Christian promise "expires, leaving the moral world in a kind of Scandinavian gloom."[3]

Deselected, unwritten plots have a more vibrant afterlife in a given narrative world than their subordinate status might initially suggest. In *Jane Eyre*, the death of Helen Burns, and Jane's removal soon after from the charity school to Rochester's mansion, indeed launches the novel on a new and generically distinctive course. The reviewer exaggerates, however, the thoroughness of the break. *Resurgam*, reads Helen Burns's headstone, and indeed she does return, if she can ever be said to have left at all. The ethical and spiritual maturity that leads Jane to resist technical bigamy with Rochester is part of Helen's legacy; Jane's need not become the tale of error and penitence her predicament renders all too possible precisely because of the abbreviated conversion narrative in which she has already taken part. Later, the interlude in which Jane contemplates going to India as the missionary wife of her cousin St. John Rivers revives the specter of a legitimate alternative to Rochester, one that privileges a model of development rooted more in the spiritual autobiography than in the nineteenth-century marriage plot. Although Jane chooses Rochester, St. John remains an influential force in the novel. The Rivers detour is not, like an episode in a picaresque novel, a relatively self-contained vignette, but a competitor plot that, beyond testing our predictive powers, changes our perception of the dominant narrative.

Jane's eventual marriage to Rochester owes as much to notions of revelation and sacrifice—ideals cultivated by her relationships with Helen and St. John—as it does to the erotic and romantic. Their union, in which Jane acts as combined lover, savior, and nursemaid to her reformed and weakened husband, allows Jane to strike a middle course between the marriage bed and a life of Christian vocation. But more than that, we are left to the last line of the novel with the lingering resistance presented by St. John's less compromising vision of what a narrative of development should properly be. We end, not with the image of Jane and Rochester's achieved bliss, but with St. John's triumphant prophecy of his own death in service to Christ. If, despite these last words, "Reader, I married him" wins out over "Come, Lord Jesus" as the novel's dominant assertion, it has been a narrow victory rather than an inevitable rout.

The Victorian novel is created out of the interaction between its written and its unwritten plots. The reader of *Jane Eyre* reads a tale of a humble governess's marriage to her wealthy master, but also, if only prospectively and hypothetically, the tragedy of a young girl who succumbs to a rake's blandishments and the redemption narrative of a woman who subsumes her unruly passions in a perhaps more enduringly satisfying life of Christian vocation. *Jane Eyre* is a less self-evidently realist novel than its distant cousin *Middlemarch*, which will take up more explicitly the gap between the domestic and the (also religiously informed) heroic in its paean to the belated Saint Theresas who found no outlet for their noblest impulses. What they share, however, is both an aesthetic that fosters the multiplication of non-nominal narrative possibilities and an awareness that the interaction between these possibilities will create a more difficult, less purely satisfying, but perhaps richer and more authentic novelistic universe than a more generically uniform iteration of a sentimental love plot, Gothic romance, or conversion narrative would have. Among several reasons why the dominant plot of *Jane Eyre* cannot be read simply as the leveling fantasy of the Cinderella story, one less-recognized reason is that readers have been teased with the possibility of another, equally culturally resonant option whose denial tints the chosen outcome with at least a shadow of regret.[4]

The unwritten plot is thus both a byproduct and an agent of Victorian realism. Born out of the characteristically realist expansion of possibilities, unwritten plots flourish in texts that invite us to consider multiple, mutually exclusive outcomes as narratively viable. Impossible in the generically stable and predictable world of the allegory or moral fable, such plots are a consequence of realism's attempt aesthetically to capture the uncertainty of ordinary life. Paradoxically, however, once-dominant plots become unwritten in part because the possibilities they offer are only an illusion; though they remain "in play" for the genre-savvy reader, they belong to modes becoming increasingly untenable for authors newly committed to principles of moderation, probability, and compromise. Jane Eyre's life includes events at the extreme edge of ordinary human experience, but in the end, the madwoman in the attic is killed and the religious enthusiast kindly refused and packed off to India so that a middle-class heiress can marry a country gentleman. A precondition for the victory of class-affirming domestic realism over the aberrancies of madness, bigamy, and martyrdom is the activation of the very plots the novel must then work to expel and suppress—plots that we cannot help but imaginatively set against what may even seem a comparatively pallid dominant one.

If the pressures and possibilities of realism gave rise to unwritten plots, so too did the unwritten plots themselves help delimit the boundaries of realism. Within what was and would remain a porous, contested, and hybrid genre, rivalries between plots and their associated paradigms reflected a real tension, one in which, in some cases, the outcome was long uncertain to author as well as reader. By the middle of the nineteenth century, even the more sensationalistic of canonical writers, along with most of their reviewers and critics, had accepted as an aesthetic ideal a certain type of mimetic fidelity to the actual conditions of life. What remained to be determined was what a narrative world based on such a principle could and could not accommodate. The answers to this implicit question were not always consistent or fully decisive. Yet by tracing the unwritten plots of Victorian novels, we can gain insight into the dynamic struggles through which authors reached at least provisional conclusions about the nature and possibilities of realism. In the invocation and rejection of unwritten plots, we find Victorian authors solidifying the boundaries of realism by formally expelling the generic remnants they find compelling yet untenable. In the durability of these plots, however, we also see a more complicated resistance to the very conventions realist novelists were inscribing—and, ultimately, a possible path to expanding the range of both representative and social possibility.

A Brief History of Nothing

The study of nonevents has a surprisingly robust, interdisciplinary history, from counterfactual histories to the hypotheticals presented in legal case studies to the Many-Worlds Interpretation of quantum mechanics, which holds that every moment of choice generates multiple competing realities, each equally valid from the perspective of those who inhabit it.[5] Necessarily speculative, these branches of inquiry have often been dogged by a skepticism that recalls earlier debates over the value of fiction itself. The psychology of counterfactual thinking, however, suggests the underlying logic and utility of such investigations. The research of cognitive scientists has uncovered a remarkable consistency in the kinds of unrealized possibilities people are likely to entertain (Roese and Olson, *What Might Have Been;* Kahneman, Slovic, and Tversky, *Judgment under Uncertainty*). The appeal of wish-fulfilling fantasies notwithstanding, our hypothetical and counterfactual formulations are notably *not* fanciful: by and large, we imagine plausible future outcomes and create alternative realities out of those past situations that seem most susceptible to revision. A blowout defeat is embarrassing; a one-point loss will generate hours of wistful retrospections on what might, very nearly, have been. When we model hypothetical scenarios, we tend to envision and negotiate between attainable possible futures, while even counterfactual scenarios, which involve completed events that cannot actually be altered, typically replay situations that might plausibly have turned out otherwise had we behaved differently. If articulating these possibilities will not change the past, the process of reflecting upon them may at least guide our actions in similar circumstances in the future.

Early intersections between literary studies and the investigations of other disciplines into non-actual events involved the capacity of such approaches to address long-standing concerns about the nature of fictional reference: when speaking of a literary text, what does it mean to say that an event "happened" at all?[6] Especially influential, in this respect, was the system of modal logic developed by Saul Kripke and used by proponents of the Many-Worlds Interpretation.[7] Adapting traditional propositional logic to statements of uncertainty and qualification (in other words, statements involving such words as "might," "probably," or "could"), modal logic, among other advantages, acknowledges the possibility of referential contexts other than that of a shared, unitary reality. Those elements of our world that are only *possibly* true, rather than *necessarily* true in all conceivable realities might, in fact, have turned out quite differently in other, equally valid spheres of existence; truth is referentially pegged to a particular reality, rather than absolutely valid for all possible realities with which we might, for philosophical or scientific purposes, wish to concern ourselves.

The applicability of this framework to literary worlds was obvious. In the mid-1970s, the philosopher David Lewis and the literary critic Thomas Pavel separately employed modal logic's possible-world semantics to justify treating the worlds of fiction as autonomous referential entities about which meaningful truth claims could be made (Lewis, "Truth in Fiction"; Pavel, "'Possible Worlds'"). While classical logic would, in Lewis's example, require us to treat both the statements "Sherlock Holmes lived at 221b Baker Street" and "Sherlock Holmes and John Watson were identical twins" as necessarily false—Sherlock Holmes never really lived anywhere—modal logic permits us to follow our intuition in treating the former as true and the latter as false. *Within the possible world in which a detective named Sherlock Holmes existed,* the detective lived at 221b Baker Street, sometimes with his friend John Watson, who was decidedly not his identical twin.

Beyond treating literary worlds as a species of Kripkean possible world, a group of scholars led by Marie-Laure Ryan employed modal logic to represent individual literary worlds as the centers of a wider multiverse. The Many-Worlds Interpretation envisions an actual world orbited by an infinite number of satellite worlds that correspond to unrealized possibilities. These unrealized possibilities can be evaluated on the basis of their closeness to our reality, where those that deviate least from a given state of affairs are deemed to be more probable than those that deviate more sharply. When we encounter a literary text, we rather imaginatively "recenter" our perception of reality around a textual actual world (TAW) that may be wildly different from our own (Ryan, *Possible Worlds* 24). This world will, in turn, generate its own satellites, whose potency will be judged according to the standards and conventions of the TAW, rather than of the reader's extra-textual reality.

The satellite worlds that Ryan identifies are created by the more or less explicitly articulated wishes, hopes, regrets, and fears of characters. In mapping a narrative multiverse, the TAW consists of those events that actually take place, while the satellite worlds consist of possibilities contemplated but never fulfilled. Eliot's *Adam Bede*, for instance, features an actual world in which Hetty Sorrel is sentenced to transportation for leaving her newborn baby to die and a wish world in which she marries Arthur Donnithorne. Other studies of literary nonevents—most of them less taxonomic than Ryan's, and often drawing more proximately from discourses of counterfactual history and thinking than from modal logic—identify additional types of unrealized plots. Robyn Warhol's "narrative refusals" occur when a text uses subjunctive or negative language to describe what it is *not* going to narrate, creating an alternative sequence designated as unreal relative to the plot that actually plays out ("'What Might Have Been'"). Andrew Miller has read the multiplot novel's juxtaposition of different characters' trajectories as a means of representing unrealized versions of a hero or heroine's life story. Hilary Dannenberg, crucially, has expanded the category of counterfactual plots to include what she calls the liminal plot, a possibility created out of readers' narrative expectations rather than by any overt counterfactual or hypothetical framing within the text.

At this point, a brief note on terminology may be in order. As we have just seen, critics have developed several terms to refer to plot events that are referred to, anticipated, or imagined but do not take place. Among them, Dannenberg's "counterfactual" plot comes closest to my notion of the "unwritten" plot, and indeed I used the term myself in previous work on the subject. Yet ultimately, counterfactuality seems an inexact lens through which to view the phenomenon I am describing. Many existing treatments of literary counterfactuals limit themselves to the study of explicitly counterfactual formulations: *if* some event had not occurred, things *would have* turned out otherwise.[8] Others, naturally, involve select genres—primarily science fiction and alternative history novels—that enable the "what-ifs" of counterfactual thinking to be played out in parallel with the events of a dominant timeline (or, in the case of alternative history, with our knowledge of actual past events); a recent example of this type is Catherine Gallagher's *Telling It Like It Wasn't: The Counterfactual Imagination in History and Fiction*. Even Dannenberg's broader use of the term occurs in the context of a much larger study that devotes significant attention to these more traditional categories of the counterfactual.

My own focus is the reverse: while unwritten plots may be advanced or represented by the particular grammar of the counterfactual, neither counterfactual grammar nor other overt introductions of plot possibilities that will not be realized (for instance, the appearance of a rival suitor) are critical to their existence. Indeed, many of these more overt framings do not create what I will call "active" unwritten plots at all. When Lady Catherine declares that her daughter, had she learned to play an instrument, would have displayed great talent, the counterfactual, comic as it is, adds to the rich cognitive landscape of *Pride and Prejudice* and supports the immersion-promoting impression that its denizens are free agents whose lives are, like ours, contingent and uncertain. There is, however, no associated plot possibility involved, or, at least, not one that bears the slightest bit of narrative weight. Similarly, the structure of the text does not leave us in any real anxiety that Elizabeth will marry Mr. Collins, even though this is a possibility that is represented within the text and one that several characters take seriously. Such explicitly articulated possibilities *can*, of course, create unwritten plots, but the unwritten plot arises from a condition of prolonged tension that relies on more than the existence of what may be token plot alternatives.

My coinage of the term "unwritten plot" reflects as well my desire to tell the particular story of how a wide range of non-actual plots became a key shaping force behind the rise of Victorian realism. Critics have long associated counterfactuality and counterfactual plots with a type of literary realism. In any kind of fictional universe, Dannenberg suggests, the creation of possible worlds that are fictional relative to the TAW tacitly upgrades the status of that world. Not all fictions are created equally; the TAW, when placed within a universe of unrealized possibilities, reads as at least more real than these others, establishing an *ontological hierarchy* of more and less substantial fictional worlds. The proliferation of counterfactuals in nineteenth-century realist novels, specifically, reflects the increasing cognitive complexity of these texts, which grant to characters an interior life rivaling that of actual persons, counterfactual thinking not excluded (Warhol, "'What Might Have Been'"). It would be scarcely credible if a woman who had rejected a proposal from one of the richest men in England did not, as Elizabeth Bennet does, spare a thought for what her life with him might have been. Dannenberg further treats the nineteenth-century counterfactual plot as an agent of realism that works against the competing pressures of the coincidence plot: while the "romance-oriented convergence" of coincidence draws attention, in its unlikelihood, to the plottedness of a novel, the counterfactual suggests that the fates of the characters in a text are as free and unpredictable as our own.

Yet this account of the role of alternative plots largely limits itself to a discussion of their role in the broad tradition of *mimetic* realism—in other words, in the representative mode established by Richardson and Fielding and adopted across the genres of canonical eighteenth and nineteenth-century fiction. Dorothea Brooke is a more psychologically complex protagonist than Tom Jones, and George Eliot's a more sophisticated narrative voice than Henry Fielding's. Fundamentally, however, the notion that the credibility of a narrative world could be enhanced by investing fictional characters with qualities and thought patterns that resembled those of actual people was by the Victorian era no longer an innovation. Rather, Victorian realism is defined by a sustained, troubled questioning of what a literature recognized as part of and committed to reflecting an embedded social reality could and should be. It is in the process of determining the parameters of such realist worlds that the unwritten plot plays such a crucial role. Unwritten, these non-realized plots are also, perhaps, ultimately unwritable in the realist novel as its authors are coming to understand it: the alternatives they represent cannot be actualized while remaining faithful to emerging principles emphasizing the probable over the exceptional and compromise over either wish fulfillment or epic tragedy. Yet rather than nominal strawmen, unwritten plots reflect—and only partly resolve—a persistent tension that suffuses Victorian realism. As such, they become double agents of narrative design, policing the borders of realist possibility while implicitly agitating against the very strictures they have imposed. In contrast to the backward looking temporal orientation of counterfactuals, unwritten plots thus look to the future as often as they do to the past. Eliciting regret for what seemed possible but ultimately could not be, they expose the limitations of not only realist narrative order but also the actual world that in part dictates those limits. Unwritten plots represent what is not, narratively or socially, possible—but also model what, in some other reality, perhaps could be.

Active Possibilities

Unwritten plots, I have suggested, represent "active" narrative possibilities, those that seem plausible enough that we could conceivably imagine them fulfilled. But what makes a possibility active—and, more specifically, what makes a possibility "active" in the context of a realist novel?

When we contemplate uncertain possibilities in our own lives, as studies have shown, our analysis tends to follow predictable patterns based on an intuitive, probabilistic analysis of the likelihood of certain events: we expend the majority of our mental energy on realistic potentialities rather than magical thinking. Even documented, pervasive cognitive errors in such analyses are exceptions that prove the rule, suggesting the extent to which we judge probabilities in light of their "representativeness"—in other words, how well they match up with our empirical understanding of the world. In one of their well-known studies on the decision-making process, Daniel Kahneman, Paul Slovic, and Amos Tverksy asked subjects to rank the probability of two scenarios: given a family with six children, is it more likely that the precise gender breakdown among those children will be GBGBBG or BGBBBB? As the probability that any given child will be male or female is independent of the sex of other children in that family, both outcomes are in fact equally likely. Yet consistently, subjects ranked the first as more probable, which Kahneman, Slovic, and Tversky explain by noting that the first outcome is more *representative* than the second. The likelihood of arriving at the particular sequence GBGBBG is no greater than that of arriving at the particular sequence BGBBBB. Because, however, most potential configurations of gender and birth order will result in a more even distribution of girls and boys than the one represented by the latter, the family with three girls and three boys comes closer to our (accurate) sense of what a typical family of that size will look like than the family with five boys and only one girl. While intuitive logic fails in this specific case to grasp the subtleties of statistical analysis, normally, Kahneman, Slovic, and Tversky maintain, this attention to representativeness serves us well in assessing the plausibility of various outcomes: "Probable events," they write, "are usually more representative than less probable events" (*Judgment under Uncertainty* 89).

A similar pattern guides our analysis of literary worlds—but only up to a point. For all our ability to imaginatively recenter our perspectives, even at our most engaged with a textual world, we never really forget that we are dealing with a work of fiction; we may feel fear or grief as we read, but we will not hide ourselves from a marauding dragon or close our Victorian novels to avoid exposure to a character's smallpox. A slightly more advanced manifestation of this recognition is our awareness of narrative conventions that render the probabilities of a constructed literary world very different from the ones governing our own, an upending of ordinary calculations of likelihood that Robert Newsom has called "the antinomy of fictional probability" (*A Likely Story* 9). From the perspective of the young Jane Eyre, a character designed as a fair portrait of what a girl in such a situation might think and do, the death of her uncle (not to mention her parents) is a tragic accident that she can imagine undone. From the perspective of the reader, aware of Jane as a character in a novel that depends on her unhappy orphanhood, it is rather an absolute necessity of the textual world in which she finds herself, what D. A. Miller might call a precondition of her story's "narratability" (*Narrative and Its Discontents*). Nobody wants to read, or write, about a Jane Eyre who lives quietly with her parents before marrying her childhood best friend.

If everyday assessments of probability are governed by our lived experience of the world, our assessments of narrative probability are derived from our prior experiences with other narrative worlds. More precisely, our assessments of the possibilities available in any particular narrative world will be grounded in our experience of other narrative worlds of its kind. When a character dies in a fantasy novel, readers familiar with the genre might plausibly wonder if the character will be brought back to life with a spell or continue his or her adventures as a ghost or vampire or mystical guide. If a character dies in a soap opera, viewers might consider the possibility that the character has faked his death, or that the body buried under his name belongs to his long-lost twin brother. But the first set of alternatives will read as impossible, and the second as at least highly unlikely, to a reader encountering a character death in a realist novel, with its more restrained set of plausible options.

Yet judgments about what is and is not possible in a given literary text are not always straightforward. Indeed, the plot I just rejected as unnarratable in the case of *Jane Eyre*—that of a young woman who lives happily with her parents and then marries a close friend—*has* been narrated, and quite successfully; what I have described is, more or less, the plot of *Emma*. This apparent contradiction, too, can be accounted for by genre: the plots of the early nineteenth-century novel of manners were not imported wholesale into the bildungsroman of the next generation, with their different scope and set of concerns. This difference, however, is not one that will be readily apparent to a reader just beginning the novel, for whom the plot could as easily play out entirely within the boundaries of the Reed estate as it can move to Lowood, Thornfield, and a lonely night on the moors. The serial form of so many Victorian novels exaggerates this disjunction by creating a tangible structural separation between what may be generically variable plot developments. The reader of the first installment of Elizabeth Gaskell's *North and South*, for instance, which finds Margaret Hale, educated in London with her rich cousin, rejecting a wealthy suitor and returning home to her father's humble country parsonage, will be as surprised as Margaret herself when the novel soon launches her into the world of gritty urban realism.

The most generically stable texts, to be sure, admit of relatively few active possibilities. In allegory, where characters are assigned fixed semantic identities, there is little room for uncertainty: of course a pilgrim named Christian will fight through the Slough of Despond to arrive at the Celestial City. Even as comparatively sophisticated a text as *Pride and Prejudice* is so perfect an exemplar of its kind that the alternative plot possibilities it introduces serve as formal mechanisms that highlight the inevitability of the very outcome they appear to challenge. The rival suitors Wickham and Collins represent elements of Darcy and Elizabeth's marriage plot rather than genuine alternatives to it; their presence creates complications for the couple, but neither, to varying degrees, could plausibly serve as the hero of a marriage plot novel with Elizabeth Bennet as its heroine. At the other extreme, a text might introduce so many and such discursively negligible possibilities that it discourages serious predictive analysis. The adventures of Tobias Smollett's aptly named Roderick Random are often great fun, but very few have a discernible effect on our hero's character or, ultimately, his fate. He makes fortunes, and loses them, and wins them back again. He fights under one flag and then another. He falls earnestly in love in one chapter and resumes hunting silly heiresses and moneyed old maids in the next. As far as the plot of the novel is concerned, the only potentially consequential question is whether he will finally be restored to his rightful place as a gentleman, a result that would affirm both the importance of a good pedigree and, as if by way of compensation, the virtues of decidedly ungenteel exercises in Scottish masculinity. Yet while this outcome is, theoretically, a matter of anxiety for the novel, Smollett does not ask readers to expend much emotional energy anticipating Random's fate. The breezy insouciance of the narration militates against the possibility of any serious disaster; the apparent death of a friendly companion is more surprising than his eventual reappearance, while the timely discovery of Random's wealthy, long-lost father, when it finally comes, is more matter of course than source of relief. The range of possibilities in Smollett's globe- and class-trotting novel—and in the picaresque genre more generally—are unusually wide, but comparatively empty; in the world of *Roderick Random*, unwritten plots can only be nominal.

In the nineteenth-century realist novel, the question of what might happen becomes both a weightier and a more difficult one as the hybridity of Victorian form resists the genre-savvy reader's normal predictive processes. In his *Good Form: The Ethical Experience of the Victorian Novel,* Jesse Rosenthal observes that even the most sophisticated contemporary analyses of Victorian novels presume a shared notion of narrative "rightness" that would not have been obvious to their original readers. If what constitutes a narratively fitting turn of events seems obvious to us, it is only because of a group of Victorian writers committed to inscribing a narrative order that reflected their evolving moral sensibilities. This was a fundamentally educative process that required upsetting nineteenth-century readers' ethical and formal assumptions, often through the deliberate undermining of existing narrative conventions. Yet even from the vantage point of our own day, the critical tendency to treat certain outcomes as inevitable is, for Rosenthal, a retroactive simplification that underplays the range of active possibilities at work in Victorian realist fiction. Even within the careers of individual authors, he notes, we see meaningfully different approaches to such crucial issues as the role of providence in human affairs and the tension between individual happiness and communal obligation. This in turn renders suspect any assertion that one particular, value-laden outcome was necessarily more appropriate than a contrasting, equally value-laden outcome. Gwendolyn Harleth winds up alone because, in *Daniel Deronda,* Eliot is telling a story in which the larger national concerns represented by Daniel's embrace of his Jewish heritage win out over purely personal narratives of progress. In many other Victorian novels, including some of Eliot's own, the moral arc tends otherwise and might be satisfied most thoroughly by the marriage of a now ethically mature Gwendolyn's individual striving to Deronda's more diffuse sense of collective responsibility. Until we arrive at the decisive moment, there is nothing in the novel that would require one outcome over the other, and indeed, Rosenthal outlines how assiduously Eliot plays upon and encourages readers' reasonable expectation that the novel is preparing, like so many of its generic peers, for a more conventional marriage plot.

Accompanying Rosenthal's moral ambiguities was an ambivalent sense of what fidelity to representing the possible, the probable, and the ordinary actually required. By the middle of the nineteenth century, Victorian aesthetic theory and criticism, as it appeared in essays, reviews, and letters, reflects a consistent concern with whether the events of novels are "probable," "likely," or "true," to the point where even authors of sensation novels—Wilkie Collins foremost among them—can be found arguing for the essential plausibility of their stories (Kent, "Probability, Reality, and Sensation"). Yet the very existence of such defenses reveals a lack of consensus about the nature and boundaries of probability. Dickens's infamous insistence that spontaneous combustion was, in fact, a real scientific phenomenon, justifying its inclusion as a plot point in Bleak House,[9] is one extreme example of a problem that pervaded Victorian intellectual life, where new scientific and mathematical understandings offered often conflicting accounts of the most fundamental aspects of human identity and progress. The effect on Victorian literature of Darwinism, with its replacement of providential teleologies with a narrative of biological contingency, has been well studied, most notably by Gillian Beer. The more recent work of Michael Tondre and Adam Grener has emphasized the additional influence of a roughly contemporaneous "probabilistic revolution" in which statistical thinking became dominant in both the social and biological sciences.[10] The availability of comprehensive statistical data on the particulars of daily life, from marriage rates to the number of Britons who could be expected to die in carriage accidents in a given year, offered an empirical portrait of a perhaps non-providential, but still highly predictable, reality. In place of a fuzzier sense of truth, novelists could thus point to—or be limited by—quantitative evidence of what constituted typical experience.

Yet the study of aggregate data also drew attention to the presence of statistical outliers that provided a model for assimilating the atypical and the bizarre as part of the range of ordinary existence: the unlikely, and even the *very* unlikely, still lie within the boundaries of measurable probability. On a macro level, the appetite of nineteenth-century journalism for the criminal, the scandalous, and the unexplained could create the impression that such outliers were far more common than they actually were, justifying the inclusion of sensationalistic incidents in novels purporting to represent life as it was. And as social science painted a portrait of a grimly regulated reality, the application of statistical thinking in biology and physics, Tondre suggests, rather exposed the probabilistic—and therefore potentially tenuous—nature of self, society, and species alike: the world as it is represents neither the world as it had to be nor the world as it could still become. Realist novelists, in Tondre's reading, were engaged with scientists in a joint project to transcend purely empirical understandings of the world and probe what was in fact a range of possibilities at the level of both individual human subjects and the larger worlds they inhabited. Grener adds that while realist authors were invested in contemporary probability theory, their priority was, more often than not, to *resist* what appeared to be the totalizing abstractions of mathematics and social science, preferring to represent the particular exceptions than the masses who obeyed the rule.

For several reasons, then, it is very difficult to determine what can and "can't" happen in Victorian realist fiction, creating an ideal atmosphere for the generating of active plots, which arise out of situations of legitimate uncertainty between explicit or implied narrative alternatives. Indeed, unwritten plots associated with models in currency before the Victorian period would often have read to original audiences as *more* viable than actual plots committed to violating preexisting conventions. The thwarted marriage plot, for instance, identifiable in retrospect as a relatively common Victorian realist type, often met with popular chagrin in its own day and was regarded as so formally disjunctive as occasionally to warrant ameliorative editorial interventions.

In the Victorian era, the rules of the traditional novel were still under negotiation, and at higher stakes than at any previous period. It was a time in which novels had acquired the cultural capital to be taken seriously as agents of social and intellectual progress, and in which authors themselves reflected self-consciously on the parameters of their chosen medium; in which the genres of the novel had grown up enough to be identifiable, stale enough to be challenged, and loved too much to be dismissed unmourned. At once sprawling and controlled, formulaic and innovative, new and familiar, the Victorian novel seemed to contain innumerable possibilities but led its reader, masterfully and inexorably, to what could in retrospect read as a foreordained, tightly plotted conclusion. As the by now highly conventionalized genres of long-form prose—the conversion narrative, the didactic novel, the Gothic melodrama, the picaresque romance—gave way to the inherently hybrid genres of realism, the question of which of a variety of possible narrative models a text would follow became more uncertain and correspondingly more fraught. What if we couldn't be sure that Christian would reach the Celestial City at all? Even ostensibly "realist" novels could not only suggest but also enact plots more consistent with the principles of romantic idealism than of realist compromise. But so too could they disrupt apparently conventional romantic plot paradigms with actual plots that subverted the very expectations they had knowingly activated.

Yet despite this uncertainty, one of the central claims of this book is that the choice of one plot over another is not, ultimately, random, but a function of the particular aesthetic priorities of Victorian realism. On one hand, the genre accommodates an almost unlimited variety of narrative events, including highly melodramatic and sensational ones. If a nineteenth-century novel is not set in the distant past or a utopian future or a fantasy realm, if it does not include overt supernaturalism or either allegorical or radically experimental modes of representation, it is presumptively realist—or at the very least, it is available for use in conversations about Victorian realism whenever needed. Thus *Middlemarch*, perhaps the pinnacle of the form, contains such elements as a murder plot and the revelation of long-hidden family scandals, while many novels collected under the broad banner of realism involve even more improbable events: a father's drunken selling of his daughter and wife, an English gentleman's fateful meeting with a Jewish mystic, leading up to the discovery of his own hidden Judaism, and any number of cases of attempted, threatened, or actual bigamy.[11]

While all these events can and do happen in the nineteenth-century novel, however, the movement of Victorian realist narrative is toward what might be called a condition of plausibility. As I have already observed in the case of *Jane Eyre*, realist novels tend to eliminate their most radical possibilities. Jane does not become a missionary to the Punjab. Dorothea Brooke lives a tempestuous eight hundred pages but settles down into a famously un-epic existence; Pip's great expectations—in both of the novel's written endings—peter out into what is at best a compromised peace following the systematic suppression of all the novel's most fantastic and anti-realistic elements. The other possibilities exist, in a sense, to be purged: the realist novel ends not simply when it has exhausted narratability, but when it has defused its most romantic possibilities in favor of a deliberately nonideal compromise.

This pattern does not, it is important to emphasize, mandate any particular outcome. Rosenthal is quite right both that the conclusions of Victorian novels would not have been apparent (and, indeed, demonstrably were not apparent) to Victorian audiences and that even sophisticated modern readers tend to overstate the supposed inevitability of certain narrative turns. Yet in the nineteenth-century novel, apparently disparate resolutions can achieve similar formal ends, allowing us to maintain a coherent sense of what a characteristically "realist" plot requires. In Rosenthal's example, *Daniel Deronda*'s outcome is indeterminate because the most active alternative to its eventual ending—the marriage of Daniel and Gwendolyn—would follow the rules of a tried-and-true Victorian paradigm, one that Eliot herself had made use of in *Middlemarch*: Dorothea makes a mistaken, bad marriage, recognizes her error, and is rewarded for her growth with a second, happy marriage. But *Middlemarch*, too, involves a compromised ending, one in which (even leaving aside the far unhappier Lydgate plot), Dorothea's greatest ambitions are thwarted. Even her indisputably successful love match with Ladislaw is not, the narrator acknowledges, "ideally beautiful," an assessment that many readers, then and now, have shared.[12] Conversely, Eliot's Romola, who finds the purpose that Dorothea lacks ministering to survivors of the plague and selflessly helping to raise the children of her late husband's mistress, is given no second chance at romantic love, representing another possible resolution to the tension—present in all three novels—between individual desire and communal obligation.

A resolution in which Gwendolyn and Deronda married might have been possible, then—but at a price. While Gwendolyn, Dorothea, and Romola, Eliot's three major heroines, live out markedly different destinies, all three plots reflect an aesthetic of imperfection, of moderation, of nonideal lives in nonideal worlds. The women represent a range of plausible outcomes, but each of these outcomes, for all the drama that may have preceded them, is resolutely plausible, distinguishing them from the more perfect unions of the eighteenth-century novel. This is not to say, of course, that a woman might not become a secular saint while also finding ultimate romantic fulfillment—simply that this is not the kind of possibility that most interests either George Eliot or, by and large, the Victorian realist novel.

To a certain extent, a focus on unwritten plots leads us to an essentially end-directed definition of Victorian realism, one in which realist plots finally outcompete their generic rivals in what amounts to a belated revelation of a novel's formal commitments. Realism is not, in this account, a matter of what a novel contains, but of who wins. The definition indeed has a certain practical merit, given the sheer expansiveness of realism as a genre and the significant stylistic overlaps between the Victorian realist novel and other nineteenth-century forms. It is implicit, too, in several standard accounts of the genre. No man, Herodotus warns us, can say, until the end of his days, whether he is happy; so too with novels. If the key attribute of the Victorian novel is social compromise or romantic disillusionment, we will have to wait some time to learn whether we are to compromise or be disillusioned. Even Thomas Hardy, after all, gives us a few successful marriage plots, albeit ones more dotted with corpses than the average Jane Austen novel.

Yet the dynamic between actual and unwritten plots is more complex than a thoroughly end-directed model would suggest. Any account of Victorian realism that presumes—as this one does—that the form is associated with the deflation of idealist possibility runs up against the obvious fact that many, if not most, major Victorian novels have happy endings, and that many of those are far less alloyed than *Middlemarch*'s exquisitely measured compromises. It is not enough merely to deem a novel "realist" when it ends poorly, and "romantic" when it ends well. Certainly, there is a substantial category of realist novels in which an actual plot involving a tragic or at least less-ideal possibility defeats an unwritten plot that maps more neatly onto the declining genres of romanticism; my next chapter is devoted to precisely this realist type. But even when this is not the case, the unwritten plots endemic to Victorian narrative are in themselves agents of realism. By evoking a denied alternative—*even when that alternative is not obviously preferable to the actual plot*—unwritten plots infuse even the happiest realist novels with a characteristic consciousness of irrevocably diminished possibility. Austen's Marianne Dashwood, unlike Richardson's Pamela Andrews, does not marry her reformed rake, although *Sense and Sensibility* activates this possibility in a scene in which a penitent Willoughby petitions for a meeting. She is, almost certainly, much better off with the older, thoroughly decent Colonel Brandon, for whom she develops a "respect and esteem" that deepens into a kind of love. But our happiness in the pairing is dimmed by its comparative lack of passion; we, like Marianne, have been readers of romances and long for that more perfect fulfillment they promise. Colonel Brandon, one cannot help think, would have been better appreciated by the more rational Elinor, who herself deserved better than the milquetoast Edward Ferrars.

Eliot and Charlotte Brontë again provide instructive models of the different ways that unwritten plots contribute to realist plotting. Both pen major novels (*Deronda* and *Villette*) in which the heroine winds up alone, and major novels (*Middlemarch* and *Jane Eyre*) in which the heroine winds up in satisfied domesticity. The former novels deliberately deny readers the ending that convention has taught them to expect. The latter novels provide that ending—but against the backdrop of unwritten plots that undermine its sense of unqualified rightness. Realist plotting is not, then, engaged in simple nostalgia for the paradigms that its formal commitments have forced it to abandon. Though in abeyance, the plots of romantic idealism are not themselves impossible within the world of the Victorian novel. What has become untenable is rather belief in them as anything other than a compromise.

Reader, Did I Marry Him? The Case of *Villette*

In one respect, the sense of the compromise inherent even in seemingly ideal outcomes may be no more than an acknowledgment of the common truth that options always narrow over time, that every path taken is a path missed. Andrew J. Miller's work on unled lives has evolved, over his career, from a particular examination of a Victorian plot structure to a larger meditation on the intersection between literary counterfactuals and the denied possibilities of our own lives: from "Lives Unled in Realist Fiction" (1998), he arrives at *On Not Being Someone Else: Tales of Our Unled Lives* (2020). "Lives unled" to "our lives"; the novelistic gesture to the intimately personal sense of loss. "Successful works of art," he writes in the later work, "leave the debris of discarded possibilities behind them, like so many cast-off clothes, or lovers" (16). Yet the glooming peaces of Victorian realism also intersect with the particular social claim of Victorian fiction to question existing conditions. If the frequent inability of realist narrative to locate or credibly enact any fully satisfying option acknowledges present limitation, the wealth of unwritten plots model, not a now-unavailable literary past, but a potentially achievable social future. If unwritten plots must be discarded as incompatible with a world of realist possibility, if, more radically, the rivalry between competing plots will expose as fatally compromised the actual plots we have been taught to desire, it is because of a surrounding reality that leaves us with poor and limited options. If the world changes, so, too, can the novel that purports to represent it; correspondingly, changing received notions of novelistic and social rightness can work to model a different kind of extra-narrative reality. Change the world, change the novel; more attainably, change the novel and provide a template for at least envisioning a different and more possibility-laden world.

Villette offers an especially compelling instance of the use of unwritten plots to challenge both literary convention and Victorian values. The novel often appears in studies of literary counterfactuals because of its final passage, which seems to leave the reader suspended between two possible endings. After describing her fiancé's ship caught in a devastating storm at sea, Lucy Snowe abruptly cuts off her narration: "Here pause: pause at once. There is enough said. Trouble no quiet, kind heart; leave sunny imaginations hope. Let it be theirs to conceive the delight of joy born again fresh out of great terror, the rapture of rescue from peril, the wondrous reprieve from dread, the fruition of return. Let them picture union and a happy succeeding life" (555). The uncertainty of the passage, however, is only feigned. If Lucy does not tell us that M. Paul has died, theoretically we should, as she suggests, be free to imagine whatever we please of his future fate, just as we are free to imagine that Lucy's absent father was named Robert or William or, for that matter, Xerxes. In fact, since she does narrate, if only in the subjunctive tense, a rescue but not a drowning, the happy conclusion is invested with greater reality than the tragic one. Nonetheless, we cannot really believe that M. Paul has survived, any more than we actually think it remotely probable that Lucy was fathered by a man named Xerxes Snowe. The passage seethes with contempt for the reader who still has the luxury of such delusions, Lucy's words a final sneer at an audience with whom she has always maintained an oddly passive-aggressive relationship. The survival of M. Paul is thus properly an unwritten plot, and not simply one option in a presciently postmodern denial of fixed meaning.

Beyond the falseness of the supposed choice offered, focus on this closing scene—even in its proper sense, as an instance of a grimly realist plot decisively overcoming a more romantic rival—can mask the novel's more sustained and complex employment of unwritten plots. Most obviously, when two characters in a nineteenth-century novel, after a long period of denial and misunderstanding, discover their love for each other and make plans to marry, our default assumption should be that they will do just that. That this does not happen in *Villette* leaves the putative marriage to stand as a strong alternative to the tragedy that actually plays out. Marriage to M. Paul, however, is far from the only possibility in play. When the novel begins, it is not immediately obvious that Lucy is to be our heroine at all: while she narrates the novel from the beginning, the principal character in the first chapters is Paulina Home, a young girl left temporarily in Lucy's godmother's care by her grieving father. Lucy, in these chapters, is neither an active participant in events nor an immediately compelling central consciousness: it is Polly whose sad history she details, Polly who delights and disconcerts those around her with her uncanny precocity, and Polly who initiates her own marriage plot through her unusual friendship with the much older Graham Bretton.

The rest of Polly's story takes place largely off-page. Within a few chapters, we have left her behind to follow Lucy Snowe, the drab observer who has not seen fit to confide her own history to the reader. We do not see the peculiar child grow into a beautiful and polished heiress, and when she reappears years later in that capacity, it is quickly to marry Graham after a courtship that Lucy can narrate only from a distance. Yet her story serves as a counterpoint to Lucy's own. From childhood tragedy to a refuge with the Brettons to a life abroad, the journeys of the two women are in several respects parallel; between Paulina's two appearances, Graham Bretton even emerges as a potential love interest for Lucy. Polly's progress, however, is a charmed version of Lucy's: her inadequate father is loving and returns to her; she appears in the Rue Fossette as a privileged pupil, rather than a humble teacher; her loves are fortuitously timed and undramatically consummated.

In another kind of narrative, this opposition might read as quasi-allegorical, or, in a less aesthetically minded text, act as a conduct-book parable setting the success of a ladylike sylph against the failure of a prickly and opinionated rebel. *Villette* suggests a more complicated relationship between the two lives. In theory, Paulina's plot is, like the image of a returning ship reaching the shore, a knife-twisting evocation of what could have been. Yet the novel leads us, too, to question the value of what convention has persuaded us to desire. Though the stories of Lucy and Paulina share a dynamic similar to that of two strands in a multi-plot novel, the structure of this novel only allows us to take the analogy so far: Polly may be more successful in life, but it is Lucy who wins out as the indisputably primary figure in the narrative. Not content simply to assert, in the manner of a home epic, the parity between Lucy's story and Paulina's more conventionally narratable one, Brontë suggests that Lucy's tale may in fact be the only one worth telling. Polly is good, Polly is kind, but we cannot escape the sense that Polly is a little bit trivial, for all that. Her naivety has the power to wound ("Why do you go on with [teaching]?" she asks Lucy, and is shocked to learn that money has anything at all to do with it); her charm is a function of an extended childhood (321). Her love problems are fleeting and largely of her own invention. For his part, Graham seems unlikely to encourage any great development in his wife. Like Paulina, he is thoroughly decent, and thoroughly insubstantial; his fault is not simply that he does not love Lucy Snowe, but that he lacks all capacity to understand her, as Lucy herself ultimately realizes. His assessment of Lucy as "inoffensive as a shadow" is both insulting and excessively kind; she is more interesting than the docile nurturer he and the other members of the Bretton circle assume her to be, and less good. The description would be better applied to Graham himself, whom Lucy calls, with her own, far more conscious mixture of praise and censure, "gracious to whatever pleased [him]—unkindly or cruel to nothing" (356). Significantly, while Graham's lack of interest jettisons their potential marriage plot, it is Lucy who finally rejects the possibility of any place in his world. The last time she sees the Brettons, they are, with Paulina's father M. de Bassompierre, unaware of her presence. Mrs. Bretton and M. de Bassompierre, their kindness ever too simplistic to absorb Lucy's suppressed bitterness and resentment, regret that they have forgotten to invite her to a public entertainment, delighting in the sight of their "steady little Lucy . . . so quietly pleased; so little moved" (513–14). Graham, however, seems to catch her eye. It is unclear whether he has finally seen her or again misunderstood. In either case, as in the beginning of the novel, Lucy cannot long remain a minor character in the narrative of another. Refusing his glance, she leaves, acting out the farewell that she has already privately articulated: "Good-night, [Graham]; you are good, you are beautiful; but you are not mine" (410).

Lucy's narrative primacy comes at a high price. In theory, any number of plot possibilities are available to Lucy Snowe. She could be, like Paulina, the heroine of a conventional marriage plot narrative, marrying the handsome, noble doctor she has known since childhood after a fortuitous encounter. She could be, like Jane Eyre, the focus of a less typical romance, the difficult woman finding her idiosyncratic happiness with a less than eligible bachelor. Recurring rumors of a ghostly nun haunting the Rue Fossette introduce a potential Gothic plot, which continues when Lucy's romance with M. Paul is threatened by a sinister Catholic cabal straight out of the pages of an Ann Radcliffe novel. Not only do these plots remain unwritten, however, but the text treats them dismissively, almost satirically. If Graham does not prove himself a scoundrel in the manner of a Willoughby or Wickham, he does reveal a subtler source of unworthiness. M. Paul, petty, harmless despot of his schoolgirl kingdom, is a quasi-comic descent from Byronic Rochester, more likely to inspire a smile than a swoon. The nun's ghost solidifies into a cross-dressing count, while the attempts of Madame Beck and Père Silas to guilt M. Paul out of marriage to a Protestant are a pale shadow of the bloody persecutions of their zealous ancestors.

Lucy might, for all that, have been perfectly happy with Graham Bretton, and even more so with M. Paul. Instead, her fate is sealed and her options restricted by the pressures of narrative. The failure of any of the novel's alternative plots to become actualized suggests Brontë's own exhaustion with the paradigms that produce them. The precocious waif, the chance meeting, the mysterious apparition, the gradual softening of an irascible heart—each of these elements of the novel evokes the outline of a fully developed unwritten plot. Yet none of them proves capable of bringing to satisfying conclusion the story of Lucy Snowe, whose life is finally defined by failure and alienation rather than a more familiar triumph and integration. The destiny of narrative, D. A. Miller tells us, is its own destruction, to reach a point of closure in "a quest after that which will end questing" (*Narrative and Its Discontents* 272). This finality represents an achievement, but also a sacrifice. We tell stories about characters because their lives are not settled, because something in them is itself untamed and seeking. They lose this quality, when they marry or solve the case or even die, finding a peace that both completes and betrays the journeying self. The rebellion of the social upstart ends with a kiss; the ungovernable temper is appeased, and in turn appeases.[13] The first-person narrator complicates this model. In a first-person narrative, the last act of the story is its own telling. On one level, this changes nothing; either way, the tale plays itself out and is done. Yet if what drives narrative is a fundamental incompleteness, the choice to tell one's story would seem itself a sign of something yet unsatisfied.

There are perhaps few characters of whom this is truer than Lucy Snowe. Once we have finished the novel, we understand clearly enough why this would be so. Yet if the disappointments and tragedies of Lucy's story explain the bitterness of its telling, so too does the bitterness of its telling prefigure these calamities. As Lucy's final, mocking refusal to narrate M. Paul's death suggests, the unlimited possibility of the novelistic world is an illusion: we know that the ship is lost even as the text authorizes us to bring it imaginatively to shore, and we can read at each stage of Lucy's narration the promise of some unhappy end. A content Lucy Snowe would not have told her own story as she has done, with her passive-aggressive narrative refusals and barely suppressed contempt, not only for the base, but for the happy.

The hostile undertone of Lucy's narration does not mandate any particular story event, but it does *preclude* some. Even when a relationship with Graham seems most possible, Lucy's discursive choices imply the failure of that marriage plot at the very moment of its activation. The coincidence of their chance meeting awakens our expectations; such an obvious contrivance suggests a narrative design to bring these two together, and a similar accident will, in fact, later lead to the marriage of Graham and Paulina. Yet we learn about the significance of the encounter only well after the event, as Lucy neglects to tell us that the handsome Doctor John is actually (John) Graham Bretton until a meeting with Mrs. Bretton makes it impossible to sustain the deception. Lucy's unwillingness to reveal her own identity to Graham is odd but not unaccountable: clearly attracted to him, she has no desire to awaken his memories of the plain girl he had largely ignored in childhood. Her unwillingness to confide in the reader is a more striking violation, an act that elicits stunned betrayal rather than pleased surprise. "I first recognized him" she tells us coolly, "on that occasion, noted several chapters back" (200), her reference to the novel *as* a novel highlighting the extent of her manipulation. Whether we immediately recognize it or not, it is our clearest sign that the plot the encounter evokes will remain unwritten. This is not the way one narrates a key event in a successful romance; it is the half-vengeful bitterness of the disappointed. The specter of a marriage, insubstantial as the ghostly nun who never haunted the Rue Fossette, is raised and banished in a breath.

By historical accident, we have, in the case of *Villette*, more evidence than we normally do of what motivated an author's choice of one plot over another. According to her biographer Elizabeth Gaskell, Brontë said that "she could no more alter her fictitious ending than if they had been facts which she was relating." She included the passage suggesting that M. Paul might have survived only out of deference to her father, who "disliked novels which left a melancholy impression upon the mind; and . . . requested her to make her hero and heroine . . . 'marry, and live very happily ever after'" (392). Perhaps Patrick Brontë really did use the precise phrase "live very happily ever after," an especially poignant wish for a man who had already buried a wife and five children. But while the sentiment may be accurate enough, the language seems likelier to have been Charlotte's telling paraphrase. By the mid-nineteenth century, "happily ever after" had already become a cliché. In the context in which Brontë is speaking, the use of the phrase serves as a scornful synecdoche for the kind of novel she is not writing. Her scorn is not because the prospect of Lucy marrying M. Paul is particularly improbable, in any real-life calculus; certainly, it would be less unlikely than his dying in a shipwreck. Rather it is because such an outcome would violate the discursive logic of this particular novel. More than that, it would be generically discordant with Brontë's enactment of a distinctly realist narrative of failure. The uncomplicated lives and loves of a Paulina are still possible, perhaps, but they are not the lives or loves that should interest the writer—or reader—of the realist novel. Whatever we have been trained to desire, we would not want Lucy, finally, married to an anodyne Graham or become a species of untroubled Paulina. Neither, in the end, can the ideal reader of *Villette*, the one even Lucy Snowe could not scorn, want her married to M. Paul.

The marriage plot is, for Brontë, a disappointment masquerading as fulfillment, an indication, even at its best, of the relative poverty of options available to heroines whose inner lives are too expansive for the worlds that must contain them.[14] In *Jane Eyre*, she compromises: her plain heroine marries her always imperfect, now broken hero and is happy. But choosing happiness, too, involves sacrifice. In a happy, rich Jane Eyre, loved and loving, we lose the inspired saint of the Indian mission and the raging orphan of the red room.¹⁵ Come Jesus, come what may, Jane will be content and settled.

Villette is what happens when Brontë rejects this compromise. The path of M. Paul and the path of Paulina are both threats to the grim autonomy of Lucy Snowe. The narrator we meet is not Lucy Snowe embittered, it is Lucy Snowe untamed. In another generation, in another world, there may have been more congenial fates available for her, ones in which marriage would not threaten a woman's selfhood, nor her opportunities be so restricted outside it. But right now, there are none that satisfy Brontë. She tries one marriage plot, she tries two; she puts a ghost in the wings and a counter-heroine in the margins, but Lucy will have her disappointments, and her say. Reader, she sneers, you should have known better.

Looking Forward, Looking Back

The chapters that follow identify and outline three major categories of unwritten plots found in the Victorian realist novel. The first, and the subject of chapter 1, "Seeing Shadows: The Romantic Underplots of Victorian Realism," is the *shadow-plot*. The broadest category of unwritten plot, it is also the one that has figured most prominently in this introduction, comprising novels in which a main plot, associated with one narrative paradigm, is shadowed by an underplot associated with another. In particular, I suggest, this is a dynamic that sets the emerging plots of the realist novel against the still-potent tropes of romance. Beginning with an account of the relationship between these two genres, the chapter illustrates the role of the shadow-plot through an extended analysis of its use in the novels of Charles Dickens, whose shifting formal allegiances make his works an ideal case study for a consideration of how generically opposing shadow-plots both confirm and challenge the conventions of realist narrative.

Chapter 2, "Raising the Veil: Horror by Proxy in the Sensation Novel," introduces a form of unwritten plot I call the *proxy narrative*, in which an actual plot serves as a stand-in for an implied but otherwise unnarratable alternative. While in the case of the shadow-plot, the strong alternative must ultimately give way to the domination of its rival actual plot, the proxy narrative reverses this dynamic: in proxy narratives, it is the *unwritten* plot that, while necessarily suppressed by a range of internal or external pressures, succeeds in fulfilling a text's discursive logic. In a proxy narrative, the unwritten plot is not, in the manner of subtext, merely another meaning to be added to a surface understanding, but an incompatible alternative that must be superimposed over a problematic actual plot if we are to make sense of the novel. This dynamic is especially prevalent in the sensation novel; extending my argument about the unwritten plot's role in the formation of realism, I suggest that climactic but inadequate scenes of revelation in Maria Elizabeth Braddon's *Lady Audley's Secret* and Wilkie Collins's *The Woman in White* should be understood as proxies for unwritten scenes belonging to a deselected genre. The dynamic between the actual and unwritten plots created by the proxy narrative reflects and finally resolves the sensation novel's competing alliances with the eighteenth-century Gothic and the Victorian marriage plot novel.

Chapter 3, "'A Thing Quite Other than Itself': Henry James and the Proxy Narrative," turns to the proxy narrative in the works of Henry James, particularly *The Ambassadors*. The late Jamesian aesthetic, in which the representative failures of language so often obscure an actual state of affairs, fosters a gap between content and meaning in which the proxy narrative thrives. This is never truer than in *The Ambassadors*, in which a series of substitutions reach their apotheosis in a final scene that can be read most productively as, in James's words, "[a thing] quite other than itself" (*The Art of the Novel* 324). Unable plausibly or ethically to depict a renunciation scene between Strether and Madame de Vionnet, James uses a proxy scene between Strether and Maria Gostrey to enact a discursively necessary outcome that the logic of story otherwise precludes. Addressing a long-standing critical debate about the otherwise narratively baffling scene, my reading suggests the potential of the category of the proxy narrative to confront narrative difficulties and radically alter our interpretations of familiar texts.

While both shadow-plots and proxy narratives may resist the domination of the actual plot, both finally involve an acknowledgment of narrative limits. In my final chapter, "Fancying the Delight: Hypothetical Realism in *The Woodlanders* and *Mary Barton*," I consider unwritten plots that rather seek to expand the limits of both narrative and social possibility. Focusing on novels of reform by Thomas Hardy and Elizabeth Gaskell, I argue that these works envision possibilities that are currently inaccessible but potentially attainable in an improved future; they are, in other words, *hypothetically realist*. In such a future, the possibilities of realist narrative will be expanded as plots that would in the present be classified as utopian fancy become compatible with the project of social realism. It is thus the responsive reader who can most successfully thwart the mandates of formal constraint, working outside the world of the novel to actualize the unwritten plots that, whether active or not, can never quite overcome the pathos of their own untenability.

The study concludes with an epilogue that traces the afterlife of the realist unwritten plot in contemporary postmodern fiction. "Returning Dickens to the Map" highlights a type of modern unwritten plot intimately related to its Victorian antecedent. In a subset of late twentieth- and early twenty-first-century postmodern novels, I suggest, we find a surprising revision of the Victorian shadow-plot. David Foster Wallace's *Infinite Jest* (1996) and Paul Beatty's *The Sellout* (2015) both reject traditional plotting for a style dominated by fragmentation, pastiche, and metafiction. Yet in both cases, these aggressively self-conscious gestures, I argue, mask a neo-realist counternarrative struggling to emerge amid the postmodern pyrotechnics that surround it.

My argument thus, in a sense, comes full circle. Here and in chapter 1, I suggest that some of the most active unwritten plots in the nineteenth-century novel are the restive, still-powerful losers of a generic struggle that has resulted in their own displacement: they are potent because we recognize them from romantic narrative modes, but they must remain unwritten because they are incompatible with the emerging forms of realism. If the shadow-plot is a relic of the past, the hypothetically realist plot I discuss in chapter 4 is a portent of a possible future, while the shadow-plots of my epilogue replicate in reverse order of priority the generic struggle found in their Victorian ancestors. The realist plot, demoted from main plot to underplot in the course of literary history, becomes the upstart challenger reasserting itself against a latterly dominant form.

It is important to note, however, that the proper metaphor is the circle, and not the straight line. Genres do not evolve by natural selection: the unwritten plot is so significant in part because it preserves as potentially possible even that which is not currently accessible, challenging the realist order it has helped to establish. Different stories, and ways of telling, are dominant in different times, and few have been so thoroughly rejected that they could not and do not emerge again, modified but still recognizable.

Change the tense, and prophecy becomes elegy; change it again, and it is prophecy once more—of another death, on a yet unbloodied battlefield.

From the possible worlds of literary fictions to the alternative realities of the physicist's multiverse, claims of the value of unreal worlds have always depended upon those worlds' relationship to our own: the image they reflect of what we are, the story they tell about what we could be. Any good author knows this; it is the reason that even the characters of the most elaborate fantasy world are ruled, like the rest of us, by death and desire. If a god cannot die himself, he falls in love with a human and learns in that way the urgency born of mortality. Unwritten plots map onto narrative worlds even less real than the novels in which they are contained; if fiction, in Plato's critique, is a second-order imitation of the world of true forms, the unwritten plot must be at least half a step hazier and more distorted. Yet ultimately, the unwritten plots of the Victorian novel are vital to the development of a genre invested precisely in negotiating the relationship between literary fiction and the world around it. At a time of general agreement about the value of what we now call "realist" plotting, but widespread uncertainty about what fidelity to the real actually required, the unwritten plot helped delimit the expansive borders of realist possibility. Unwritten, these plots may represent the formal expulsion of an attractive but generically impossible narrative outcome; still implicitly present, they can nonetheless protest against the very logic—narrative and social—that has defeated them. At times, they cannot be said to have been defeated at all, continuing to operate as covert agents of narrative meaning. In a world of romance, they might have been possible without subterfuge. In a world of reform, it might take no romanticist to activate them once again.

What, in the realist novel, is possible? Several generations of post-realist literary genres later, we must look back to the Victorians for the answer. But among the several possibilities this book poses is one that saw the Victorians rather looking ahead to their readers, if perhaps not quite so far ahead as the possible future that we ourselves inhabit. What is possible, and what mere fancy, which plots are to be revitalized, and which laid forever to rest? It is for you and me, Dear Reader, to decide.

1

Seeing Shadows

The Romantic Underplots of Victorian Realism

In the long critical history of British literary realism, two views have emerged by consensus: that it was a vitally important aesthetic movement, and that it may not have existed at all. Certainly, it did not exist as a coherent or consistent set of conventions. Some Victorian authors thought of themselves as realists, but their definitions varied, and many other authors whose works are commonly included in the genre had no such explicit ideological commitments. Post hoc critical attempts to define realism have been at least as wide-ranging. For Ian Watt, realism existed primarily as a representative mode that emphasized "particularity of description" over the aestheticized vagaries of allegory or romance: in the realist novel, we find mappable physical spaces and individuated characters whose lives unfold in extended chronological sequence (*The Rise of the Novel* 56). For Harry Shaw, it resides in the historical specificity of its content and the fundamentally anti-romantic drive of its plots, which stage the collision between individual desire and social existence as invariably disillusioning. Some bound the term's potential expansiveness by limiting its historical range either to the years of Victoria's reign (1837–1901) or to a more compressed span between roughly 1840 and 1880, while others restrict it even more narrowly within this period to works displaying, in addition to the other attributes of realism, formal sophistication and "moral seriousness" (Leavis, *The Great Tradition* 30) or those explicitly "engaged in debates about realism" (Claybaugh, *The Novel of Purpose* 42). Rae Grenier has tied realism to the inculcation of sympathy, while Caroline Levine traces it to the forces of narrative suspense, which compel readers to defer judgment and set aside prior assumptions. Elaine Freedgood, perhaps most radically, treats the phenomenon as a critical "invention" that has achieved unwarranted cultural primacy at the expense of other literatures and forms.

The limitations of any of these approaches become evident in the difficulty we encounter constructing a persuasive canon from them. One would be hard-pressed to find any major novel of the eighteenth and nineteenth centuries that has not, at one time or another, been considered part of the realist tradition, including such seemingly obvious exceptions as *Frankenstein* and the historical romances of Sir Walter Scott.[1] Indeed, almost all models of realism raise the question of why any number of texts would be logically excluded: plenty of contemporary literature and fantasy novels, for instance, also feature some combination of descriptive particularity, sympathy, suspense, and romantic disillusionment. Conversely, many novels that are universally considered to be realist contain highly sensational elements; if we were to limit our definition of realism to those novels that eliminated such melodramatic staples as secret relatives, coincidental meetings, bigamy, and murder, we would be left with a canon indeed little larger than Trollope's Barsetshire novels. Despite the widespread association of the realist novel with depictions of ordinary life, it is not until the modernist era that everyday existence becomes truly narratable. More typically, the realist novel functions by subjecting characters whose lives bear some kinship to our own to the pressures of extreme and unusual circumstances, further obscuring the boundary between the realist novel proper and its rough generic contemporaries. There is thus often no clear consensus on the classification of a particular novel; the same works may be classified, alternatively, as picaresque and protorealist, Gothic and (realist) anti-Gothic, sensation fiction and "sensational realism."

Even in less ambiguous cases, the nature of narrative design militates against the stability of the form. At minimum, realism is generally perceived to be characterized by mimetic fidelity to the conditions of actual life. Yet no matter how much comprehensive detail and acute psychological insight realist novelists bring to bear upon their subject, one condition they can rarely replicate is the inherent plotlessness of human existence. We do not expect the lives of real people to meet standards of narratability or provide satisfying closure. Our futures are not foreshadowed, nor our chance encounters assumed to be invested with deep significance; the gun shown in the first act may lie dormant in a safe through the final curtain.

Adoptees do not routinely find their birth parents among their existing set of acquaintances, and the likeliest culprit is, more often than not, indeed the guilty party, and not a red herring. Hilary Dannenberg has written on the methods that realist novels use to "domesticate" these improbabilities within an internally consistent, immersive narrative universe (*Coincidence and Counterfactuality* 5), while George Levine and, more recently, Audrey Jaffe have treated the attempt to surpass the inherent distortions of language as a definitional aspect of the genre. Yet even when we accept the contrivances of plot as an organic part of the reality of a textual world, we remain aware on some level that a novel, no matter how exhaustively it details the minutiae of daily life, is liable to explode into melodrama or collapse into implausibility—that realist novels, whatever else they are, can never be quite real.

The boundaries of realism can often be usefully delineated as much via negative definitions as through positive ones. A novel, even a realist one, is not an autobiography or a historical record; if it *is* a realist one, we know that it will not, at the very least, also be a work of high fantasy or science fiction. The utility of negative definition, however, is most apparent in the far less obvious case of romance, the form out of which the novel emerged, and against which nineteenth-century fiction began increasingly to define itself. As the tension between what might be called realist and romantic plot possibilities is a key element of Victorian plotting, generating a larger number of unwritten plots than perhaps any other dynamic, distinguishing more firmly between the two genres is crucial to this project.

The Novel and the Romance

The term "romance," of course, has itself gone through several permutations, from its origins in the Middle Ages referring to a long-form verse epic of chivalric deeds, to its somewhat later incarnation denoting a prose account of a series of adventures, often fantastic or highly dramatic in nature, to its modern use to describe a particular, rather low-brow genre of fiction centered on at least mildly erotic depictions of romantic relationships. That the novel was not, in its earliest days, well-differentiated from the romance is obvious from the fact that the word for "novel," in many languages, is *roman* or a close variant; even after a distinction between the two emerged in English in the late seventeenth century, critical references to the two terms continued for at least half a century after that to demonstrate a high degree of overlap.² Yet by the middle of the eighteenth century, novelists had begun routinely to invoke, in idea if not always by name, a difference between prose fiction involving epic or otherwise sensational events, unfamiliar and exotic settings, and highly idealized, usually aristocratic heroes and heroines and a newer class of novel focused on non-noble, contemporary individuals living more or less ordinary lives. From the earliest days of Richardsonian-style English realism, then, the difference between the novel—or, more specifically, what would be later recognized in the dominant critical tradition as the *realist* novel—and the romance was linked to the former's nonideal and anti-epic qualities. "When I read for Entertainment," complained the playwright Richard Sheridan, in an early comparison between the two modes, "I had much rather view the Characters of Life as I would wish they *were* than as they *are*: therefore I hate Novels, and love Romances" (*Letters* 61).

Ideal, however, can be a relative term. Certainly, Tom Jones is a less perfectly noble figure than Amadís of Gaul. Yet the eighteenth-century novel is still comparatively didactic; Tom is wild and prone to excess, but he is a thoroughly good sort, after all, and—born on the wrong side of the blanket or not—of good old English pedigree to boot. He may need some chastening, but by the end of the novel there is little doubt that he has received his just reward, while his worthless cousin has received his equally merited punishment. If eighteenth-century novels don't always end well, they do, as a rule, end *right*, their characters' fates reflecting a moral order consonant with the presumed values of their readership. Even when readers showed willingness to tolerate a more flexible ethic, authors themselves sometimes demurred, as in the famous case of Richardson, who repeatedly reedited *Clarissa* to quash a burst of unanticipated popular enthusiasm for the villainous Lovelace. It is perhaps unsurprising, then, that while Fielding and Richardson are most prominent as founders of the realist tradition, a substantial body of criticism treats their works primarily as romances.³ Without committing herself to a single generic label, Patricia Meyer Spacks, in her account of the eighteenth-century tradition as a whole in *Novel Beginnings: Experiments in Eighteenth-Century English Fiction* (2006), begins by "bracketing the issue of realism" (4), a term she regards as an inexact simplification. If the eighteenth-century novel is "realist," it is so only to a point:

> It is primarily because [eighteenth-century] novels depict characters
> with physical needs and ordinary occupations in relatively familiar set-
> tings that they have so often been described as realistic. Moreover . . .
> novels of this period also reflect in recognizable ways the assumptions
> and disturbances of the society from which they emanate. The facts of
> the world we inhabit measure reality for most of us, and eighteenth-
> century fiction frequently draws on facts of experience. Yet to call it
> realistic for these reasons requires ignoring a great deal that it also
> does: for instance, the degree to which it relies on palpable artifice,
> trades in wish fulfillment, and depends on plotting that is too neat to
> correspond to the course of actual lives. (2–3)

For Spacks, the Watt-derived identification of the eighteenth-century novel with the origins of realism has distracted from attention to prominent aspects of the form that fail to conform to such generic expectations.

Again relevant is the divide between eighteenth-century and Victorian realism. As I outlined in the introduction, the tradition of mimetic realism described by Ian Watt and traced to the eighteenth-century masters is by the middle of the nineteenth century too ascendent to be especially useful as a means of textual typology, at least in conversations about British fiction. Instead, Victorian realism, in addition to adopting the eighteenth-century novel's non-epic focus and attention to authenticating detail, displays a fundamentally *anti*-romantic tendency to subvert idealized conventions, including many of those that dominated earlier "realist" fiction. Narrative rightness is not moral rightness; a character's fate will be properly determined by the probabilities governing his or her circumstances, which are likely to be too variable to admit of unqualified triumph.

The "romantic" mode against which this new brand of realism was defined encompassed three main types, only one of which was in conflict with the principles of eighteenth-century realism. The first was the form of romance Richard Chase prominently associated with the American tradition, which self-consciously rejected the principles of mimesis.[4] Less invested than their British counterparts in the authenticating detail and naturalistic characterizations of realism, the masters of the American Renaissance dealt in more broadly drawn, often deliberately exaggerated character types, larger-than-life figures who represented truths of human nature via metaphor and allegory, rather than through faithful reflection of an extra-novelistic reality. An encounter with Ahab, in the pages of *Moby-Dick*, might lead us toward a more refined understanding of human psychology, but we wouldn't (one would hope) encounter anyone quite like Ahab in the streets of New Bedford.

"Romance" in Victorian Britain, however, more often referred to works with less lofty aspirations than *Moby-Dick*. Realism, in all its permutations, still accommodated a large number of improbable and sensational events. Yet these works were distinguished from those involving experiences and modes of life that fell inherently outside the scope of conventional experience (and, often, that took place outside of an immediately familiar social reality). A realist novel might contain a bigamy plot or a murder; novels comprised chiefly of naval adventures, an expedition to the Far East, the travails of a Scottish patriot during the Battle of Culloden, or the career of a notorious highwayman—all of which adorned popular genres over the course of the nineteenth century—were generally regarded as romances, and judged accordingly by Victorian reviewers.[5] A late-century romantic revival, represented by works as varied as the socialist-inflected fantasies of William Morris, both Robert Louis Stevenson's boys' adventure novels and his allegorical psychodrama *Jekyll and Hyde*, and the "imperial romances" of H. Rider Haggard and Joseph Conrad, forcefully asserted the form's claims to continued critical relevance. These works, however, were by and large published after the peak years of Victorian realism, during the literary interregnum out of which classifications such as "fin de siècle literature" and "protomodernism" were born.[6] They possess as well a more intense self-consciousness than their eighteenth-century forebears, positioning themselves deliberately against the dominant mode of Victorian social realism. The most sophisticated imperial romances, Edward Said has argued, in fact subvert their own apparent romanticism, a gesture that he associates less with eighteenth-century romance than with "the easily recognizable, ironic awareness of the post-realist modernist sensibility" (*Culture and Imperialism* 188).

So far, these distinctions between realism and romanticism are fully congruent with the conventional definitions of mimetic realism. Both eighteenth- and nineteenth-century realist novels are committed to representation of particulars, sustained attention to the lives and thoughts of ordinary characters inhabiting socially recognizable realities, and at least relative avoidance of narratives primarily invested in the fantastic extremes of human experience, technically possible or not. It is in this sense, according to Patricia Meyer Spacks, that the eighteenth-century tradition is indeed realist. The sense in which it is not is rather in the form of its plots.

The word "plot," as I am using it, is not a synonym for story. "Story" refers simply to the events of a novel: Rachel Verinder is given a precious stone, her cousin Franklin Blake steals the stone under the influence of opium, a detective comes to investigate, a maid is suspected, and so on, until Franklin discovers that he himself has been the unwitting culprit. "Plot," on the other hand, has the added sense of design and intention, comprising not just a sequence of events, but the causal connections between them and the meaning they combine to make.⁷ The Moonstone's marriage plot brings together Rachel and Franklin in a union that is not only personally satisfying but socially affirmative, expelling the threats of foreignness and criminality that have dogged the domestic sphere throughout the novel; simultaneously, its imperial plot interrogates the British colonial enterprise through the story of the moonstone's original theft from India and ultimate repatriation, while a detective plot tests the limits of Victorian rationality. These plots are all, as a matter of course, comprised of story events, yet incidents that play a major role in one plot may be tangential to the progress of another, while some events—for instance, the evangelical Miss Clack's comically ineffectual attempts to force moralizing tracts on several other characters—take up narrative space without achieving significance in any of The Moonstone's main plots. Stories may be innocent, but plots never, performing, whether they wish to or not, a particular function within the culture in which they are embedded.

It is on the level of plot that nineteenth-century realism distinguishes itself from its eighteenth-century predecessor. The major novelists of the eighteenth century saw themselves as committed to a project of realist representation. Their successors in the nineteenth century sharpen this form with increasingly sophisticated depictions of consciousness, most notably free indirect discourse, and correspondingly more psychologically credible characterizations. Yet the clearest demarcation between them—the difference of kind, rather than degree—is in the disposition of their plots. The plots of the Victorian realist novel and those of its eighteenth-century predecessors, to be sure, often share significant structural similarities. The sentimental novels of Richardson, Burney, and Eliza Haywood feature love plots complicated by class and money; so, too, do the domestic dramas of Eliot, the Brontës, and Thackeray. The picaresque sets a naive, struggling young hero on a series of formative adventures; so, too, does the bildungsroman. Yet ultimately, these two models represent markedly different worldviews and, crucially, offer a range of markedly different possibilities. The former genres are ultimately romantic in their orientation; the characters of these novels live in a recognizable world without being fully subject to its limitations. Heart and virtue, the saintly and the reformed, will ultimately win the day. The latter, by contrast, are fundamentally realist; though their characters may and usually do inhabit stories full of melodramatic promise and romantic expectation, the course of those characters' lives will be determined by an array of forces that sharply curtail their options.

This disparity is evident in eighteenth-century authors' own declarations of their formal priorities. Richardson, Fielding, Burney, and other eighteenth-century authors wrote disparagingly of the romance, which they associated with a moral frivolousness that stood in sharp contrast to their own literary mission. This criticism was grounded less in any especially immoral content found in "romances" than in a sense that they focused on fantastic themes that excited readers' passions without providing any compensatory ethical value. In the preface to *Evelina*, for instance, Fanny Burney warns readers that they should not "entertain the gentle expectation of being transported to the fantastic regions of Romance, where Fiction is coloured by all the gay tints of luxurious Imagination, where Reason is an outcast, and where the sublimity of the Marvellous rejects all aid from sober Probability" (7). Without gainsaying the appeals of romance, Burney offers a more substantial fare; the focus on more ordinary events and subjects allows for a practical modeling of virtuous behavior, one that sacrifices the pure play of romance for the educative possibilities of the novel. Richardson, despite some period-typical slippage in his use of the words "romance" and "novel," lays out more explicitly the moral possibilities of this newer mode of writing in a letter about the then in-progress *Pamela*: "[*Pamela*] might possibly introduce a new species of writing, that might possibly turn young people into a course of reading different from the pomp and parade of romance-writing, and dismissing the improbable and marvellous, with which novels generally abound, might tend to promote the cause of religion and virtue" (qtd. in Eaves and Kimpel, *Samuel Richardson* 89).

This is not, plainly, yet Lukács's epic of a world abandoned by God. Neither does the world of the eighteenth-century novel bear much resemblance to Harry Shaw's site of inevitable disillusionment or Caroline Levine's suspense-driven deferrals of certitude. Despite the formal debt the Victorian realists owe to their eighteenth-century forebears, their narrative priorities are rather defined against the Richardsonian model, replacing an ethos in which plots reflected a Providential working out of difficulties with one in which the mandates of realism required a more measured assessment of the possibilities and limitations available to socially imbricated individuals. "Romance," as an alternative to nineteenth-century realism, therefore comprehends both the allegorical and sensational modes against which the early novel emerged and the wish-fulfilling, conventionalized plots of the early mimetic realists.

The Demotion of Romance

The romantic plots of the eighteenth-century British novel do not simply disappear in the nineteenth century. This is, in the most obvious sense, because many Victorian novelists were not realists at all, and even those who were realists were not consistently so. In *Good Form,* Jesse Rosenthal observes that only a tiny fraction of works published during the nineteenth century were what we today regard as "Victorian [realist] novels" (192). By his count, the number of genuinely "Victorian" novelists is twenty-six; in several cases, he counts only portions of those authors' oeuvres ("most of Gaskell, some of Gissing"), and a number of Rosenthal's judgments are in any case debatable (he treats *Wuthering Heights* as a realist novel, excludes most of Thackeray, and includes Bram Stoker, most of whose works, even apart from *Dracula,* contain heavy supernatural elements). Such taxonomical questions notwithstanding, Rosenthal's list underscores the extent to which later critical focus on a small number of canonical and semicanonical writers has obscured the realities of Victorian literary culture. In the nineteenth century, the *Middlemarches* and *David Copperfields* of the day shared column space and public attention with any number of less heralded works, many of them far more likely to cater to continuing appetites for the sensational, the didactic, and the ideal—and some of them written by the same authors.

Neither were the "realist" novels of these twenty-six writers—or perhaps twenty-two, or thirty-four, depending on who is counting—free of some of the same impulses that drove their romantic cousins. Despite the tendency of many accounts of realism—including, at times, this one—to treat realism as a teleological fulfillment of the promise of a more primitive literary form, romance is a tradition with its own competing aesthetic claims, one that realist writers, too, appreciated. As noted an advocate of realism as George Henry Lewes complained of a timid, "coat-and-waistcoat realism" that replaced the emotional intensity and imaginative possibilities of melodrama with "scenes of drawing-room existence" (*The Principles of Success in Literature* 187). If most works in the Victorian realist tradition did not merit such scorn, it is because they had *not* sacrificed such romantic staples at the altar of probability, by and large reconciling their commitment to faithful representation of the usual with conventional standards of narratability privileging atypical experiences and unusual events.

Victorian realist novels do not spurn the tropes of romance; they demote them. Despite the evident difficulties of both later critics and the authors themselves in determining exactly how much melodrama, intrigue, and sheer contrivance a "realist" novel could contain while remaining within the generic framework, it is possible to identify in the relatively small Victorian realist canon (and, to a lesser extent, in the eighteenth-century realist tradition) at least a greater degree of narrative restraint than we observe in literary romances of the same and previous eras. Yet when it comes to content, at best, the difference between realism and romance is defined less by a binary than across a spectrum.[8] Perhaps the most significant difference, again, is the one between the didactic, wish-fulfilling impetus of eighteenth-century plots—evident in both romances and novels of period—and the ethically fraught, compromise-driven ones of the nineteenth. Written and read in the context of expectations raised by the conventions of the former, the nineteenth-century realist novel inescapably evokes, but ultimately rejects, the paradigms of romance and, in doing so, clarifies its own aesthetic priorities.

The romantic plot possibilities of the Victorian realist novel are not fulfilled. They are, however, activated, remaining present in the text as unwritten plots whose formal displacement clarifies the emerging principles of Victorian realism. In sharp contrast to the conventionalized world of the romance, which cannot, morally or aesthetically, contain the possibilities of realism, the realist novel is committed to containing within it the possibilities of romance. An inherently hybrid form, the realist novel emerges precisely from a tension between competing modes. Pushing back against the generic consistency of the more stylized forms of the picaresque and the sentimental novel, Victorian realist novels evoke these plots and their associated possibilities as part of a complex negotiation between the still-vital principles of romance and the ascendent claims of a realism sensitive to and reflective of the actual probabilities governing human existence.

The attitude of realist novels toward their dominant real and unwritten romantic plots is not consistent. Sometimes the victory of realist over romantic plotting is triumphant. This is especially true in instances in which the type of unwritten plot that I call the romantic shadow-plot is affiliated with the frankly anti-realistic genre of the Gothic, where the banishing of horrific possibilities allows for a purgative restoration of the mundane and the domestic. Yet at least as often, the defeat of romance is a more equivocal accomplishment. True, most obviously, in Lukács's plots of romantic disillusionment, even the cozy domesticity of the marriage plot novel can be seen through its shadow-plots to be a loss as well as a gain: there remains with us the memory of the spurned suitor, the abandoned journey, the heroic life that went contentedly but still wistfully unlived. The very endurance of romantic plotting among authors formally committed to realism suggests a reluctance to abandon entirely even the most conspicuously anti-realistic impulses of narrative. In the end, romance will give way to the competing pull of the ordinary, the probable, the *real*—or as near as any author can get to it. But realism, in these cases, is less a goal than a verdict. Victorian novelists dispel their romantic possibilities, not because they want to, but because they must: representing authentic experience, with its disappointments and qualified triumphs, is not a matter of desire, but the function of the ethical imperatives of a body of authors often at least as committed to social change and inculcating empathy as they ever were to the aesthetic principles of realism.

What we witness in the Victorian novel's continued tension between romantic and realist modes is an earnest, sustained struggle to determine what, in fact, *was* possible in this new narrative and moral landscape. Far from obvious, as we have seen, even in retrospect, the boundaries of realism were, in the nineteenth century, still in flux. Romantic plots, even if they were destined to remain unwritten, were at least still alive enough in the libraries and the memories of realist authors and readers alike that they could only be read as active: the journey could end in unalloyed, exuberant triumph; the hapless victim of social circumstance might yet find her virtue rewarded. Having accepted the premise that the novel had some responsibility to reflect life as it was, it was not obvious what, precisely, this obligation entailed. We thus find in the plots of the Victorian realist novel a preview of much later critical debates over the genre. Did the realist experiment extend to plot at all, or was it merely a matter of detail-rich setting and convincing characterization? How much contrivance—and, perhaps, how much happiness—could the genre accommodate before losing its moral and artistic credibility? To the extent that romance was to be sacrificed, *was* it a sacrifice, and if we were losing something of value, how to compensate for its lack? Most commonly, as I have been suggesting, the result of these questions was a dominant realist plot and a strong, unwritten shadow-plot whose existence satisfied the psychological and emotional needs of the romantic imagination as its displacement satisfied the logical, aesthetic, and ethical demands of realism. Yet in the extended combat between these generic rivals, we see as well a subtler negotiation of formal parameters, one that would both solidify and challenge the emerging conventions of the British realist novel. For the remainder of this chapter, I examine in more depth the function of the shadow-plot in the novels of Charles Dickens. An author whose place in the realist tradition has, despite his towering status in Victorian fiction, been consistently ambivalent, Dickens is nonetheless an ideal test case for discussion of genre and unwritten plots in the realist novel. In the very hybridity of his works, Dickens is in many respects the most representative figure in a tradition marked by formal inconsistency and generic tension. Far more than Trollope or even Eliot, Dickens developed an unapologetic blend of the real and the romantic that tested and helped define the form in which he would become so dominant a force.

Dickens's Genres

The story of the American release of the last installment of *The Old Curiosity Shop* is one of the best-known pieces of Dickensian lore.[9] At the end of the previous segment, Dickens had left his readers at the threshold of Little Nell's cottage, where the child lay silently abed. Was she dead or sleeping? Time—and the next chapter—would tell, but for the moment, her fate, as far as readers knew, was undecided. Certainly, they behaved as if it were, inundating Dickens with "imploring letters recommending [her] to mercy" (*Letters* 153). When the ships carrying the novel's final installment arrived in New York harbor, the story goes, readers crowded the docks, crying out "Is Little Nell dead?" (Ackroyd, *Dickens* 337). The answer, of course, was yes, as it had been since long before the ships had set sail or the precise words of her doom had been written. Yet until that moment, Nell had been, in the minds of the readers, if nowhere else, suspended between two narrative alternatives. One was destined to be realized, and the other to be discarded. For a time, however, both were possible, and so the letters were written and the vigils kept as readers prayed for a girl who, if only they had known it, had been dead all along.

Dickens is only sometimes treated as a realist author, and even then, it is often with an asterisk. F. R. Leavis pointedly left him out of *The Great Tradition*, declaring that despite his obvious brilliance "his genius was that of a great entertainer, and he had for the most part no profounder responsibility as a creative artist than this description suggests" (30). More appreciative later readings—including Leavis's own in *Dickens the Novelist*, written twenty years after *The Great Tradition*—decisively refuted the notion that Dickens was insufficiently serious or aesthetically sophisticated to merit sustained critical attention.[10] Even so, the extent of Dickens's realism remains a subject for debate; Peter Brooks, for instance, included Dickens in his 2005 *Realist Vision*, but prefaced his discussion of *Hard Times* with a caveat: "I am of course not sure that it is right to talk about Dickens in the context of realism at all, since so much of Dickens appears as the avoidance or suppression of realism" (40).

Some critics have dealt with Dickens's intermediate status by noting the easy divisibility of his career into early and mature stages that correspond roughly to the period's larger cultural transition between romance and realism.[11] While Dickens's early works are steeped in the conventions of his eighteenth-century antecedents Fielding and Smollett, his later novels are characterized by an increasing social and psychological complexity. Triumphs become less complete and social problems more pervasive; heroes gain flaws and miss opportunities. More and more prominent characters are left out of the joyful final tableaux, which are themselves often harder won and more compromised than their counterparts in earlier novels. In *Nicholas Nickleby*, the world of the novel is remade in the image of its dashing hero's exuberant goodwill; by *Our Mutual Friend*, it is only through giving up for lost the other members of a venal social chorus that a stolid band of refugees can make for themselves a separate peace.

Yet as Brooks's hesitation suggests, Dickens's conversion to realism was always ambivalent. Pip and Louisa Gradgrind and Arthur Clennam possess more developed interior lives than their predecessors and must contend with novelistic worlds whose constraints are subtler and more inexorable than an evil uncle's antipathy or the deceptions of a pickpocket gang. These worlds simultaneously, however, accommodate hosts of characters and situations that seem imported from the realms of the Gothic melodrama and the moral fable. Alex Woloch has written in *The One vs. the Many* of the way in which Dickens's protagonists frequently risk being "engulfed" by more prepossessing minor characters, the grotesques and eccentrics that readers often remember even after more prominent figures have been forgotten. Aimless barristers encounter sinister foreign schemers and doomed, angelic waifs; middle-class strivers collide with clairvoyant crones and resolutely noble fallen women. Dickens's plots, too, strain the limits of realist credibility. Fundamentally ordinary conflicts are created by overtly literary contrivances: Pip's story about the disappointment of bourgeois desires relies on a convict's largesse, an old woman's pathological vengeance, and a series of coincidences that drive and unite the various parts of the narrative. Like the victories of their protagonists, the triumph of realism in the later novels of Dickens is often compromised and incomplete.

Dickens's evolving use of unwritten plots reflects the romantic shadowplot's role in addressing the persistent question of just how realistic a "realist" novel could be. On one level, narrative alternatives, as Hilary Dannenberg has suggested, enhance a novel's reality effect by producing the impression of openness within a fixed narrative universe. This illusion of openness is perhaps most apparent in the well-known phenomenon in suspense in rereadings of texts, in which the outcome is known, but readers may nonetheless perceive as possible events that they know will not actually take place (N. Carroll, "The Paradox of Suspense"). But even when outcomes are not known, the discourse of a text may practically preclude events that are theoretically possible: Thomas Hardy could, of course, have finally left Jude Fawley as the successful head of a thriving family, just as he could have had him ascend spontaneously to heaven in the manner of a

García Márquez character, but neither one nor the other would be consistent with the novel's established formal and thematic concerns.

Unwritten plots thus get at the heart of the critical question of how deterministic literary structure finally is. Are the fundamentals of any particular plot determined by formally and culturally generated deep structures, or are they the results of conscious and changeable authorial will? Is, in other words, the use of unwritten plots a tactic employed to create the illusion of uncertainty, or the mark of legitimate doubt, on the part of authors as well as readers? To the extent that discursive logic impels texts-in-progress toward certain fixed outcomes, even the most potent unwritten plot exists only to be eliminated, to give the appearance of freedom in the face of constraint. But to the extent that those outcomes may be obscured by real uncertainty over the possibilities available in a given textual world, unwritten plots pose a more serious resistance to the constraints of form. If the author of a half-written serial can mull his options and undo his designs, then the events of the most artfully contrived narrative world exist, like those of our own lives, as the non-inevitable products of circumstance and choice.

Appropriately enough, the unwritten plots in Dickens's novels, which tread so closely the generic boundaries between romance and realism, themselves embody both possibilities. Little Nell's death in *The Old Curiosity Shop* was—apart from its fame as a cultural phenomenon—a reflection of Dickens's growing acceptance of the constrains of realist plotting. Still grounded in a tradition that permitted the improbable and the fantastic, Dickens himself was, for a significant portion of the novel's composition, unsure that Nell had to die. Yet as his narrative grew from the short story Dickens had originally intended to the novel he wound up writing, it became obvious that Nell's death was the only logical end to her journey. I ultimately suggest, however, that in its most sophisticated form, Dickens's realism was on the contrary characterized by a resistance to the formal imperative toward closure. If the romanticism in his early works could be read as a sign of his lingering immaturity as a writer, by his late works, the maintaining of romantic possibility had become rather a conscious revolt against the new conventions of realism.

The Unexpected Novel

Dickens's novels reflect a particular preoccupation with alternative possibilities. In his 2007 article "Lives Unled in Realist Fiction," Andrew Miller discusses Dickens's tendency to confront his characters with visions of alternative selves who serve as counterfactual possibilities for their own lives: Edith Dombey, had she not been sold in marriage by her scheming mother, might have been the innocent Florence; Sydney Carton, had he put his talents to better use, could have lived Charles Darnay's life instead of suffering his death.[12] Beyond haunting characters with images of alternative selves, Dickens also raises the specter of alternative novels. David Copperfield, whether or not he is the hero of his own life, is certainly the hero of *David Copperfield*. But the novel's opening chapter, "I Am Born," is also the story of a misbirth: after being congratulated on her new nephew, David's eccentric Aunt Betsey storms from the home, mortally offended that David's mother has given birth to a boy and not the girl she has preemptively adopted as goddaughter and namesake. Throughout the novel, Dickens will periodically raise the question of what kind of a story this might have been had Betsey Copperfield been born that night and David left "forever in the land of dreams and shadows" (12). For his part, fact-minded Thomas Gradgrind would never have considered the qualities and capacities of George, Augustus, and John Gradgrind, all "suppositious, non-existent persons" (3). But Dickens does, and opens the second chapter of *Hard Times* by raising the specter of the rejected Gradgrinds who, he imagines, might have turned out more flexible than their stern counterpart.

In *David Copperfield* and *Hard Times*, Dickens's evocations of unwritten narratives reflect on the circumstances that constrain our possibilities: whether one is born a boy or made a Benthamite, the conditions of our birth and upbringing foreclose, or at least threaten, the realization of certain potential outcomes. When it came to the process of writing his own novels, however, Dickens was notably open to the possibility of revision and alteration; each of his novels, to a greater or lesser extent, contains within itself the specter of its own discarded alternatives. The most famous instance of Dickens's malleability is his decision to replace the original ending of *Great Expectations* after Edward Bulwer-Lytton suggested that it was too depressing, but there were other changes as well. When the obvious original of *David Copperfield*'s dwarf hairdresser Mrs. Mowcher wrote to complain about her portrayal as an unscrupulous flatterer, Dickens transformed the character into an unlikely heroine (*Letters* 674–75). After initially intending *Dombey and Son*'s Walter to serve as a cautionary tale of youth corrupted by greed, he found he couldn't bring himself to carry the plan through, displacing the original subplot onto a minor character and leaving Walter to serve instead as a cautionary model of a rather bland leading man (J. Forster, *The Life of Charles Dickens* 2:341). And, on the "valued suggestion" of his best friend and first biographer, John Forster, Dickens decided, well into the writing process of *The Old Curiosity Shop*, that his child-heroine Little Nell would have to die (Forster 1:211).

Even before Forster's intervention, *The Old Curiosity Shop* had undergone radical changes. The novel began not as a novel at all, but as one of the tales in *Master Humphrey's Clock*, a weekly periodical in which Dickens used the meetings of kindly Master Humphrey and his small circle of acquaintances as a nominal pretext for introducing a series of otherwise unconnected stories. A combination of poorer than expected sales and enthusiasm for the story—at that point really no more than a sketch—of a little girl living with her grandfather in a curio shop induced Dickens to extend his tale into a full-length novel, and thus *The Old Curiosity Shop* was born, "with less direct consciousness of design" than perhaps any other of his novels save *The Pickwick Papers* (J. Forster, *The Life of Charles Dickens* 1:202).

Conscious or not, Dickens's shift from one formal category to another necessitated changes to his original plans, such as they were, for Little Nell's story. This is most apparent in his clumsy abandonment of the first-person narrator of the opening chapters, whom readers of the periodical would have recognized as Master Humphrey; even worse was his attempt, after the close of the novel proper, to claim retroactively that Humphrey had returned in the person of an entirely different character (*Master Humphrey's Clock* 105), an assertion that fails under even the most casual logical analysis. Dickens's original intentions for the story remain too obscure to say with certainty what other elements of his initial design might have been altered to accommodate the significant expansion of the tale. One point that seems clear from Forster's account, however, is that the short story version of *The Old Curiosity Shop* was not to have been a tragedy ending in the death of Little Nell.

Forster places great emphasis on his own contribution, proclaiming "I was responsible for its tragic ending," and claiming that Dickens "had not thought of killing her" until Forster himself suggested it at about the novel's halfway point (1:211). The tendency toward self-promotion is typical of the biographer; elsewhere he pauses during an account of the publication of *Pickwick* to note the remarkable coincidence that both of the most important events in Dickens's pre-fame (and pre-Forster) life, his marriage and his encounter with the model for Pickwick, were, by some "shadowy association," linked to Forster himself: he married on Forster's birthday, and the inspiration for Pickwick shared his name (*The Life of Charles Dickens* 1:112–13). Yet even Forster stopped short of claiming that the suggestion was a product of his own creative insight, presenting it rather as the natural consequence of what Dickens had already written: "I asked him to consider whether it did not *necessarily belong even to his own conception,* after taking so mere a child through such a tragedy of sorrow, to lift her also out of the commonplace of ordinary happy endings so that the gentle pure little figure and form should never change to the fancy" (1:211, emphasis added). However late he may have come to the realization, by the time he was at the point of actually concluding the novel, Dickens, too, had begun to speak of Little Nell's death as a tragedy beyond even his power to remedy: "I am slowly murdering that poor child, and grow wretched over it," he wrote to the actor William Macready. "It wrings my heart. Yet it must be" (*Letters* 180). A second letter sent shortly after the publication of the novel's final number was more explicit in its assignation of blame: "That Nellicide was the act of Heaven, as you may see any of these fine mornings when you look about you" (228).

Such professions of inevitability, in the mouths of authors, come off as slightly disingenuous: who, if not the author, controls the progress of the narrative? In the case of *The Old Curiosity Shop* the claim that Dickens was somehow compelled to kill Nell is particularly difficult to accept. For a significant portion of the novel, he had evidently been capable of imagining an ending in which Nell lived, and even afterward, the novel seems to be preparing her for a reprieve. While the villainous dwarf Quilp seeks her, so too does the mysterious single gentleman, whose designs, it transpires, are far more benevolent. Indeed, there is no shortage of candidates for a timely rescue: from the family's loyal servant Kit to the long-vanished narrator to the poor schoolmaster who takes pity on the child and her grandfather, any number of possible heroes lies in wait to bring Nell her richly deserved reward. If ominous reminders of Nell's growing weakness make her death always a potent possibility, this host of potential saviors makes her survival at least as foreseeable an outcome, up until the moment that the cottage threshold is crossed and the angel-girl's bower revealed as her deathbed.

All the same, Nell dies. Something in the shift from the short story, in which Nell would have lived, to the novel, in which she must die, has proved so fatal that even her own creator cannot mitigate her doom. That element, I would suggest, is genre. Certainly, realism is, at first glance, not much in evidence in *The Old Curiosity Shop*, an early Dickens novel and probably his most overtly fantastical. Even after his reassessment of Dickens, F. R. Leavis, for one, couldn't bring himself to expend much critical energy on the novel, considering Nell herself a "contrived unreality" wholly detached "from any perception of the real" (Leavis and Leavis, *Dickens the Novelist* 298). Continually associated with the otherworldly, Nell lies on "a little bed that a fairy might have slept in" and appears "as if she had been an angel" (5, 318). The world she inhabits is, if usually more grotesque than ethereal, in many respects no less unreal: having grown up among a collection of "curiosities," Nell escapes from a dwarf, hides out with the performers of a circus freak show, and briefly finds refuge as a keeper of the grim human parodies of a waxwork.

At the same time, there is a very real horror at the heart of her experiences. Ian Duncan notes that Nell's essentially romantic identity is perpetually threatened by the workings of the materialist commodity culture that surrounds her. Her grandfather's gambling debts leave Nell vulnerable to Quilp's sexual exploitation, symbolized by his occupation of Nell's old room—including that fairy bed—as soon as he takes possession of the Trent home, while her brother offers her hand to Dick Swiveller as a cynical attempt at securing her (presumed) fortune. Even the thoroughly benign figure of the old uncle, who comes bearing Nell's rightful inheritance, is in this context as much threat as benefactor: only death saves Nell from initiation into the necessarily corrosive world of money and the marriage market. For every nightmarish figure that Nell encounters in her travels, she also meets more commonplace victims of a social order as brutal as any fairy-tale villain: the promising young scholar, dying of overwork and want, the orphan sisters, separated by the poverty that has left them to lives of lonely drudgery. Nell's problem, however, transcends the commonplace struggles of the innocent waif in a cruel world. Rather, as Duncan's reading suggests, hers is a formal crisis of a character being forced into a generic paradigm for which she is fundamentally unsuited. Nell may be a child of romance, but the journey that turns her tale from a short story to a novel removes her from her proper sphere into a realism she was never intended to encounter. While Dickens may not initially have recognized it, embedded in the structure of his narrative was a conflict between two literary modes that could be neither reconciled nor easily dismissed—one that would doom the survival of Little Nell to the realm of the unwritten.

The Perils of the Road

Superficially, *The Old Curiosity Shop* appears to be, like its immediate predecessor *Nicholas Nickleby*, a picaresque novel on the model of *Tom Jones* and *Roderick Random*, launching a hero out onto an open road filled with adventure and peril. The wanderings of Nell and her grandfather are episodic and often aimless. The tension of her plight comes from external circumstances: we wonder how Nell will dodge her avaricious pursuers, not whether she herself will give in to temptation; her moral virtues never in question, the weakness Nell succumbs to can only be a physical one. Yet the journey of *The Old Curiosity Shop* differs fundamentally from that of its antecedents. One characteristic that distinguishes the picaresque, a romantic form, from its realist equivalent the bildungsroman is its attitude toward social possibility. The hero of the picaresque must confront the unpleasant aspects of his world: imprisonment, impoverishment, and mishaps comical and serious are all staples of the genre. Finally, however, reality will bend to accommodate the needs of the hero. Nicholas must undergo the injustices of Dotheboys Hall and the indignities of life on stage, but he will finally and improbably emerge triumphant: the wicked uncle will die; the benefactor will appear; the day will be saved and the girl won. Even the poor schoolboys belatedly get their due: their tyrannous master Squeers is imprisoned, and Dotheboys Hall, as they exultantly cry, is "broken up" for good.

The bildungsroman inverts this relationship between self and society: rather than triumphing over his world, the hero must be reconciled to it (Redfield, *Phantom Formations*). Nicholas Nickleby can give the schoolmaster Squeers a good thrashing in the first third of the novel, secure that his actions will be validated by the wider world in the last. His descendant David Copperfield must instead seethe quietly when he unexpectedly encounters his stepfather Mr. Murdstone, the man he holds responsible for his mother's death; when David last hears of him, Murdstone has just married a second and still younger wife. Accepting the world as it is is part of the process of maturation for the hero of the bildungsroman; he may triumph within that world, but only by learning to negotiate the rules of a reality that will always be more limited than his desires would have it.

The realism of the bildungsroman, rather than the romantic possibility of the picaresque, ultimately determines the course of Nell's tragic journey. Surrounded by the fantastic, Nell is nonetheless unable to wrest control of her fate from the unforgiving world around her; poverty, cruelty, and illness will not in this case be overcome by virtue and faith. The reason for this failure is not any harshness inherent in the form; most bildungsromans end happily enough. Rather, Nell's failure is determined by an incompatibility between Nell herself and the paradigm into which she has been inserted. Nell is forced into the trajectory of the realist novel, but it does not follow that Nell herself is a realist hero. In part, this is function of age and gender: the protagonist of the classical bildungsroman, by the time his journey begins, is typically a male on the brink of adulthood. Throughout the novel, characters comment on the incongruity of Nell's task: "[These paths were] never made for little feet like yours" (333), says one sympathetic stranger. "One of you is a trifle too old for that sort of work [walking through the night], and the other a trifle too young" (321), remarks another. Nell is a little girl undertaking what should, both practically and narratively, be a young man's journey, and her failure is in this context just punishment for her transgression.[13]

Yet her unsuitability runs deeper than her physical unfitness for her task. One aspect of Lukács's definition of the "novel of romantic disillusionment" that holds largely true for the English realist tradition is his sense of the novel as a playing out of the essential incommensurability between an interior life and material reality. In the novel, "a purely interior reality which is full of content and more or less complete in itself enters into competition with the reality of the outside world . . . the failure of every attempt to realize this equality is the subject of the work" (Lukács, *The Theory of the Novel* 112). But while Nell is unquestionably at odds with her environment, she lacks the complex interiority of Lukács's hero. "She seemed to exist," says Master Humphrey, speaking for Dickens, "in a kind of allegory" (10). The hero of the bildungsroman may die, as Julian Sorrel does in *The Red and the Black,* but he can also mature, assimilating the lessons of experience with the impulses of nature to achieve an integrated, socially tenable selfhood. Nell, however, was never meant to grow up. Conceived as a romantic symbol of innocence and goodness, she cannot hope to profit from a journey that could only diminish her idealized nature. In the world of romance, she might have lived; in a world of realism, she must not.

All the same, romantic possibility is by no means at an end for Dickens. It remains, in the first place, in the persistence of the fantastic imagery that continues to challenge the dominant realist mode. Once we have recognized—as Dickens did—that Nell's road is the bildungsroman's path to realism, her fate is sealed. But the fairy-tale features of Nell's world continue to the end to work against encroaching realism: if we are in a world of dwarves and giants, angels and monsters, we may also be in a world in which Nell can be saved. Realism will finally defeat her, but not without resistance from the genre that lives on to protest its displacement and testify to the road not taken.

Romantic possibility lingers as well in a subplot that plays out a version of Nell's narrative of victimized innocence to radically different effect. Jerome Meckier has observed that focus on the suspenseful pause between Kit's arrival at the cottage and the discovery, in the next installment, of Nell's death has failed to account for the much longer delay—nine weeks, in total—between that moment and her last living appearance in the novel. In between, readers committed most passionately to following Nell's narrative are instead taken on an extended detour into subplots that Meckier sees as "counterpoints" to Nell's actual fate. Though, in Meckier's analysis, Nell's impending death should by now be obvious to readers, Dickens's use of these alternatives, which see several instances of threatened innocence rescued and virtue triumphing over vice, "unsettled the serial reader's certainty that Nell was doomed" by presenting readers with seemingly parallel cases that turned out otherwise ("Suspense in *The Old Curiosity Shop*" 200).

These "counterpoints" function as romantic shadow-plots to Nell's own. The most significant of these is the story of the young girl called The Marchioness, the serving drudge of a sadistic mistress who houses her in the cellar on a near-starvation diet. Alone and abused, without even a proper name to call her own, the child initially seems, far more than Nell, to be firmly situated among the realist elements of the novel, a pathetic victim of the social order smuggled into the tale from one of Dickens's journalistic street sketches. By the end of the novel, she has instead become a case study of the transformative power of fancy. The girl's wretched lot first changes when she is befriended by Dick Swiveller, a sympathetic tenant of the repulsive Miss Sally. Like Mr. Dick, *David Copperfield's* mad would-be author, this literary Dick acts as a diffracted version of Dickens's own imagination and, specifically, as a figure of romantic fancy. "Left an infant by my parents, at an early age . . . cast upon the world in my tenderest period . . . who can wonder at my weakness! Here's a miserable orphan for you" (172), he proclaims, in a typically melodramatic revision of his really quite tolerable childhood. Sally Brass and her brother Sampson are, as their surname suggests, steeped in a culture of base materialism of which the Marchioness is only the most immediate victim. But Dick can infuse even their grim existence with romantic interest: "This is a most remarkable and supernatural sort of house! . . . She-dragons in the business . . . plain cooks of three feet high appearing mysteriously from under ground" (258). It is he who dubs the little servant the Marchioness, treating her with the exaggerated courtesy of a knight addressing his lady, and he who, finally, ensures that her trajectory will be the reverse of Nell's. Having entered the novel as a potential suitor of Nell, he exits it by marrying the Marchioness, whom he formally renames Sophronia Sphinx as a nod to her obscure origins. These, however, are perhaps less mysterious than he supposes: she is, it is heavily implied, the illegitimate child of Miss Sally, always portrayed as a mannish, sexless figure, and Quilp. With this revelation of her grotesque descent, the Marchioness completes her transformation from figure of realism to figure of romance: for her, the rescuer has arrived just in time rather than moments too late.

The Marchioness and Nell never meet. Rather, they operate in parallel, one a figure of romanticism imported into a fatal realism, the other a figure of realism initiated into a saving romance. Yet the two women are not equals. The Marchioness is, essentially, the heroine of a short story played out within the body of the larger novel. Unusually for a character in a Dickens novel, her plot is comparatively self-contained; it influences other narrative strands, but does not depend on them, and has only the most indirect relationship to Nell's story. Within this curtailed form, romance can still triumph, and the fancy of a fairy godfather turned lover can transform an urchin into princess and riddle and bride all in one. But when the romantic fancy Dickens can still sustain for the length of a tale is tested against the expanded world of the realist novel, it collapses, and that is the world in which Nell must travel. Had she remained at home—remained ensconced in the few chapters containing Master Humphrey's fond recollection of a chance meeting one night in London—she, too, would have been saved: her long-lost uncle, in the form of the single gentleman, would have found her at home when he came on his first fruitless call, bearing the fortune she so desperately needed. But unlike the Marchioness, whose glimpses of the world are taken furtively through the keyhole of her cellar door, Nell seeks out a wider plane of existence. Not knowing she was only ever supposed to be an allegory, not knowing that the rules of the journey have changed, she departs on what she believes to be the well-worn path of the picaresque: "'Dear grandfather,' cried the girl with an energy which shone in her flushed face, trembling voice, and impassioned gesture ... 'Let us walk through country places, and sleep in fields and under trees, and never think of money again, or anything that can make you sad, but rest at nights, and have the sun and wind upon our faces in the day, and thank God together! Let us never set foot in dark rooms or melancholy houses, any more, but wander up and down wherever we like to go'" (71).

A world without money, or pain, or grief. It is Nell's proper sphere, but it is not one available to the earthly traveler. Unable credibly to achieve the necessarily compromised maturation of the realist hero, she must settle for the apotheosis of the romantic saint. The reader's path, unrelieved by any such ascension, is perhaps a sadder one. Lulled by the survival of the romantic shadow-plot as a legitimate possibility, we have hoped for an ending that was never really an option at all; we do enter the dark room of the melancholy house, and realize too late that we have been reading a tragedy all along.

The Failed Scheherazade

Yet although Nell's fate is tragic, that of the community surrounding her is not.[14] In the first stage of Dickens's career, characters by and large get the endings they deserve. By *Great Expectations* and *A Tale of Two Cities*, protagonists, no matter how sincerely penitent or belatedly heroic, will find themselves unable to compensate for initial failures of heart or will; as comparatively early as *David Copperfield*, a good portion of the novel's supporting cast has to be shipped off to Australia to find even qualified happiness. The early novels, by contrast, end in the creation of small-scale, utopian versions of English society in which the good are rewarded, the evil are punished, and members of all classes are left, with a very few exceptions, to live harmoniously within their respective stations. Normally, the protagonist is instrumental in securing this ideal. In *The Old Curiosity Shop*, however, it is only the death of formally problematic Nell that enables the achievement of a perfected social order. In dying, she frees up Dick for the Marchioness and Kit for the pretty housemaid Barbara, who can better tolerate her husband's continuing infatuation with a dead child than with a living woman. The single gentleman, thwarted in his original mission of mercy, uses the money intended for Nell to dispense charity to her various helpers: from the poor schoolmaster who provided her final resting place to a furnace keeper who offered a night's shelter from the cold, all get their just reward. Even angelic Nell, the novel's final chapter suggests, is perhaps not lost but rather restored to her proper sphere. Sacred in Kit's fireside tales, Nell is remembered and revered by all who knew and loved her; her tragedy is muted by the sense that she is more suitable as presiding deity than as living member of a human society.

Yet this is, as Dickens himself felt so keenly, a poor consolation, and the difficulty of achieving even this compromise reflects the formal struggles of an author beginning to chafe against the restrictions of his chosen genre. In *Nicholas Nickleby*, *The Old Curiosity Shop*'s immediate predecessor, it is Nicholas's energy and virtue, his "life and adventures" that bring about the novel's final settlement. In *The Old Curiosity Shop*, the absence of an adequate hero instead forces Dickens to abandon the attempt at fictional immersion and conclude his narrative with a self-conscious authorial intrusion: "The magic reel, which, rolling on before, has led the chronicler thus far, now slackens in its pace, and stops. It lies before the goal; the pursuit is at an end. It remains but to dismiss the leaders of the little crowd who have borne us company upon the road, and so to close the journey" (547). Replacing the literal journey with the narrative one, Dickens concludes the novel without fully confronting the generic problem posed by the protagonist who would not be a romantic and could not be a realist heroine. His awareness of what "must be" having led him grudgingly to his great "Nellicide," he finally returns to a model of storytelling in which the unrestrained play of fancy can turn a drudge into a marchioness or a dead child into an immortal angel. The declining potency of this romantic imagination is reflected in the transformation of charming fabulist Dick Swiveller, several novels later, into the madman Mr. Dick. For now, however, it will suffice to stave off, for a time, the pressures of realism.

Or, it will suffice up to a point. Before the end comes, Nell herself makes a last attempt to change her story. In the final, most desperate leg of her journey, she tries belatedly to reinsert herself into a series of more appropriate generic paradigms. Having fled from her last refuge after her increasingly senile grandfather has fallen under the sway of another group of gamblers, Nell tells the old man that they must fly from "the horrible dream" she cannot bear to dream again. It is a recasting of her story as fantasy, a desperate retreat back into the paradigm she has so fatally abandoned. But even as she weaves the fancy, she cannot forget the reality that overwhelms it: "This dream is too real" (318), Nell says to urge her grandfather to leave. Next, she takes shelter in a furnace room, where the forbidding industrial fire, its flame hidden through "iron chinks," its ashes falling into a "bright hot grave," surrounded by the "unearthly noises" of machinery, becomes a hideous parody of the domestic hearth that might, in another life, have one day been hers to tend. Finally, she finds herself on a ship, surrounded by a group of rough sailors who ask for her to pay for her passage with a song. While she claims not to know any, the man persists: "You know forty-seven songs . . . Forty-seven's your number. Let me hear one of 'em—the best. Give me a song this minute" (324). The frightened girl searches her memory and finds one song, then another, and then another. All night long she sings, and by this expedient "[keeps] them in good humor" (324).

The scene of Little Nell singing, as if for her life, among the threatening men recalls the story of Scheherazade, who each night staved off death by plying her murderous husband with her tales. It was one of Dickens's childhood favorites, a romance that captivated him long before he discovered the picaresque of *Humphrey Clinker* and *Roderick Random*.[15] Scheherazade's stories would have been worth listening to even without the threat of the sword hanging always above her neck as she spoke. But the most exquisite thrill came from the knowledge of that other, awful possibility: one day, the blow might fall, as it had on so many less gifted wives. Of course, it was only the storyteller's art that made the threat seem real; Scheherazade could not die if the tales were to go on, and no reader would believe in a sultan who could listen for one thousand nights unmoved. By the time her tales finally ran out, if they ever did, he could not help but love her; we too had listened, for all those nights, and knew how such stories went. But Nell, try as she might, cannot hope to match the power of that ancient princess. While Scheherazade must call upon inventive powers, Nell's task involves an appeal to memory; the songs are not Nell's own, and her recitation is compulsory. For Scheherazade's one thousand and one tales, Nell has forty-seven songs, an arbitrary number that Nell approaches only by repeating the same old tunes again and again. Nell mimics Scheherazade, but she, like the songs she recalls imperfectly, is no more than an echo of a lost past, the shadow of a romantic heroine who once found salvation in stories.

Two paths lie before the sultan: death or the story. He chooses as he must, and so does Dickens. But in Dickens's case, both choices, death and the story, arrive at the same end. The romantic shadow-plot—where the story stopped at chapter 3; where the angel-child stayed home and left another to serve as hero; where Little Nell was only sleeping—still lingers at the margins, because the triumph of realism could never be easy or complete. Yet choosing the story, in *The Old Curiosity Shop*, means choosing the novel as Dickens was coming to understand it, and this meant that Little Nell had to die. We mourn her bitterly and sincerely. But for the sake of the novel, we cannot wish her death undone. The sacrifice of romantic allegory would, later in Dickens's career, later in the nineteenth century, lead to heroes with an interiority that Nell could not have developed while remaining Little Nell. We leave the child to her little bed, a lasting reminder of the narrative direction that Charles Dickens might, in another life, have taken.

Seeing Shadows

Dickens's account of Little Nell's death emphasizes the necessity of the tragedy; among many theoretical possibilities, only one was ever really an option. The emerging realist Dickens *cannot* save Little Nell; the novel's end is the single natural and fitting consequence of the narrative that has preceded it. In this model, shadow-plotting creates a graveyard of jettisoned plots and inaccessible genres, a place where Dickens can raise the ghosts of romantic possibilities but never quite recall them to life. Yet Dickens's own career provides an obvious contradiction to this account of narrative construction in the two endings of *Great Expectations*. Since Forster first published the original ending of *Great Expectations* in his biography of Dickens, readers have been left with the evidence that Dickens found himself capable of writing two crucially dissimilar endings to the novel, challenging any impression of compulsion. As D. A. Miller has commented, the very existence of a second ending requires a text open-ended enough to have produced both: "if either ending wholly regulated the narrative leading up to it, Dickens would simply have been *unable* to change the original without substantially revising the rest of his novel" (*Narrative and Its Discontents* 273–74).

Nonetheless, partisans of both endings have argued their claims precisely on the grounds of the fundamental narrative rightness of one or the other of the conclusions; Dickens might have been able to write another ending, but only one could be a *proper* ending.[16] Advocates for the first conclusion even have a ready-made scapegoat for Dickens's defection from the paths of narrative virtue in Edward Bulwer-Lytton, the friend and fellow writer who suggested the change. Although Dickens does not enumerate the "good reasons" Bulwer-Lytton offered for revising the original ending, his inducements for providing a happier ending to Pip and Estella's story have often been assumed to be more commercial than literary.[17] Dickens's letter announcing the change to Forster, to whom he had already sent a draft of the novel with the original conclusion, provides additional ammunition to those who would interpret Dickens's decision as a crass and grudging concession to public taste: he says that he has no doubt the change will be "more acceptable," and evaluates the result with the somewhat backhanded boast that he has "put in as pretty a little piece of writing as I could" (J. Forster, *The Life of Charles Dickens* 3:369).

Far more convincing are the aesthetic arguments in favor of the canceled conclusion. Forster sets the tone for later uncharitable readings of the alteration by calling it a "summary proceeding" and maintaining that the first ending "seems to be more consistent with the drift, as well as natural working out of the tale" (3:368–69). For all its "prettiness," the happiness of the second ending feels unearned. This is not entirely a matter of genre: literary realism can coexist with the happy ending, as it does routinely in the case of the marriage plot. What a realist novel does require is a sense of causal sequence taken to its logical conclusion—or, at least, *a* logical conclusion. The marriage of David Copperfield and Agnes, insufferable as it may be in other respects, undeniably arises out of the structure and constitutes an essential element of that particular novel: David seals his development as an adult by his recognition of Agnes's virtues.

The logic of *Great Expectations* dictates precisely the opposite of what transpires in the published ending. Pip's central mistake has been bound up with his love of a woman who represents the falseness of the world toward which he strives. We need not be censorious enough to demand that Pip, at twenty-three, resign himself to a life of penitential celibacy to be convinced of the narrative impropriety of his marriage to Estella; it is one thing to accept Pip and a softened Estella shaking hands in a street in Piccadilly, another to tolerate them joining hands in the ruined garden of Satis House. A brief meeting with Estella can be assimilated into a general sense of lost expectations that include and are represented by but do not end with her. A longer and more lasting encounter requires that she assume a function absolutely antithetical to the one she has occupied throughout the narrative in order to become an appropriate locus of desire. It is a transformation that we are, as Forster reminds us, expected to accept in two pages in which Pip and Estella's reflections on the states, past and present, of their respective hearts must serve as validation of what is in her case an entirely off-page metamorphosis.

There are also, however, strong stylistic reasons to prefer the Satis House ending. Jerome Meckier notes that the revised conclusion returns, as the original had not, to patterns of imagery—particularly those involving clasped hands and rising mists—that have recurred throughout the novel. The logic of these images, Meckier suggests, properly dictates a reconciliation that is not a romantic rewarding of reclaimed virtue, but a realist embrace of a drastically reduced set of possibilities. The image of Pip and Estella leaving the ruined garden of Satis House among the evening mists recalls both the mist-strewn atmosphere of Pip's own earlier departure from the forge and the final line of *Paradise Lost,* in which Adam and Eve leave Eden "hand in hand, with wandering steps and slow" (XII.648). Satis House itself, of course, was never more than a false Eden—in the world of this novel, Eden was the forge, where another Pip, in the form of Joe and Biddy's child, now occupies our hero's forfeited space. For Pip and Estella, the world behind them and the world before are both compromised. It is the evening mists, and not the morning ones, that rise over their departure; they may yet be happy, but it will be the happiness of fallen people, in a fallen world.

The leading merit of the Satis House ending, however, is an ambiguity that contains within it the conclusion it purportedly displaces. Pip and Estella themselves remain, at least for the moment, divided in their understanding of the reconciliation:

> "We are friends," said I, rising and bending over her, as she rose from the bench.
>
> "And will continue friends apart," said Estella.
>
> I took her hand in mine, and we went out of the ruined place; and, as the morning mists had risen long ago when I first left the forge, so the evening mists were rising now, and in all the broad expanse of tranquil light they showed to me, I saw no shadow of another parting from her. (460)

That *Pip* believes that this moment of empathy can be sustained as a more lasting relationship does not guarantee that his hopes will be realized; Pip does not, after all, have the best track record when it comes to expectations. Yet even many critics who praise the second ending for its ambiguity cannot resist arguing either for or against Pip and Estella's marriage. John O. Jordan acknowledges the indeterminacy but also articulates a defense of the Satis House conclusion that reads it as, effectively, an expanded version of the original in which Pip and Estella merely part a moment after, rather than a moment before, the close of the narrative: "If Pip and Estella had remained together after they left the ruined garden, if they had subsequently married . . . Pip would in all likelihood say so" ("Partings Welded Together" 29). Meckier takes the opposite position, emphasizing the ingenuity of Dickens's resistance to cheap novelistic closure before declaring confidently that the Pip who narrates the novel can only have been one who has been long married to Estella.[18]

This critical tendency reflects an inherent difficulty in the second ending, whose ambiguity is at once obvious and implausible. There is actually very little room for doubt about the primary interpretation of the scene. Readings that assume Dickens intended us to read past the clear implication that Pip and Estella are to marry turn Dickens into a motiveless cryptographer out to deceive an unsuspecting audience. At the same time, the effect of the conjunction of Estella's final rejection and the negatively stated, subjectively framed closing line cannot be discounted. If Dickens wanted to marry off the two characters, he had plenty of less ambiguous ways of doing so; in many of his other works, Dickens is so thorough in his wrapping up that not even family pets or childhood acquaintances escape his telescopic gaze. Here, he will not definitively project even his main character into any future beyond a present moment understood in light of Pip's uncorroborated belief. That belief is cast into further doubt by the novel's pattern of dividing Pip's experiences into what Peter Brooks has called "official" and "repressed" plots (*Reading for the Plot* 117). Repeatedly, Pip assumes that his life is following a path that corresponds to his desires (Mrs. Havisham is his benefactor and intends him for Estella), only to be confronted by a reality that reflects his latent fears (his benefactor is the convict who awakened his guilty consciousness in childhood). Pip making a similar mistake at the very end of the novel, however disappointing to his narrative of development, would be fully in keeping with this precedent.

What we are left with, then, is something resembling a dominant and a shadow-plot. Pip may see "no shadow of another parting," but, in fact, the rejected first ending is precisely that, a different parting in which we are left in no doubt that the separation between the two is to be final. Only by chance did the original ending survive to become a literal unwritten—or, at least, unpublished—alternative to the chosen conclusion, preserved alongside its rival in afterwords and footnotes. Yet in leaving his readers with the ambiguity of the final line, Dickens transfers to the published page the shadow-plot inscribed in the two endings: the first conclusion is not so much rejected in favor of the second as it is incorporated within it.

Dickens refuses, however, to establish these two alternatives as part of—to borrow Dannenberg's phrase—a stable ontological hierarchy. What Dannenberg calls counterfactual plots typically promote novelistic realism by giving priority to the actual world of a text. If the only point of reference for a textual actual world were our own, it would be more difficult cognitively to suspend the dichotomy between fiction and reality. By contrast, surrounding the events of a novel with counterfactual alternatives creates an internal frame of reference in which, for instance, Nell's death acquires a reality that her survival does not. In the case of the death of Little Nell, the persistence of a seemingly viable unwritten plot in which Nell lives also helps to maintain the illusion that his characters are free, their fates not constrained by the laws of narrative logic: Dickens ultimately recognizes as binding a formal imperative to kill Nell, but constructs competing mechanisms temporarily to mask his design and keep active the possibility of her survival. *Great Expectations* lacks any such clear delineation. Dickens does not, in the manner of some postmodern authors, leave the novel in such uncertainty that there can be no distinction made between the various possibilities it raises: the prospect of Pip and Estella's marriage is clearly dominant, and that of their final separation subordinate.[19] But here, unlike in *The Old Curiosity Shop*, neither does he fully exorcize the unwritten plot he has in this case only seemingly discarded. Rather, in the unwritten plot he finds a mechanism for inserting realist-associated doubt into an otherwise romantic plot development, embedding within an ostensibly romance-oriented actual plot the layers of compromise and qualification that are so characteristic of realist narrative.

Fighting Closure

The function of the unwritten plot in *Great Expectations* is thus not to solidify an absolute outcome, but to define a range of possibility. Some options, by necessity, lie outside this range as surely as Nell's survival ultimately did. The last chapter of *Great Expectations* closes with an unwritten plot, but it also—in both versions—opens with one. Returning to the forge of his childhood after years away, Pip finds Joe, Biddy, and their son, whom they have named Pip. The older Pip observes a remarkable similarity between himself and his namesake: when he enters the room, he sees "sitting on my own little stool looking at the fire . . . I again!" and finds later that he and the child "[understand] one another to perfection" (457). Indeed, given that the two Pips are not, in fact, biologically related, the resemblance is not just remarkable but uncanny. Dickens's emphasis on their similarity reinforces the sense that the child is, for Pip and for the reader, simultaneously the actual son of Joe and Biddy, a reminder of the son Pip himself might have had, had his life gone differently, and a version of Pip whose path in life will not be thwarted by the burden of spurious expectations. In this case, the unwritten plot indeed represents a lost possibility, an unfulfilled promise that can no longer be redeemed. The possibility that does remain, that Pip will find peace with Estella, can assuage but never fully compensate for this loss. Whether it is the most likely or even appropriate outcome of all that has preceded it, the compromised happiness of the second ending represents the outermost limit of what is narratively possible for this novelistic world.

Yet if the negotiation between competing plot outcomes underscores the closing of certain possibilities in *Great Expectations*, it also opens others. Pip cannot finally return to the forge and marry Biddy for the same reason that Nell cannot survive: in a realist novelistic world, characters must contend with the constraints and limitations faced by actual people. There is a different limitation, however, that is imposed, not by the conditions of our world on that of the novel, but by the form of the novel on the lives it contains. Part of the attraction of fiction is its promise of endless possibility, its ability to suspend the laws of nature and physics and, perhaps above all, of the probabilistic logic that tells us most lives will be ordinary and unremarkable. But while this is true in theory, every novelistic world finally establishes its own boundaries. When we open a realist novel, it very quickly becomes apparent that the hero will not be able to resolve his problems by performing a spell or traveling back in time, even though there are fictions in which we might accept either of these solutions as plausible. The life of a realist hero is also limited in ways that do not constrain those of actual people. As improbable as it is that anyone who does not happen to be a character in a spy novel will discover that his or her otherwise friendly and unassuming neighbor is secretly a foreign agent, it remains—if barely—in the realm of the possible for a real person. It would, on the other hand, be virtually impossible for Pip to make such a discovery about his flatmate Herbert, as such a turn would be incompatible with principles of narrative design that preclude any such random turn of events.

This limitation obtains equally with more plausible possibilities. Novels, even when they are not neatly moralistic, cannot avoid saying *something* about the reality in which they operate. Authors choose not only between outcomes but between paradigms. Is this a world constructed to emphasize the triumph of the good, or its frustration? Is our tale one that suggests human capacity to change, or argues against it? We name an allegorical hero Everyman, and a realist one Pip, but Pip, too, must carry the burden of representation: strip away the convict benefactor and the bitter old woman in the wedding dress, and we are reading a tale of utterly ordinary ambition and ingratitude. I have said that Pip could not have married Biddy, and on one level it is true, but on another, of course he could have. A man might conceivably return home, penitent, to a woman he has previously rejected and not find her already married, just as, indeed, a sickly, almost impossibly good fourteen-year-old might in fact survive difficult circumstances to make a decidedly non-picturesque marriage in a disappointingly imperfect world. Pip cannot marry Biddy, rather, because the characteristic attribute of realism is that, no matter the improbabilities that might appear in the story, the plot that is being constructed is not, finally, the most extraordinary but the most fitting. A Pip might have returned to marry Biddy, but *this* Pip cannot, because to do so would undermine the novel's established belief in the inability of penitence ever fully to repair the past.

In this context, the second ending of *Great Expectations* is preferable, not because it is plainly the most fitting conclusion, but because it seems not to be. In the romance, narrative's drive toward closure produces outcomes that correspond to the longings of readerly—and writerly—desire. In the realist novel, as Dickens had discovered so painfully in the writing of *The Old Curiosity Shop*, the same impulse leads more often to denial of our dearest wishes, no matter how fervent our prayers and how faithful our vigils. Yet, paradoxically, the sacrifice that realist plotting demands is grounded in fundamentally anti-realist principles of design. If life will not, in all likelihood, offer most of us the wish-fulfilling fantasies of romance, neither can it preclude as absolutely as the realist novel does the possibility of a wholly unplotted reprieve. By preserving the original ending of *Great Expectations* as a shadow-plot within his second, Dickens renegotiates the terms of realist plotting without giving way to the competing lure of romance. Choosing for his dominant plot the less narratively suitable, romance-oriented conclusion, he evades the inherently unnatural conventions of even realist fiction. In shadowing that plot with the remnants of the canceled alternative, however, he avoids the trap of replacing this most narratively basic level of artifice with the more overt contrivance of romance delivered without the mediating forces of imperfection and doubt.

The original ending, in which Pip and Estella part forever, extends the logic of the earlier loss of Biddy: Pip has erred, and the consequences are unalterable; it is, as Forster rightly noted, the conclusion toward which the novel has always been tending. The second resists that logic: Pip has erred, and the consequences are unalterable, but only some consequences, and only sometimes. It is perhaps no coincidence that Bulwer-Lytton had in *Paul Clifford* engaged in a similar reversal, taking us almost to the point of his hero's hanging before instead telling us of his escape to a useful, honest future. We will never know with what reasons Bulwer-Lytton argued so forcefully to persuade Dickens to revise his ending, but among them was perhaps this one: "who does not allow that it is better to repair than to perish?" (*Paul Clifford* 309). Dickens was a far more sophisticated writer than his friend, and he would not reverse Pip's fortunes so completely. But after considering the competing options, he found that he could give him, at least, the peace of the fallen—the fallen, and the free.

Free, because the ambiguity that Dickens preserves in his final line represents a far more radical resistance to, not just the inevitability of narrative design, but the impulsion toward narrative closure. While the indeterminacy of the revised conclusion may not quite constitute a protomodernist gesture of openness, *Great Expectations*—in both versions—is, by Dickens's standards, comparatively inconclusive; there are no conspicuously loose ends, but the knots are not tied as tightly as they might be. Dickens does not, for instance, take the opportunity of Pip's return to England to provide an update on significant minor characters such as Jaggers or Wemmick or Pumblechook. By comparison, in *David Copperfield*, his only other novel in which a first-person narrative structure precludes an omniscient glimpse into futurity, Dickens still manages to fill us in on the fates of such essential figures as David's primary school teacher, the servant of a former friend, and a second friend's wife's sister, whom David has never met.

Great Expectations, however, is in this respect less anomalous than it may first appear. In the latter half of Dickens's career, even his most comprehensive endings are often complicated by unwritten plots that unsettle our sense of a theoretically closed text. These alternatives do not operate by preventing the story from coming to a decisive conclusion—*Great Expectations* is the only Dickens novel that could invite comparisons, however imperfect, to the postmodern, choose-your-own-ending twist at the end of John Fowles's *The French Lieutenant's Woman*.[20] Rather, their function is more akin to that of the strategies that, as Rachel DuPlessis and Susan Fraiman have demonstrated, female writers have used to subvert traditionally male conventions. Yet this is not so much a matter of, in DuPlessis's phrase, "writing beyond the ending"—or even writing "around" it in Hilary Dannenberg's emendation (*Coincidence and Counterfactuality* 4)—as it is of bifurcating what precedes it, forcing the actual world of the novel to expand to accommodate its own unwritten alternative.[21]

In *Hard Times*, Dickens can achieve this effect only by invoking the nonfictional world to set against the more constricted novelistic one upon which it intrudes. After definitively answering a series of questions about what is and is not to come to pass in his characters' futures, the narrator tells the reader that is up to him or her whether such things are to be in their own lives. Mobilizing the unwritten plots he has denied his characters into an exhortation to his readers, Dickens revives the possibilities he has just rejected, dividing the actual world of the text into a closed fictional realm and an open-ended real one. In the case of *A Tale of Two Cities*, the fictional sphere itself is more susceptible to confusion between an actual and an unwritten scene. Everyone remembers Sydney Carton's noble last words as he goes to the guillotine: "It is a far, far better thing that I do, than I have ever done; it is a far, far better rest that I go to than I have ever known." The problem is that he never said them—his speech is introduced with the qualification "If he had given any utterance to his [thoughts], and they were prophetic, they would have been these" (357). As any film or stage adaptation of the scene will indicate, what is clearly delineated as counterfactual is simultaneously perceived as actual, permitting Dickens to strike a middle course between the self-indulgent heights of historical romance and the more wistful tribute he actually offers.

The unwritten plot that closes *Hard Times* projects the narrative into an unconstrained future; its counterpart in *A Tale of Two Cities* divides it into two parallel moments of the present. In *Little Dorrit*, our heroine enacts a more active liberation from the impositions of narrative closure in a gesture that attempts retroactively to cancel a previously established textual reality. The final chapters of the novel have introduced a particularly lugubrious bit of narrative contrivance: Mrs. Clennam is not her son Arthur's biological mother, having wrested custody of him from a singer with whom her husband had had an affair. More than that, in a fit of guilt over the subsequent death of the singer, her husband arranged for a sizable bequest to be left to the youngest daughter of a teacher who had supported the young woman—or, if he had no daughters, to his youngest niece, who conveniently turns out to be Amy Dorrit herself. This history, the reader recognizes at once, has been the hidden machinery driving much of the narrative: Arthur and Amy, now on the point of marriage, met because his mother, in an attempt at partial recompense, had hired her as a seamstress. Almost as soon as it has been revealed, however, this plot is formally nullified. Immediately before Amy and Arthur leave to be married, she makes an unusual request:

"I have taken such an odd fancy. I want you to burn something for me."

"What?"

"Only this folded paper. If you will put it in the fire with your own hand, just as it is, my fancy will be gratified."

"Superstitious, darling Little Dorrit? Is it a charm?"

"It is anything you like best, my own," she answered. . . .

"Is it bright enough now?" said Arthur.

"Quite bright enough now," said Little Dorrit.

"Does the charm want any words to be said?" asked Arthur, as he held the paper over the flame.

"You can say (if you don't mind) 'I love you!'" answered Little Dorrit. So he said it, and the paper burned away. (825)

The reader understands what Arthur does not: the paper is the proof that would allow Amy to claim her inheritance, Mrs. Clennam having confessed the deception to her, and only to her, just before dying. Little Dorrit can do nothing to change the effect the other woman has had on the course of her life and story: there are consequences to our actions, and they are unalterable. But not all consequences, and not always. In burning the document, Little Dorrit, so far as she is able, vacates the force of her discovery, forfeiting the legacy and ensuring that Arthur will never know the truth. In effect, she has unwritten an actual plot in favor of its alternative—and, as far as Arthur is concerned, in favor of an endlessly open set of possibilities, a cliffhanger that will never be resolved with the next installment. For Arthur, the world of the novel will always be the world as it was for the reader three chapters earlier, a world of suspicion without proof and expectations not yet gratified. He has learned that some scandal in his mother's past has left her prey to a blackmailer; he has even suspected that it might have some connection to Amy, to whom his mother has shown unwonted generosity. He has seen the clues and held the last one in his hand, yet he will never solve the case. It is a fate common enough in our world, but rare in that of the novel; meaning eludes him, and he eludes meaning.

For in asking Arthur to destroy the paper, Little Dorrit does, for herself and for him, what Little Nell could not. Some of the same conditions that doom Nell might have applied equally to Amy. Little Dorrit, too, has been the angelic mainstay of a broken-down old man, too pure for her surroundings, seeming at once younger in appearance and older in strength of character than her actual age would suggest. But while Nell becomes a tale in the end, Amy passes out of one. In part, this has again been a battle between romance and realism. Immediately after burning Mrs. Clennam's papers, Little Dorrit signs her marriage license, the transition between the two documents suggesting the replacement of the byzantine contrivance of high melodrama with the naturalized conventions of the marriage plot: Arthur asks for magic words, and Amy answers, "I love you." Beyond that, however, is the struggle of realist narrative to surpass even its own artifice. Romance and realism are too closely linked; Amy and Arthur's union is itself made possible by an improbable series of events played out long before her birth. For Little Dorrit, the old uncle with his money was never the savior, but the threat, bringing her the proof that in a novel, two people never marry except by grace of another's will. So she does what she can, burning the papers in an act that turns the apparatus of fiction against itself. She gathers the powers of fancy, does her charm and, Prospero-like, burns her book. In our last image of her and Arthur, they are walking away from their own story:

> They all gave place when the signing was done, and Little Dorrit and her husband walked out of the church alone. They paused for a moment on the steps of the portico, looking at the fresh perspective of the street in the autumn morning sun's bright rays, and then went down.
> Went down into a modest life of usefulness and happiness.... Went quietly down into the roaring streets, inseparable and blessed; and as they passed along in sunshine and shade, the noisy and the eager, and the arrogant and the froward and the vain, fretted and chafed, and made their usual uproar. (826)

There are doubtless stories to be told among that crowd, stories to be designed and plotted and wrapped up. But Amy's will no longer be one of them. She has the secret, after all, of frustrating such plotters, for what power would any story have if we refused to tell it?

The ending of *Great Expectations* creates a parallel effect. To the extent that Pip and Estella have overcome their pasts, it is through escaping the grand designs of master plotters. Estella has not, as Miss Havisham intended, gone on to wreak revenge on the hearts of men; Pip is no longer the rich gentleman Magwitch had contrived to make him. Even now, the two are where they are because of their benefactors, but they belong to them no longer: they have come to the old house to leave it behind, and indeed, Estella, after holding on to Miss Havisham's property for years, tells Pip that she has finally sold it. Pip does his part by, like Amy Dorrit, keeping silent. As he and Estella sit in the garden, his mind turns naturally to Magwitch's death, specifically to "the pressure on my hand when I had spoken the last words he had heard on Earth" (459). Those last words had been about Estella: "'You had a child once, whom you loved and lost.... She lived, and found powerful friends. She is living now. She is a lady and very beautiful. And I love her" (436). It is the natural moment for Pip to make an equivalent revelation to Estella herself, but he lets it pass, leaving Estella to break the silence that has fallen between them.

What is the reason for Pip's forbearance? Once before, he had chosen to keep the secret out of concern for Estella's social standing and her pride, but by now, the former would not be jeopardized nor the latter revolted by such a disclosure. Neither can Pip feel the need to purge Magwitch's ghost as they are purging Miss Havisham's: his intentions may not have been wholly selfless, but there is nothing in Magwitch's actions to compare to the sustained, destructive malice of his counterpart's. It is not Magwitch, but a higher authority that Pip thwarts. When Pip tells the dying Magwitch that he loves Estella, he compassionately leaves him free to draw the inference that Estella loves him too. It is the natural conclusion for him to come to; even the illiterate Magwitch cannot fail to grasp the poetic rightness of the notion that the boy he has turned into a gentleman will wind up with his own lost daughter. This coincidence is, indeed, one of the reasons why the second ending has been read as so excessively neat, actualizing the "conventional romantic fairy-tale ending" that Pip is by then wise enough to offer Magwitch only as a knowing fiction (Brooks, *Reading for the Plot* 137). By sharing this information with Estella, Pip could not avoid imposing a similar burden of narrativity on Estella's own response: it would reinforce the sense—already acutely felt in the coincidence of their finding each other again in the garden of Satis House ten years after last leaving it—that there is a fatality driving them toward each other.

But there is, of course precisely such an external force bringing them together. Within the textual world of the novel, Pip can indeed lessen the effect of history and circumstance, at least as far as Estella's choices are concerned, by declining to reveal this additional layer of connection between them. The piling on of these coincidences, however, reminds the reader of the presence of the author who engineers them; whether Pip speaks or does not speak, marries or stays single, is all owing to an act of manipulation. It is one thing to suspend disbelief, and another to keep faith once the conventions have been laid bare before you; in both *Little Dorrit* and *Great Expectations,* one half of the couple lives in an unwritten plot sustained by a partner's silence, while the other can only will forgetfulness of prior initiation into an actual world of narrative convention. The only way for Dickens to allow Pip and Estella the freedom they are seeking is thus through not choosing, or at least not completely. Dickens brings Pip and Estella together again. He removes a second husband who, in the first ending, had precluded entirely the possibility of their finding a future together. He even signals, in the way in which he leaves them, his own conviction that, for these two, the ending of compromise is preferable to the rejected one of denial. Yet having been reminded so recently of Pip's last words to Magwitch, we know that the most narratively desirable inference is not always the correct one. And so we are left with an unwritten plot that will not be entirely erased. Among rejected endings and untold histories, we see it still, the shadow of another parting, ever secondary, but ever possible.

The Final Mystery

Dickens's works exist at the formal borders, between romance and realism, between openness and constraint. Part of this intermediate quality comes from the time during which he wrote and the artistic background out of which he emerged. But part of it, as well, came from his own belief that the events of the actual world could be as strange, as unlikely, of those of any novel: "On the coincidences, resemblances, and surprises of life, Dickens liked especially to dwell, and few things moved his fancy so pleasantly. The world, he would say, was so much smaller than we thought it; we were all so connected by fate without knowing it; people supposed to be far apart were so constantly elbowing each other; and to-morrow bore so close a resemblance to nothing half so much as to yesterday" (J. Forster, *The Life of Charles Dickens* 1:112).

The circumstances of Dickens's death perhaps bear out his conviction of life's novelistic quality. Dickens died of a stroke on June 9, 1870, having completed only half of *The Mystery of Edwin Drood*. A novel left unfinished by an author's death is always fertile territory for speculation, and never more so then when that novel has declared itself a mystery. *Edwin Drood* is no exception; one theory on the mystery has an Indian death cult mixed up in Drood's murder,[22] while another of the most popular, at least through the mid-twentieth century, involves Edwin escaping the attempt on his life, disguising himself as an elderly detective, and returning to town to solve the mystery of his own supposed murder (Lang, *The Puzzle of Dickens's Last Plot*). A majority of critics, however, now accept a more restrained version of events suggested by both the evidence of the existing chapters and comments Dickens had made about his plans for the ending: Edwin was, as he appears to have been, killed by his jealous uncle John Jasper, who will finally be found out and executed for the crime.[23]

It is a plausible ending and, probably, the right one. Readers who believe that Edwin Drood would have returned triumphant to solve the crime and claim his bride are fundamentally misreading the shift that had occurred over the course of Dickens's career. A "shallow, surface kind of fellow," Edwin, with his brash enthusiasm and skin-deep flaws, is as inappropriate a hero for *Drood* as Nell had been for *The Old Curiosity Shop*. Jasper, whose divided, tormented psychology was evidently to have furnished much of the interest of the novel, would indeed more properly have assumed that place: Edwin is a picaresque hero transplanted into, not just a realist novel, but a protomodernist one, more important in death than in life to the narrative that bears his name, but is not his story. An ending that leaves him to rest is, as Foster said of *Great Expectations*, "more consistent with the drift, as well as natural working out of the tale," than any of the other alternatives.

Even so, perhaps the most "natural working out of the tale" comes after all from a far humbler source. In the unapologetically campy Rupert Holmes musical *Drood*, audience members are given the chance to vote on their favorite ending. There are over four hundred possible configurations, and audiences tend to favor the least obvious, pairing the lovely Rosa Bud with the street urchin Deputy and pinning the crime on the thoroughly upright (and thoroughly motiveless) Reverend Crisparkle (Weltman, *Victorians on Broadway*). The ending, however, is always the same. Edwin Drood emerges alive, a better man ready to share his hard-won wisdom with the audience:

> I have read the writing on the wall,
> And it's clearly spelled out
> For those who've held out
> That holding on to life is all. . . .
> If you hear my voice, then you're alive
> What a bloody marvel we survive . . .
> Try to live forever
> And give up never
> The fight—you'll need the wherewithal! (Holmes, "The Writing on the Wall")

It is an ending that Dickens could perhaps no longer have written, had he lived: he knew by then that writing, whether it appeared on the wall or on the manuscript, could hardly be so easily erased. The latter half of his career is marked by gestures against closure—the abandoned character, the cut-off sentence, the burned plot, the double ending—but the sad irony suggested by *The Mystery of Edwin Drood* is that the only way of truly preserving possibility, of setting free a character from his own creator, is through a more radical incompleteness. Authors must die and novels must end, except when the author dies and the novel hasn't, cutting his characters free and adrift in a world of unwritten alternatives. Like the figures on the Grecian urn, they remain suspended in their eternal moments of uncertain action, and like the figures on the Grecian urn, win a prize that is not worth its price. Better to choose the compromise of that gentler sort of unwritten plot, which can only exist in the face of an opposing ending, yet may still live on to remind us that no ending short of death need be quite final; who knows, really, but that Dickens, too, might not have been preparing Edwin for a reprieve? Still, there is a value in an *Edwin Drood* unfinished. Dickens believed that the worlds of life and the novel were not as separate as most people supposed. In the sudden death that left the only work he had advertised as a mystery incomplete, Dickens's life ended with the dramatic irony of a novel, while *Edwin Drood* assumed—forever, but never at last—the plotlessness of an ordinary life.

2

Raising the Veil

Horror by Proxy in the Sensation Novel

For most of Mary Elizabeth Braddon's sensation novel of the same name, Lady Audley's secret isn't much of one. The former Lucy Graham's hidden crimes are appropriately dreadful: having bigamously married her wealthy second husband, she murders (or, it transpires, attempts to murder) the first when he reappears inconveniently. The novel, however, takes few pains to conceal this dark history. Our hero, Robert Audley, arrives to visit his uncle and his beautiful, obscurely born new wife. En route, he discovers his old schoolmate George Talboys, who has returned to England after a long absence to learn that his own lovely young wife has died. It becomes quickly apparent, to the reader, if not yet to Robert, that the two women are one and the same: when George arrives at Audley Court with his friend, the lady of the house makes strenuous efforts not to see him, while George falls ill with shock upon seeing a picture of her. When he disappears mysteriously the next day, there can be little doubt that innocent little Lucy is to blame.

But Lady Audley's secret is neither bigamy nor murder. Once Robert is satisfied that his amateur detective work has not led him astray, he confronts his aunt with his evidence. Our femme fatale folds like a cheap corset, helpfully confessing—to hereditary madness. *That* is her secret, and it is at least an unexpected one; the novel can now be absolved of telegraphing the solution to its central mystery. It is also nonsensical. Lady Audley's actions are evil, but comprehensibly so. Left impoverished by an absent husband, she positions herself to find a richer one. When the return of the first threatens her improved social position, she murders him. When Robert seems poised to expose both crimes, she takes equally extreme measures to protect herself, trying to preempt any disclosure by claiming to her husband that *Robert* is mad and then burning down an inn in an attempt on his life. Her behavior, however horrific, has been at every turn consistent with the cold logic of rational self-interest. Madness, a malady that strikes unpredictably and renders the sufferer's actions morally void, seems both too tawdry and too easy an explanation for behavior that has been represented in the language of conscious evil.

Braddon has, it might seem, traded one aesthetic mistake for another, replacing a too-obvious secret with a patently unconvincing one. Yet the novel's open acknowledgment of the implausibility of its climax suggests that the inadequacy of the revelation is a feature, rather than a flaw, of the narrative's design. When Robert tells a doctor about his aunt's disturbing confession, the doctor dismisses Lady Audley's self-diagnosis as unfounded; she is guilty of no motiveless crimes or random aberrancies. After an off-page examination, he hastily reverses his position. This cannot, however, diminish the force of the original objection, which has been articulated at greater length and far more convincingly than his vague confirmation of "latent insanity" (385). Lady Audley knows a hawk from a handsaw: she is passionate, she is violent, but when the wind blows southerly, she is sane all the same.

The unwritten plot, as we have seen, arises out of limitation as much as it does out of possibility. If our sense of narrative freedom permits us to consider multiple future outcomes, our awareness of convention, by sharply curtailing a given text's range of possibility, is what allows certain unwritten plots to assume priority over others. It is limitation, in turn, that ultimately forces the underplots of realist fiction to remain unwritten: the shadow-plot for a time appears plausible but proves finally inconsistent with the formal priorities of realism. We could not, midway through the novel, imagine a version of *The Old Curiosity Shop* in which Nell and her grandfather escape to South America and join Simón Bolívar in liberating Peru, a technically possible turn of events that would violate entirely our intuitive sense of narrative logic. We *can* imagine a version in which Nell is rescued by the timely intercession of a long-lost relative, an outcome the text itself implicitly entertains, and one that would follow a familiar novelistic paradigm. Such a conclusion would not, however, be ultimately consistent with the discursive aims of the particular world of *The Old Curiosity Shop*.

That we—and Dickens—recognize this only belatedly makes the novel's formal imperatives no less binding. The openness of a fictional text is only virtual; that anything can happen in a novel does not mean that it should. It is part of the pact the reader makes with the author: we will suspend disbelief through any number of fantastic events as long as a text obeys its own internal logic. The inherent hybridity of most works of Victorian realism—whose generic affiliations may be indeterminate until late in the novel and often remain a matter of critical dispute—allows them to accommodate an unusually wide range of unwritten plots. But even the majority of their associated possibilities, as we have seen, are more imagined than real. The good reader of *Villette* would not, in the end, be satisfied with the marriage of Lucy and M. Paul, an outcome fundamentally at odds with the conspicuous reserve and suppressed bitterness of Lucy's narration. Only this recognition exempts us from the scorn reserved for "quiet, kind heart[s]" that cannot face the final tragedy (555). Let the rest retreat into the delusive promise of an ever-active counterfactual; we know better, though we, too, are tenderhearted and mourn for Paul and Lucy. We see it now, though we did not a moment earlier; it would have been the fulfillment of our hopes, and not their disappointment, that constituted Brontë's greatest betrayal.

The next two chapters describe what happens when a text violates this pact. In some cases, of course, a work's failure to fulfill its own discursive promises may be no more than an aesthetic mistake: there are flawed novels, and bad ones. But in other novels, I argue, a development that could be taken for such an error is rather a crucial element of the narrative's design. A proxy narrative, as I call it, emerges out of a moment of dissonance or difficulty. Perhaps the happy ending seems not quite earned, or the climactic scene involves a matter too trivial to merit the seriousness with which the narrative treats it. Maybe a significant character has been too hastily cast aside, or minor one been elevated past her station. Yet the proxy narrative, unlike the merely faulty text, embeds a correction within the novel itself: as well as telling us what has happened, the text suggests what *ought to* have happened—indeed, what we must implicitly believe happened—to avoid dissonance or disappointment. The result is a reading that negotiates between two alternatives: the scene as written, and a phantom scene that everything surrounding it suggests should have been. Reversing the usual order between an actual and an unwritten plot, in a proxy narrative, the latter, rather than the former, emerges as primary. Normally an unreconstructed warrior, conquered but still restive, the unwritten plot becomes in the proxy narrative a dark horse champion, claiming victory even as the unsuspecting herald reads out the tale of his defeat.

In this chapter, I discuss the category of the proxy narrative through readings of two sensation novels, Braddon's *Lady Audley's Secret* and Wilkie Collins's *The Woman in White*. Belonging to a genre defined by lurid shocks and horrifying secrets, the two novels might at first seem almost immune to questions of plausibility. Yet even as it hearkens back to the eighteenth-century Gothic, the sensation novel also shares a well-recognized, if always tenuous, relationship to realism. Neither sensation authors nor their reviewers exempted these works from period-typical concerns about the credibility of characters and plot; if many reviewers used these standards to condemn sensation novels, Henry James, for one, credited the works of Collins and Braddon with a "thorough-going realism," and references to "sensational realism" and "realistic sensationalism" were common throughout the genre's brief heyday in the 1860s (Allan, "Sensationalism Made Real"). Contemporary criticism has largely corroborated this judgment, emphasizing the abiding formal links between what otherwise might seem to be ideologically opposing forms.[1]

It is this tension, perhaps, that accounts for the frequency of disappointing endings among sensation novels. Dealing initially in the tropes of the Gothic, the sensation novel rather works toward the enactment of realist plots that enshrine domestic order and social regulation. At a key moment, these works must therefore betray their own discursive promises in order to effect a formal transition from one of its prevailing modes to its ultimately dominant other. As such, both *Lady Audley's Secret* and *The Woman in White* turn upon central revelations that are not so much implausible as necessarily unconvincing, even for the reader who has gamely attenuated her disbelief. This chapter suggests that these apparently discordant scenes, which bear the burden of this shift, can be productively read at once as straightforward, if disappointing, revelations *and* as proxies for phantom alternatives that are, paradoxically, at once necessary and unnarratable. Allowing a scene to do the work the novel's jettisoned Gothic plots require while simultaneously, if belatedly, fulfilling the demands of realist taste, character, and logic, the proxy narrative trusts its readers virtually to enact possibilities that cannot, even in this most hybrid of Victorian forms, be otherwise accommodated.

Reading Mistakes

The trust such texts repose in their readers is not a blind one. Narratives of all kinds take it for granted that we are capable of reading into a text events other than the ones represented there. Narrative time, we understand, is distinct from chronological time and will not encompass every moment of a character's experience over the duration of a novel. We are thus unperturbed when a character last seen preparing for bed suddenly appears at breakfast, or, under certain circumstances, if a couple we left stewing after a quarrel reappears the picture of marital amity. This is because we can infer what the omitted scene must have been from the material that surrounds it. In the first case, we do not even need context; sleep—unless it is disrupted, or plagued by nightmares, or otherwise noteworthy—belongs to what Gerald Prince has called the "unnarratable," a category that includes events too minor or routine to require representing.[2] In the second, the novel can omit the reconciliation because it has already given us all the information we need to read the absent scene into the narrative. If the two characters are comic figures, a melodramatic argument followed by ostentatious shows of affection might be part of the joke, suggesting how little has been required to smooth over the violent dispute. If they are social climbers, we may rather recognize the plain implication that their ambition has prompted a public affectation of harmony. Without representing a scene that must, logically, have occurred, the text has nonetheless provided us with the materials to compensate for that omission.

The same awareness that allows us to cope with narrative gaps can guide our response to narrative errors. When publishers discover an error after a book has gone to press, they may insert an erratum slip instructing readers to read "light" for "might" or "sail" for "snail." Yet given sufficient context, readers may make the substitution automatically, even subconsciously. Psycholinguists have shown that humans process written language by the word rather than by the letter; as long as the first and last letter of a word are preserved, changing the order of intervening letters will slow but not inhibit comprehension (Rayner, White, and Liversedge, "Raeding Wrods with Jubmled Lettres"). A minor mistake, like a single inversion of letters, or even the repetition of an entire word, may pass entirely unnoticed: we see what we expect to see, what we *need* to see if we are to make sense of the words.[3] Neither will we be at any great loss if we do observe an error. When we encounter the sentence "Mary needed milk and eggs, so *he* went to the store," unless the line appears in a very specific context, we can accurately read the line to signify that a female named Mary went to the store, rather than assuming the author has taken the opportunity to casually upend our notion of Mary's gender identity. The same context that would have permitted us to fill in the missing pronoun had the author omitted it entirely allows us to replace an incorrect one with the appropriate substitute.

A similar process plays out in the case of a different and more potentially significant type of narrative dissonance. To modern readers, the sexual mores of most nineteenth-century British novels are likely to seem prudish. At best, the chaste romances of these works may read as benignly quaint. In other cases, erotic scandals expose what should in theory be a troubling moral gap between our own and our protagonists' values. *Mansfield Park* is a comparatively rare case of a nineteenth-century novel in which the extremity of our heroine's moral standards—most notably, the priggish Fanny's objections to staging a private theatrical performance—seem meaningfully to have harmed the novel's subsequent reception.[4] But perennial favorite *Pride and Prejudice,* too, prominently features some very questionable sexual ethics. Neither Austen's text nor Elizabeth Bennet shows much sympathy for the admittedly obnoxious Lydia, whose great crime consists of a brief cohabitation with a significantly older man who has secured her consent with false promises of marriage. When Elizabeth's older sister Jane, certainly no libertine, gently suggests, once Wickham has been pressured into marrying Lydia, that the couple might "settle so quietly, and live in so rational a manner, as may in time make their past imprudence forgotten," Elizabeth—and, by inference, the text—strikes a far less compromising note: "Their conduct has been such," the idol of generations of bookish teenage girls primly replies, "as neither you, nor I, nor anybody, can ever forget. It is useless to talk of" (208). Talked of, but quickly dismissed, is the notion that a sixteen-year-old should perhaps not be compelled to marry a twenty-eight-year-old known scoundrel simply because she has been impetuous enough to sleep with him; the more sensible members of the Bennet family regret that Lydia has tied herself to Wickham, but view marriage as the only possible solution to what we might today call a case of statutory rape.

Pride and Prejudice seems so far to have survived the "Me Too" era unscathed, while even the less-beloved *Mansfield Park* has been adapted for screen, radio, and stage several times in the twenty-first century, Fanny Price's bold stance against the immodesty of private theater faithfully included.[5] In theory, such stories force readers to adopt one of two untenable positions. Either we validate a premise we must view as gravely mistaken, tutting censoriously over loose women and "natural" children, or we engage in a reading that willfully subverts the plain meaning of the text: if Jane Austen was no milquetoast Fanny Price, neither was she, at least on the evidence of her novels, of Sarah Siddons's party without knowing it.[6] *Mansfield Park* requires us to take seriously Fanny's objections; whatever *we* might think of her moral judgments, the text itself consistently validates them. Yet in practice, most readers find a middle ground that permits us to cope with our cognitive dissonance. We may call it "allowing for the era," but what we are doing, in effect, is reading the problematic scene as the moral equivalent of a more palatable alternative. In modernizations (as opposed to modern adaptations) of the novels, this technique may be literalized: *The Lizzie Bennet Diaries* (2012), a popular YouTube retelling of *Pride and Prejudice* set in recession-era Southern California, replaces Lydia's elopement with Wickham with the threatened release of a sex tape featuring the youngest Bennet, while in *From Mansfield with Love* (2014), one of *The Lizzie Bennet Diaries*'s several imitators, practical Fanny objects to the staging of a pretentious art film on account of the waste of time and money involved.

While reading the original novels, we must implicitly make a similar imaginative leap to read scenes that on their face display outmoded if not frankly destructive sexual ethics as credible markers of their participants' respective moral worth. For *Pride and Prejudice* to work, Lydia's premarital sex—and before that, her much milder teenage flirtations—must be taken as a sign of her essential frivolity and corruption, meriting the scorn of her more respectable relatives and justifying, at least in part, Darcy's resistance to marrying Elizabeth. Similarly, if we are to accept Fanny as a heroine, we must regard her puritanical rigidity as evidence of laudable rectitude. Some readers of *Mansfield Park,* and likely even a few readers of *Pride and Prejudice,* have refused to make this cognitive move, and indeed, some novels may be so inextricably bound to such repugnant values as to practically and ethically preclude such readerly legerdemain.[7] Yet those who still read nineteenth-century literature with pleasure find a compromise. Without forgetting that the scene is actually about the moral perils of staging a vaguely risqué play for one's family and close friends, contemporary readers of *Mansfield Park*, I suggest, subconsciously replace the proposed entertainment with an alternative—if not necessarily a named or fully formulated alternative—we might more plausibly view as questionable. Substituting a generic notion of immoral behavior for the specific action, we can evaluate Austen's characters without betraying either the text or our own ethical sense. Without recourse to the YouTube adapter's sex tape, we formulate a subtler compromise that allows us to read past the actual content of troubling scenes and proceed *as if* we were reading a situation that justified the response to it.

The cases of the typographical error and the moral "mistake" are so common and our responses to them so automatic that they may escape our attention. A reader flummoxed by misspellings and outraged by each ingénue could not be much of a reader at all; whether moving past such faults requires us to change a letter or tart up a marriage plot, we will not find ourselves at a loss. What we are doing in these scenarios, however, is reading by proxy, replacing—in some cases quite literally—the actual word on the page with the one that might have been there. The version of the text we absorb, in which "might" is made "right" and so is Fanny Price, may be true enough to the spirit, but not to the letters of the text as written.

Such proxy readings arise from more than offended sensibilities. Formally, the problem we confront in reading *Mansfield Park* is that of a disjunction between story, defined as the events of the narrative, and plot, defined as the narrative work being performed by those events. Because the meaning of "story" and "plot" differ, not only in colloquial and critical usage, but in different critical contexts, my use of these terms requires further explanation. In ordinary conversation—or even scholarly conversation, outside of certain structuralist and narratological analyses—we often use the words interchangeably. Even some of the commonest uses of the terms, however, reflect more specific meanings; Hilary Dannenberg notes that one would never ask someone to "tell a plot," as we do to "tell a story" (*Coincidence and Counterfactuality* 6). Similarly, the term "marriage plot" has come to signify something more than "a story about marriage," referring rather to a particular nineteenth-century narrative model in which the ultimate end is an appropriate marriage that mediates between rising concern for individualism and conservative social consciousness. A concluding marriage alone does not constitute a marriage plot and can in fact work against its aims; in *Daniel Deronda,* our hero's choice of wife signifies his rejection of his English identity in favor of a spiritual patrimony.

The particular meanings taken on by "story" and "plot" in these cases mirror the two major schools of thought on the theoretical distinction between them. Following the Russian formalists Shklovsky and Tomashevsky, story and plot are sometimes used—with their close cousins story and discourse and *fabula* and *sjuzhet*—to distinguish between that which happens in a text (the "what" of a narrative) and the way in which that text is narrated (the "how" of a narrative). This definition proves especially relevant to discussions of narrative time, in which "story" refers to a series of events in chronological sequence, and "plot" signifies the order of events as they are related to us. In E. M. Forster's classic definition, however, story and plot are less the what and how than the what and *why* of a text: "'The king died and then the queen died,' is a story. 'The king died, and then the queen died of grief' is a plot" (*Aspects of the Novel* 86). For Forster, story represents the bare bones of narrative, while plot includes the ligaments, providing the explanations and interpretations that connect event to event.

In the work of later critics such as Greimas, Propp, and Todorov, Forster's definition evolved into a more comprehensive theory of narrative meaning. Shklovsky had been concerned with the "what" and "how" of narrative, and Forster with the "what" and "why." These critics distinguished instead between what a text was *about* and what a text was *doing*. The anthropologist Claude Levi-Strauss noted that while different myths might contain any number of distinct story events, many myths across cultures nonetheless share "deep structures" that underlie widely disparate sequences (*Myth and Meaning*). There are an infinite number of stories, but only a limited number of plots, created out of common cultural pressures that motivate the production of certain types of narrative discourses. A plot, in this sense, refers less to the particulars of an individual novel—in other words, the stuff of story—than to the work being performed by them. Vladimir Propp expressed a similar idea by categorizing each story event in a series of folktales according to one of thirty-one of what are in English translated as narrative "functions": Little Red Riding Hood's grandmother falling ill and Jack's family cow running dry of milk would be in Propp's framework two different story versions of the same archetypal plot event, in which the hero is sent on a journey or quest (*Morphology of the Folktale*). Levi-Strauss and

Propp focus their discussions on myth, but their paradigms apply to more recent narrative structures as well. The marriage plot, detective plot, and bildungsroman, each with its own associated set of stock events and characters, perform functions embedded in a specific culture with a need for its own dominant narrative forms.

Normally, story and plot operate in tandem. The narrative world of a novel, more complex than the pared-down one of myth, may accommodate story events that are not strictly necessary to the progress of the plot. Similarly, more intricately constructed novels may contain many plots, not all of which will be directly served by any given event; if a plot can generate multiple stories, so too can a story accommodate multiple plots. Yet none of these events amounts to a disjunction between plot and story: a comic vignette or pathetic tableau might be extraneous to a marriage or detective plot without undermining it. More often, major story events will perform double duty as plot agents. It is not terribly important to the "deep structure" of *Pride and Prejudice* whether Elizabeth hears that Darcy has denied Wickham a living or gotten him expelled from Cambridge, as either one or the other would serve the marriage-plot function of creating a misunderstanding between the novel's designated lovers.

The difference in the proxy narrative, and the source of the disappointment or uneasiness we often feel in encountering one, is that plot and story are instead working at cross-purposes, bifurcating the narrative into an actual plot (or, perhaps more accurately, actual *story*) that fails to satisfy the demands of textual meaning and a more compelling unwritten or "phantom" plot that is never allowed fully to materialize. Unlike events that are merely additional to the requirements of plot, these disjunctions occur at moments the text has highlighted as critically important. In some cases, the moment will occur at the very end of the novel, a placement that imbues the scene as written with narrative and thematic importance that it, in these instances, fails to live up to. In others, it will, as in *Lady Audley's Secret*, take the form of a scene of revelation that, after pages of expectation, turns out to be either (or both) inconsistent with the rest of the narrative or simply unworthy of the significance ascribed to it.

The problem that creates the proxy scene in *Mansfield Park* is extrinsic to the text, created out of the gap between the novel's values and that of its reader. Judged on its own terms, the novel itself is consistent: Fanny is a moral heroine, and as such, she resists the temptation of Mary Crawford and her wicked schemes. In the proxy narrative, however, the division between plot and story is, as we have seen in Lady Audley's Secret, embedded in and even highlighted by the text itself; Braddon is as aware of the inconsistency as any of her readers. This self-awareness raises an obvious question of motive: if Braddon sees the problem, why not fix it? Answering this question, however, will require beginning with a different line of inquiry involving, not what is present in the text, but what is being left out. What revelation *would* satisfy the plot of Lady Audley's Secret? Why don't we ever receive it? And, given that we do not, why does the novel nonetheless succeed in its apparent aims?

Seeing It Through

The revelation in Lady Audley's Secret is discordant because it satisfies, if only barely, the demands of story while ignoring the demands of plot. The story works, I should clarify, not because the diagnosis of Lady Audley's madness is a sensible turn of events, but because *everything* works on the level of story, which consists of sequence detached from meaning. It takes very little to turn "the King died, and then the Queen died" into a coherent plot, and some effort to do the same with "the King died, and then the Queen juggled seven quail eggs." Both, however, are stories, chains of events that need not display any particular logic at all. By this generous standard, the relative plausibility of Lady Audley's insanity scarcely rates a mention: a bereaved monarch's turn to ovi-dexterous displays demands an explanation; the discovery that an attempted serial murderer suffers from insanity *is* an explanation. In any case, with apologies to Collins and other champions of the form, complaining about the implausibility of a Victorian sensation novel is like complaining about the prurience of a work of pornography: the criticism is at once incontrovertibly valid and utterly misguided. Of course sensation novels are implausible; that is precisely the point.

It is plot that carries with it the burden of meaning, and it is on this level that Lady Audley's Secret threatens to collapse. The plot of the novel is a version of what Peter Brooks has identified as perhaps fiction's ultimate ur-plot: the "same-but-different" plot. A "same-but-different" plot operates through the replacement of an inappropriate relationship or set of circumstances with a more palatable equivalent: the heroine of the fairy tale

"All-Kinds-of-Fur," for instance, shares an incestuous bond with her father that is eventually redirected toward a legitimate marriage with her chosen husband (Brooks, *Reading for the Plot* 8–9). Robert Audley's quest, more than to unravel a mystery, is similarly to redirect aberrant passion to an appropriate channel—and, on the level of genre, to trade the psychosexual terror of the Gothic for the domestic compromise of the realist marriage plot. Robert's oddly triangulated relationship with his best friend's look-alike sister has invited queer readings of the novel, including Jennifer Kushnier's "Educating Boys to be Queer: Braddon's *Lady Audley's Secret*" (2002) and Richard Nemesvari's "Robert Audley's Secret: Male Homosocial Desire and 'Going Straight' in *Lady Audley's Secret*" (2000). Critics have identified in the novel as well a more pervasive gender and sexual anxiety grounded in both Lady Audley's monstrous femininity and Robert's conspicuously failed masculinity.[8] A nominally employed lawyer who never seems to have turned his energies to any worthwhile pursuit, Robert has persistently avoided romantic relationships, either with his lovely, available and blatantly interested cousin Alicia, or with anyone else. The first woman he shows an unwonted attraction to is Lady Audley, who, as his aunt by marriage, would be off-limits to him even before the mounting evidence of her crimes makes her a horrific sexual choice. The second, as noted above, is the sister of his close friend George Talboys, the missing first husband of Lady Audley, who appears to attract his interest partly because of her uncanny resemblance to her brother.

Considered in outline form, this plot, too, seems to function well enough, in the sense that it performs the work it needs to do. Clara Talboys is the perfect object toward which Robert's passions can be redirected: with a strong will to match Lady Audley's own and a face genetically predisposed to recall the halcyon days of homosocial Eton, she serves as a safe alternative to the dual threats of queerness and distorted womanhood. And, indeed, Robert does finally marry Clara; once Lady Audley has been dispatched to a private asylum and George resurrected to a reassuringly desexualized role in the family circle, Robert emerges as a successful husband and provider. As part of his transition to married life, we are told, Robert bequeaths his meerschaum pipe and French novels to a bachelor friend. If the former winks at the accessory's phallic potential, the latter entails both a more general dismissal of the erotic and a specific rejection of Lady Audley:

earlier in the novel, Robert tells George, ostensibly in jest, "I feel like the hero of a French novel; I am falling in love with my Aunt" (94).

Yet while both the story and the plot of *Lady Audley's Secret* may be in themselves viable, taken together, they reveal a profound mismatch. We might accept a story about a madwoman's crimes, or a plot about the regulation of sexual desire. *Lady Audley's Secret*, however, fails convincingly to link the two, instead merely suggesting the possibility of unwritten plots that might have done so. The novel draws on three familiar plot paradigms: beginning in the world of the Gothic romance, it takes a long detour through detective fiction before wrapping up in a neat marriage plot. Yet our expectations of each of the three models are disappointed or otherwise subverted. A Gothic romance, complete with forbidding mansion, monstrous beauty, and dreadful secret, might turn supernatural or it might not, but in either case, it would seem to call for more villainy, less mania, and a foe not so easily foiled by the expedient of quietly locking her away in a Belgian madhouse to die of natural causes. By the rules of the detective plot, Robert Audley should be following clues to a logical conclusion. If Lady Audley is to be revealed as mad, we should have some preparation for that eventuality; in the absence of any such hint, we would expect a solution that follows rationally from the evidence at hand. And according to the marriage plot, we should be reading a story in which Robert and Clara are our unquestioned leads, condescending to share space with a wicked aunt or absent brother without ever ceding their essential dominance.

None of these plots, however, quite materializes. Amateur detective Robert almost solves the case, but the climactic revelation catches him entirely by surprise, as well it might, given the total lack of clues to that effect, and abundance of evidence indicating quite the opposite. Clara Talboys assumes the role of heroine, but too belatedly and half-heartedly for the ending marriage to seem anything but perfunctory. For all her passionate dedication to avenging her brother, she actually does very little to bring Lady Audley to justice, and George turns out in any case not to require quite as much avenging as she had supposed. More seriously, her attachment to Robert, and his to her, must be accepted more or less as an article of faith, as the novel devotes minimal attention to establishing any real connection between the two. Robert claims, after one meeting with George's look-alike sister, to be thinking obsessively of her, but his thoughts of her reveal themselves always to be entwined with his obsession with another. This other is not George, but Lady Audley herself. While he gives due deference to the effect his investigation of his aunt might have on his elderly uncle, Robert ultimately frames his conflict over how far he should pursue the mystery of his friend's fate as a choice between Clara, who has exacted from him a promise to expose the truth, and Lady Audley: in a typical moment of indecision, he recalls "the pale face of Clara Talboys—that grave and earnest face so different in its character to my lady's fragile beauty" (290).

The connection occurs subconsciously as well. At one point, Robert wonders why he cannot fall in love with his cousin: "Why don't I love her? Why is it that although I know her to be pretty, and pure, and good, and truthful, I don't love her? Her image never haunts me, except reproachfully. I never see her in my dreams. I never wake up suddenly in the dead of the night with her eyes shining upon me and her warm breath upon my cheek, or with the fingers of her soft hand clinging to mine." "The more he tried to think of Alicia," the narrative continues, "the more he thought of Clara Talboys" (344). Robert's language, however, suggests that his thoughts have turned in a different direction. Lady Audley's "soft hands" are mentioned frequently enough for the words to have acquired the quality of an epithet, and Robert's portrait of a beautiful woman who steals into his room by night and "haunts" his dreams applies better to the succubus-like Lady Audley than to the stern, at times almost mannish, Clara. Robert contrasts the effect of his cousin, whose image haunts him only as a reproach, to the more pervasive visitations of this other woman. Yet almost without exception, whenever Robert thinks of Clara, it is precisely in the form of a reproach; each time he is inclined to stop his investigation, the thought of Clara's upturned face, imploring him to bring her brother's killer to justice, shames him into redoubling his efforts. Clara is as unlikely a contrast to Alicia on a logical level as she is on a semantic one. Robert wonders why he cannot love his cousin, who is "pretty, and pure, and good, and truthful," a description that, in the context of what follows, serves as the first of a series of implicit comparisons between Alicia and the other woman. But Robert has no reason to assume Clara is anything but pretty, pure, good and truthful, and little reason to torment himself for preferring another eligible woman to his cousin. The intensity of his guilt makes sense only if the alternative to Alicia is a far less acceptable choice than Clara Talboys.

If *Lady Audley's Secret*'s detective plot is incomplete and its marriage plot belated, we might assume that its dominant mode must then be the Gothic, where sensation trumps evidence, and happy endings arrive as afterthoughts to horror. Even here, however, the novel disappoints our expectations. The horror of *Lady Audley's Secret* is grounded primarily in a pervasive sexual anxiety. More than a vaguely sinister figure, Lady Audley, with her crimes against husband and hearth, draws on archetypal images of the monstrous woman, the Lilith or Lamia whose sexuality entices and then destroys. A climax that turns on a confession of madness cannot bear the burden of resolving pathological sexual anxiety.[9] As far as Lady Audley's erotic threat is concerned, the scene is rather an anticlimax: instead of addressing her monstrous womanhood, the novel nullifies it. Demoting its villain from succubus to hysteric, the text trades what has so far been its operative archetype of negative femininity for a neutered alternative; as a victim of inherited madness, Lady Audley inspires Robert's pity, rather than his horror, leaving the larger psychological stakes governing their conflict unaddressed. The monstrous woman is so frightening because she plays into more ordinary male neuroses about sexual emasculation and betrayal; the woman who literally castrates or kills her lover is different in degree, but not in kind, from the woman who cuckolds or jilts him. Uninterested in engaging with any kind of sophisticated psychology of madness, the novel's diagnosis of Lady Audley reframes her as a danger like any other, an external threat to be feared simply because she is capable of acts of unpredictable violence. As soon as she is removed from the scene, her potency evaporates: we may fear a rampaging lioness, but she doesn't haunt us.

Yet this facially inadequate story event proves nonetheless capable of performing its apparent plot function. Before the revelation scene, Robert remains a fundamentally emasculated figure, sexually immature, professionally rootless, indecisive, and perhaps unstable. After it, he is transformed, taking control of the arrangements for Lady Audley's confinement, supporting his broken uncle, and quickly establishing his own home and a successful legal practice. He has become, in other words, a perfectly inoffensive Victorian realist hero.

As in *Mansfield Park*, a problematic scene—although one problematic for a very different reason—succeeds to the extent that we are capable of reading it as a proxy for the phantom one that we miss. Lady Audley's madness is not enough to explain the complete overthrow of her psychological hold on both Robert and the narrative itself. The structure of the novel does suggest, however, the kind of scene that might have effectively combated her influence. Lady Audley, with her deceptive beauty and almost preternatural sexual power, evokes, not only the suggestive specters of the Gothic, but an older model of malignant femininity: the Lovely Lady, who in legend and folklore assumes the form of a beautiful woman before unmasking herself to her unsuspecting prey, often at the point of intercourse (Doniger, *The Bedtrick* 140–44). The most well-known use of the Lovely Lady trope in English literature may be Spenser's portrait in *The Faerie Queene* of Duessa, the witch who nearly woos the Redcrosse knight from his mission. Blind to her true nature even after several warnings, Redcrosse cannot escape from Duessa's thrall until his friends conspire to have the witch stripped, revealing, among other horrors, "her nether parts, the shame of all her kind / [which] my chaster Muse for shame do blush to write" (I.viii.48). This confrontation with Duessa's "nether parts" allows Redcrosse to redirect his wayward passions toward a more appropriate object; having conquered, in Duessa, a figure of repugnant female sexuality, he is free to pursue the conspicuously nonsexual Una, who represents the true Church in the poem's extended allegory. Transmuting Eros into a romance that is itself justified as a devotional act, the stripping of Duessa successfully replaces errant sexuality with decorous affection.

The confession scene in *Lady Audley's Secret* lacks the content, but replicates the function, of the archetypal stripping of the Lovely Lady. Even Spenser is coy about the precise appearance of his Lovely Lady's sexual organs, about which his pen blushes to write. In the Victorian novel, the need for concealment is far greater. Thackeray comments on this decorousness in what is perhaps the most well-known nineteenth-century invocation of the Lovely Lady trope:

> We must pass over a part of Mrs. Rebecca Crawley's biography with that lightness and delicacy which the world demands—the moral world, that has, perhaps, no particular objection to vice, but an insuperable repugnance to hearing vice called by its proper name. There are things we do and know perfectly well in Vanity Fair, though we never speak of them . . . In describing this siren, singing and smiling, coaxing and cajoling, the author, with modest pride, asks his readers

all round, has he once forgotten the laws of politeness, and showed the monster's hideous tail above water? No! Those who like may peep down under waves that are pretty transparent, and see it writhing and twirling, diabolically hideous and slimy, flapping amongst bones, or curling round corpses; but above the water-line, I ask, has not everything been proper, agreeable, and decorous, and has any the most squeamish immoralist in Vanity Fair a right to cry fie? When, however, the siren disappears and dives below, down among the dead men, the water of course grows turbid over her, and it is labour lost to look into it ever so curiously. (*Vanity Fair* 747–48)

What Thackeray describes, however tartly, is a simple matter of narrative tact: unable to say precisely what Becky has done, he nonetheless implies quite enough for a reader to get the general idea. In *Lady Audley's Secret*, we find a more radical disconnect between what Braddon narrates and what seems, in plot terms, to have taken place. Becky's sexual adventures, modestly obscured as they may be, are part of the textual actual world of *Vanity Fair*. By contrast, there is no stripping scene in *Lady Audley's Secret*; the actual plot of the novel rather involves the revelation of madness that does nothing, on its face, to address the erotic horror that suffuses the narrative. Nonetheless, this scene serves the narrative function of the unwritten one that *would have* addressed and resolved it. Everything that precedes Lady Audley's confession suggests that a sexual unmasking must occur. Everything that follows it suggests that such a scene has already happened. Madness, in other words, has become a proxy for the monstrous "nether parts" the text is unwilling to describe. Moving up the female body, Braddon replaces the vagina dentata with the hysterical mind, rewriting the tropes of romance in the language of realism.

This relationship between the proxy and the phantom scene may appear at first to be subtextual. But as the comparison with *Vanity Fair* will have suggested, subtext, which implies a layering of meaning, is not quite an accurate description of what is happening here. When, early in the novel, we learn that Robert is a confirmed bachelor and English public school graduate with a taste for Meerschaum pipes, these details may indeed indicate an unspoken subtext of homosexual inclinations: as Kushnier's article outlines, to someone with the right cultural context for understanding them, these details carry an additional significance, one that complements, rather than undermines, their plain meaning. The difference in the proxy narrative is that it involves two meanings that are rather mutually exclusive. Whatever else the act may signify, when we glimpse Robert puffing on his Meerschaum, we can also gather that he is, quite simply, enjoying a good smoke. A cigar can sometimes be more than a cigar, but it cannot, ordinarily, be *less*. But as the text takes pains to highlight, Lady Audley's madness cannot be accepted on the level of plain meaning; common sense and discursive logic alike revolt against the attribution of her crimes to insanity. Her madness is present and impossible; her sexual unmasking absent but essential. It falls to the reader to recognize both a given that cannot be denied and a hypothetical that ought not be, reading the confession scene both as itself and as the confrontation with demonic femininity that the scene's position in the Lovely Lady narrative suggests it should be. We must train ourselves, in other words, to see double, reading both the present absence and the absence present.

Why and Why Not

If the unwritten plot is, in the proxy narrative, in fact the primary source of narrative energy, why is it suppressed in the first place? Victorian censorship provides one obvious motivation. A nineteenth-century author could skirt the unsayable through implication, but also through replacement. In her description of Dorothea Brooke sobbing during her honeymoon in Rome, George Eliot chooses the former; the passage, with its talk of "quickening power" and ideas that "urged themselves on her with [an] ache," is both a generally applicable meditation on disillusionment and a veiled reference to a specifically sexual disappointment (183–84).[10] In the *Mill on the Floss*, by contrast, the illicit boat ride that seals Maggie Tulliver's doom can be read most logically as a stand-in for a more serious transgression. If the worst Maggie has done is linger on a boat and *not* have sex with her cousin's fiancé, the intensity of her guilt, which prevents her from pursuing any option that might ameliorate her social disgrace, is another instance of a penchant for martyrdom the text has consistently treated as misguided. The novel's apparent validation of Maggie's choice, killing her off in a drowning that is as purgative as it is tragic, in that case represents a formal disjunction. Reading the boat ride as a proxy for consummation solves the problem, rendering Maggie's crime a serious enough betrayal to require a sacrifice that is not simply an extension of the Pyrrhic self-flagellation of her childhood.[11] Nothing in Eliot's notes or letters provides insight into whether she had ever contemplated another version of the scene. But the insistence of her publisher, John Blackwood, that she transform a "loosely-hung, child-producing" woman into a "prolific, loving-hearted" one suggests that a fornicating heroine might indeed have been a step too far (Tillotson, "The George Eliot Letters" 68).[12] The boat ride thus becomes the equivalent of the structurally warranted scene; indeed, several contemporary reviews of the novel portray Maggie's transgression as a sexual fall without commenting on the actual circumstances of her brief elopement, a move that may suggest less about the exacting mores of the reviewers than about the scene's role in the text.[13] Censorship, however, is only the most obvious motivation for creating a proxy narrative. One of the more recognizable uses of proxy relationships is in cases of what René Girard and Eve Sedgwick have called triangular or triangulated desire, in which a character mediates unacceptable passion by deflecting it onto a third party. Sedgwick's use of the term, probably its most famous, focuses on cases in which the unacceptable desire is homoerotic and thus unable to be represented. But triangulated desire is more than a censor's dodge. Fear of the erotic is certainly part of the reason that Miles Coverdale ends Hawthorne's *Blithedale Romance* by confessing to his love of the innocent Priscilla when it has been obvious throughout that his attraction has been to her half sister, Zenobia, a far darker figure whose presumed sexual past drives Coverdale to titillated speculation. The suppression, however, occurs purely on the level of character; the subterfuge is not the text's coy subversion of enforced standards of decency, but Coverdale's own unwillingness to own up to his desire and all it implies. The motivation for the proxy staging is in this case part of, rather than—as in the case of censorship—opposed to, the internal dynamics of the text; Coverdale's lie is not an obstacle to be overcome by readers, but a weakness to be taken into account.

The logic that relies on a proxy plot for its fulfillment acknowledges the narrative centrality of the phantom plot even as it precludes that plot's realization within the actual world of the text. Despite the novel's air of Gothic throwback, Eva Badowska has written, *Lady Audley's Secret*, in common with other sensation novels, displays a conspicuous investment in—and anxiety over—the material and psychological conditions of modernity. This affiliation with the modern, I suggest, dictates as well Braddon's range of narrative possibilities. *Lady Audley's Secret* cannot stage a Spenserian stripping scene because it is a Victorian novel, but also because it is, for all its hybridity, finally a realist novel, concerned less with creating perfect unions than with coming to socially tenable compromises. The realist novel does not deal in hags and witches, sexualized or not; it exists outside the mythological context in which the exposure of a literally grotesque sexual organ could plausibly occur. Yet the loss of the landscape in which foul Duessas and treacherous Belles Dames might have unmasked themselves does not erase the cultural need that produced them; Robert Audley must do a Redcrosse Knight's work without benefit of sword or shield. The imagined stripping scene is psychologically necessary, but practically impossible. As such, it must and will be carried out—but only as an unwritten plot. Like a text containing a shadow-plot, the proxy narrative leaves the reader suspended between two scenes, one written, and one only suggested. Yet the latter is in the proxy narrative not quite as an *unrealized* possibility. Less than an actual occurrence but more than pure potentiality, the unwritten plot alternative in the proxy narrative *is* realized, albeit not on the level of story. Rather, it constitutes a phantom narrative created wholesale from the demands of plot, a necessary projection that fills the void left by an inadequate reality. Once conceived of, its significance not only rivals but actually surpasses that of the event it implicitly challenges: Lady Audley's madness is a silly piece of melodrama; the defusing of her sexual threat is the key event of the novel.

In the Victorian proxy narrative, as in the shadow-plot, a key element in the production of an unwritten plot is the pressure of realism. Something is gained in the rise of new forms, but something is lost as well. The hero of the bildungsroman longs for the open road of the picaresque; the urban reformer mourns the politically inert pastoralism he feels compelled to condemn. When the older form emerges as dominant, as it does in *Paul Clifford*'s abrupt turn from Newgate novel to comic opera, the reversal is a self-conscious act of dissent in which the desperation of the victory cry presages the transience of the triumph. Yet if the discarded plot may at times be regretfully jettisoned, its diminishing span of possibility granted and then exhausted, in other cases, what the generic cast-off requires is not a funeral but an exorcism. In this respect, the sensation novel, a genre formally committed to its own undoing, provides among the proxy narrative's most fertile ground. In *Lady Audley's Secret,* we have seen the formal problem posed by the sensation novel's movement from the Gothic horror plot to the marriage plot. In Wilkie Collins's *The Woman in White*, we find an even richer instance of the potential of the unwritten proxy narrative to negotiate between the two, serving the dual masters of discursive need and generic limitation.

Anne Catherick's Key

The structure of *The Woman in White*—the "best and best known" of all sensation novels, and the one that, more than any other, defined the genre as a distinct form—will by now be familiar to us (D. A. Miller, *Cage aux folles* 108). Like *Lady Audley's Secret*, the novel revolves around a secret—*the* Secret—that will render all the novel's mysteries plain. The word is used first by the feeble-minded Anne Catherick, who offers the Secret, portentously capitalized, to Laura Fairlie as the key to destroying her abusive husband, Sir Percival Glyde. When it is picked up by other characters, they retain Anne's peculiar emphasis; to Laura, to her sister, Marian, to her suitor, Walter Hartright, to Anne's calculating mother, to Sir Percival himself, it remains the Secret, singular and all-important. But, as in *Lady Audley's Secret*, the solution to the mystery, when it comes, is comparatively tame. The plot of *The Woman in White* revolves around the faking of a woman's death and her incarceration in an asylum under the name of a previously unknown half sister. It includes mysterious doppelgängers, Italian secret societies, and a sinister count frequently accompanied by white mice that shadow him like a witch's familiar. Yet the revelation that promises to crown this melodramatic tableau comes to us straight from the pages of no more lurid a document than a church's marriage registry: Sir Percival was born out of wedlock and is thus not the legitimate heir to the family estate. The horror of the murdering husband and his Svengali-esque adviser Count Fosco peters out into a question of primogeniture, while the plot of the novel reveals itself as an elaborate prelude to the marriage of Walter and Laura, the two blandest characters in it.

In Victorian England, of course, the illegitimacy of a firstborn son was no minor matter, and crimes have been committed for far measlier stakes than the potential loss of a baronetcy. The problem, once again, is with the revelation's place within this specific narrative world, one in which, I suggest, the question of *Sir Percival's* legitimacy is of comparatively little weight.

In any event, whether the Secret satisfies or betrays our most lurid desires, Anne Catherick, it turns out, never knew it. Having once overheard her mother threatening Sir Percival with an unspecified secret, she has repeated the warning, convincing the paranoid baronet that continued possession of his wealth and title depends on the silence of a dangerously unstable woman. The hysterical claim that drives so much of the narrative—Laura's, and then Walter's, search for the truth, Sir Percival's elaborate attempts to suppress it—is thus, in Anne's mouth, so much sound and fury, a mindless echo lacking sense or reference. There is a secret at the heart of this text—indeed, there are many—but the Secret as we first learn of it is an empty sign that readers and characters alike only mistake for meaningful content.

Superficially, Walter's discovery about Sir Percival's birth retroactively validates Anne's message: there is, in fact, a secret capable of giving Laura power over her abusive husband. Yet if the revealed truth ratifies Anne's previous claim, so, conversely, does the revealed fiction—her fabricated knowledge of the Secret—challenge the significance of that truth. For much of the novel, Collins has encouraged us to draw an equation between what turn out to be dissimilar quantities: Anne's presumed knowledge (the Secret) is the same as Sir Percival's actual Secret, which will be the key to both saving Laura and understanding previously obscure narrative events. The collapse of the link between the two secrets, however, calls into question everything that follows from it: if the claim that has propelled the narrative is without substance, where, finally, does meaning reside?

Not, it would seem, in Sir Percival's secret. Anne's Secret, the pure verbal form, is at least as important to the novel as the facts that, in the end, only incidentally corroborate her assertion. When Laura tells her sister Marian about her meeting with Anne, she considers whether the Secret "only exist[s], after all, in Anne Catherick's fancy." Marian, normally a far more trustworthy judge than Laura, dismisses the possibility on the basis of Sir Percival's cruel and at times unaccountable behavior: "I judge Anne Catherick's words by his actions—and I believe there *is* a secret" (286). But Marian's logic for once proves faulty. Sir Percival's illegitimacy explains very little of his behavior up to that point; the initial motivation for his actions is the fairly transparent one of relieving himself from debt by getting his hands on Laura's personal fortune through marriage. There *is* a secret, and Sir Percival *has* acted with great cruelty, but no causal relationship links these two facts. While Sir Percival's later belief that Laura has learned about the circumstances of his birth influences the subsequent course of the narrative, even then the particulars of his secret scarcely matter. Laura does not escape Sir Percival because she exposes the material fraud at the heart of their marriage, but because he dies in an attempt to conceal evidence of his crime. Any sufficiently damaging revelation will do: the novel's purposes would have been served just as well had Sir Percival, rather than Count Fosco, been secretly on the run from foreign assassins. Like Anne's illusory promise, the Secret itself matters more for the role it serves than the information it conveys, generating events that invest it with an importance its content, narratively speaking, never warranted.

Ultimately, for all the focus on the Secret, the energy of *The Woman in White* lies elsewhere: in the confrontation with the instability of human identity, in the challenge of finding an appropriate direction for one's desire, and, perhaps above all, in the exorcism of the Gothic potential that the Secret, for much of the novel, seems most forcefully to represent. The substance of the secret is far less significant than its function, driving a plot that finally has only a tangential relationship to what seemed to be its central element. And Anne Catherick's Secret, the mere outline of meaning, is not an unfulfilled promise, but a warning, cautioning us about what we miss when we mistake a red herring for a smoking gun.

Or, perhaps, a smoking gun for a red herring. In theory, Anne's supposed secret is an illusory screen on which characters and readers alike project their lurid fantasies, only to be checked by the revelation of a truth that deflates their romantic speculations. But the plots activated by both Anne's hints and the semantic associations surrounding the character cannot be so easily dismissed, to the point where the actual revelation reads as hollow and disappointing. In other words, *Anne's* Secret—the array of suggestive meanings drawn largely from the Gothic tradition—serves as the site of a series of unwritten plots that will, in this case, as in *Lady Audley's Secret,* be only nominally overwritten by the actual plot delivered by the disclosure of Sir Percival's. That secret, in turn, becomes a proxy for the ones that cannot be and are never written, the ones that *would* satisfy, not the vulgar curiosity of the sensation-seeking reader, but the discursive promises of a novel that, for all the reassuring domesticity of its conclusion, has been primarily concerned with anxieties more deep-seated than that of whether a particular English baronet does or does not deserve his inheritance.

Even in the late-eighteenth century, works in the Gothic tradition from which *The Woman in White* draws had become as liable to defuse as to indulge its most extreme impulses. A genre that had begun with a giant mystical helmet wreaking bloody vengeance on the false Duke of Otronto reached its pinnacle in the novels of Ann Radcliffe, which almost invariably concluded by providing rational explanations for apparently supernatural events. Over a half-century of realism later, the sensation novel trades off the Gothic tradition without fully participating in it. The two forms contain many of the same elements: the imperiled innocent and the lonely mansion, concealed identities and dastardly schemes. Yet in the sensation novel, the range of possibility becomes more constricted. In his preface to *The Castle of Otranto*, Horace Walpole gives himself carte blanche for all manner of "miracles, vision, necromancy, dreams, and other preternatural events" by citing the work's medieval setting: "Belief in every kind of prodigy was so established in those dark ages, that an author would not be faithful to the manners of the time who should omit all mention of them" (60). Typically located in foreign lands or long-ago eras, Gothic novels could escape the growing demands of realism: what happens in Udolpho stays in Udolpho and can be believed in so long as it does so. Relocating to contemporary England burdens the sensation novel with a different set of expectations. Ghosts do not walk in nineteenth-century England, for all that Anne appears before Walter as if "sprung out of the Earth or dropped from the Heaven" (26). Instead, the Gothic-inflected expectation of the otherworldly gives way to the now-familiar trappings of domestic realism, with its drive toward conformity and social reconciliation. The *Woman in White*'s premise is thus rife with Gothic potential that it will not and cannot carry out as it performs the taming work of the marriage and inheritance plots. The novel's structure, which consists of multiple characters offering "testimony" on the events leading up to Laura's marriage and presumed death, reinforces this generic indeterminacy by challenging the notion of stable textual forms: the record begun as epitaph becomes epithalamium; the marriage record that denies legitimacy can be manipulated to confer it, or destroyed altogether.

In this context, the Secret—comprehending both Anne's unfulfilled implications and the revealed truth of Sir Percival's identity—must be read primarily, not as a carrier of content, but as a mechanism of form, the device that effects the novel's transition from Gothic melodrama to Victorian domestic fiction. The question of Sir Percival's legitimacy or illegitimacy is accompanied by a variety of practical implications for Sir Percival but possesses no real narrative stakes. The novel does, however, raise a more pressing question of legitimacy that must be in some manner addressed before it can end as it does. Laura epitomizes the desexualized romantic ideal of Victorian domestic fiction, the object of a theoretical desire that is declared but never seems deeply felt. Walter professes his love for Laura, and we must take him at his word. Yet in the uncanny resemblance between Laura, the legless angel of Victorian romance,[14] and Anne Catherick, consummate figure of the Gothic, we see a version of the "same but different" trope that negotiates between acceptable and unacceptable desire. On the level of story, this likeness is practically necessary, enabling Sir Percival to fake his wife's death and imprison her in an asylum under Anne's name. On the level of plot, it is even more significant. If the marriage plot is to defeat sensation, it must first free Laura from the shadow of Anne, thereby legitimating Walter's desire. Underscoring the shift in narrative attention away from Anne and the Gothic toward Laura and the marriage plot, the paralleling of Anne and Laura permits the novel systematically to neutralize Anne's influence, not by destroying her, but by transforming her into the heroine of the Victorian novel.

Simply by virtue of her role as the first unrelated woman encountered by the hero of a nineteenth-century novel, Anne generates what will turn out to be an unwritten plot, entering *The Woman in White* as a presumptive romantic possibility. This first meeting, in which Anne appears before Walter at night on a deserted road, dressed all in white and raving about a man who has betrayed her, evokes the melodramatic and the supernatural, but it also hints at the potential for sexual scandal and, perhaps, danger. Walter protests that, appearances aside, "the grossest of mankind could not have misconstrued her motive in speaking, even at that suspiciously late hour and in that suspiciously lonely place" (27). Yet this attempt to preempt the reader's suppositions is itself an acknowledgment of the scene's erotically charged nature, which extends beyond the possibility of prostitution. The mysterious woman who accosts young men on the road calls to mind Keats's perilous Belle Dame, or—as in the case of Lady Audley—even older destructive female archetypes. More prosaically, the most logical inference to draw from Anne's vague accusations against a baronet is that the man has, in all probability, taken advantage of his position to seduce and ruin this desperate young woman. It is worth noting here that while this proves not to be true of Anne, by the time Walter marries Laura, she will, of course, have been victimized sexually by Sir Percival; in this case, the phantom plot, in which Anne is indeed the victim, carries the burden of suggesting the largely unacknowledged experiences of Laura. At the end of the novel, Laura can still occupy the narrative role of virginal bride rather than mature and perhaps even compromised woman in part because her actual ordeal can be displaced onto the double who merely appears to have undergone it.

When Laura herself enters the narrative, it is immediately clear that she is being primed for the role of Walter's romantic interest and, consequently, the novel's putative heroine. Neither in the reader's mind nor Walter's, however, can she escape her association with the double who has preceded her. In the most obvious sense, Walter cannot confess his immediate attraction to Laura without implicitly acknowledging the far more threatening sexuality of Anne. The more time he spends at Limmeridge, the more forcefully he is impressed by the wealth of connections between them: Anne Catherick, he learns, grew up at Limmeridge and developed her mania for white clothes from Laura's mother, while Laura's betrothal to a baronet brings to mind Anne's enemy of the same rank. "Was there no possibility," Walter wonders after yet another "chance reference" linking the two, "of speaking of Miss Fairlie and of me without raising the memory of Anne Catherick, and setting her between us like a fatality that it was hopeless to avoid?" (77). The question is the central one of the novel: the issue of whether Walter can save Laura from Sir Percival is ultimately secondary to that of whether the erotic possibility activated by Anne can be successfully transferred to an almost sexually void fulfillment with beautiful, banal Laura.

The existence of a third principal woman reinforces this pattern of substitutions. Marian Halcombe, Laura's legitimate half sister, is in all ways but one a more promising candidate for the role of heroine; indeed, for all intents and purposes she *is* the heroine, except in her failure to marry the hero. While Laura remains to the end a passive doll characterized by little more than a rather insipid sweetness, Marian proves resourceful, brave, and witty, serving a crucial role in foiling Sir Percival's and Count Fosco's designs. Structurally, however, Marian is superfluous: though Walter gratefully gives her the literal last words of the narrative, she is finally relegated to life as a third wheel in his and Laura's relationship, a permanently designated godmother and maiden aunt to Walter Junior. Although Collins gains a slight logistical advantage in giving Laura and Walter a confidante, particularly once Laura's marriage has exiled Walter from the main events of the novel, most of her role could be either taken over by Walter or mooted by giving Laura a more active role in her own story.

The natural corrective to the imbalance between Laura's formal and Marian's actual prominence would be to combine the two into a single woman, a bold and intelligent heroine who could be both wife and partner to Walter. U. C. Knoepflmacher, however, has suggested that Marian is important precisely as the putative heroine of the novel's "counterworld," a space in which Victorian proprieties collapse into frank acknowledgment of the baser impulses that underlie such pretensions of civility. In this shadowy world, the hero to Marian's heroine would be, not the comparatively dull and conventional Walter, but the villainous Fosco, an Italian aristocrat whose manipulations of legal and social forms expose the hypocrisies of English society. In this reading, the superiority of Fosco to Walter is sealed by the former's open admiration of and attraction to Marian, a sharp contrast to the disgust her physical qualities inspire in Walter. At their first meeting, Walter's initial impression of her figure as she approaches leads him to expect a beautiful woman. Immediately afterward, he meets with a startling disappointment: "The lady is dark.... The lady is young.... The lady is ugly!" (37). In a reversal of Thackeray's image of Lovely Lady Becky Sharp, whose monstrous lower body, but not her angelic countenance, must be concealed beneath the waves, Marian offers a frankly sensuous body betrayed by a disturbingly masculine face that eliminates her as a romantic possibility. As a romantic possibility, but not, as Fosco's response suggests, as an erotic one. Walter, bound to an ethic in which passion must be sublimated into the desexualized aesthetic appreciation of romance, cannot acknowledge his desire for a woman whose appeal must remain erotic; Fosco, suffering from no such false consciousness, persists in his attraction.

Collins, whose own personal life was resolutely unconventional, may, as Knoepflmacher surmises, have regarded Fosco and Marion, rather than Walter and Laura, as his natural allies.[15] Yet the novel itself treats Walter's marriage to Laura as an ideal outcome that has the effect of assuaging the sexual anxieties that have dogged Walter throughout. These anxieties can be seen in both his extreme response to Marian's appearance and in his more enduring discomfort over the resemblance between Laura and Anne who, we later learn, is also a half sister of Laura's. Walter's description of Laura focuses almost exclusively on her face, the same attribute he finds so hideous in Marian. His dismissal of Marian as an object of desire carries some of the same defensiveness we find in his preemptive refutation of any improper inferences the reader might draw about Anne. Through his excessive reaction against Marian, he defuses the force of his initial attraction and quickly attaches himself to a woman whose appeal is aesthetic rather than sensual. Anne, in her similarity to Laura, presents a more vexing problem: as long as both women live, Walter can never be quite sure that his pure and innocent beloved is not the madwoman who approached him one night like a streetwalker or lamia, raving about a man who had wronged her. As with Spenser's Fidessa and Duessa, the horror of the doubled woman lies in the possibility that the apparent virgin could take off her clothes and reveal the monstrous—or, perhaps more dangerously, arousing—"nether parts" of a less virtuous simulacrum.

Marian does more, however, than highlight the tension between Laura and Anne. Possessing the outline of a beautiful woman while remaining—to Walter, at least—essentially unattractive, Marian embodies the possibility of disparity between form and substance. Her role in the novel is determined by a version of this disparity: the story that would be served best by the active but sexually proscribed Marian must give way before a plot that requires the victory of legitimate desire. While a composite heroine combining the qualities of both women might have satisfied both story and plot, dividing Marian from Laura clarifies and purifies the function of the latter. As in a Freudian act of psychological splitting, Walter's—and perhaps the novel's—own inability to cope with ambivalence manifests itself in the separation of what should be one woman into two: the intelligent and sexually charged Marian acts, while Laura remains the virtuous, pure, and, above all, safe object of decorous romantic fulfillment. More symbol than woman, Laura is reduced to her generic function as the domestic ideal capable of combating Anne's Gothic threat.

While the novel establishes a number of substantive links between Laura and Anne, the most significant connections between them lie likewise below the level of story, arising from a series of more diffuse verbal and psychological associations that precede any more tangible knowledge. The information that Laura is to be married to a baronet reminds Walter of Anne's accusations against a man of that rank who has betrayed her.

Of course, this connection will prove to be more than a free-associative blending; Sir Percival is in fact both Laura's intended husband and the man responsible for Anne's plight. Yet the retroactive validation of Walter's musings does nothing to diminish the force of the initial, unsupportable suggestion: Walter himself admits that "judging by the ordinary rules of evidence, I had not the shadow of a reason, thus far, for connecting Sir Percival Glyde with the suspicious words of . . . the woman in white" (80). In this case and others, ultimate confirmation merely corroborates what Walter seems instinctively and at times unconsciously to have known. He makes the connection between Laura's intended and Anne's baronet before he has even verified that Sir Percival is a baronet, rather than (as would be far more likely) a knight. More strikingly, his first linkage of the two women occurs before he has seen Laura at all. Falling asleep the night of his encounter with Anne, he wonders whom he shall dream about: "the woman in white? Or the unknown inhabitants of this Cumberland mansion" (36). Before the story has brought them together—as childhood playmates, as twin victims of Sir Percival, as half sisters—Walter's subconscious has done so, establishing a connective thread that precedes and perhaps surpasses the events of narrative. On the level of language, words serve both as referential signs and as discursive forms whose function operates independently of their content. In his first meeting with Anne, Walter tries to coax the mysterious woman into an explanation of her plight by "lift[ing] the veil that hung between [them]" (31). But when a veil is finally lifted many pages later, it reveals, not Anne, but Laura, who appears before Walter at her own supposed grave, garbed in clothes that recall both Anne's eccentric attire and Walter's metaphor. The veil is a tangible object *and* a component of a metonymic chain that would do the work of linking Anne to Laura, the shroud to the wedding dress, whether or not the image were embodied in the form of two white-clad women.

This privileging of the intuitive and the associative over more conventional paths to meaning points to the novel's larger generic problems. At its end, as I suggest, the novel will suppress its Gothic plots in favor of belated turn toward realism. But before this moment, the dynamic between the two has been the reverse. Like *Lady Audley's Secret*, *The Woman in White* is, at least putatively, a type of detective narrative, setting an amateur sleuth the task of unravelling an all-consuming mystery. Yet, as Ann-Marie Dunbar has noted in her comparison between the two novels, ordinary evidentiary standards ultimately prove in both texts to be inadequate to solving the case. The methodologies of conventional realism fail to account for the affective and instinctual logic of the sensation novel, a truth crystallized in the need to turn to a culprit's confession, rather than the detective's deduction, to finally solve the mystery (98).[16] These final revelations, in other words, cannot help but be inadequate because they are placed generically in conflict with the very logic that should have produced a narratively satisfying conclusion. In *The Woman in White*, this leads to an especially complex play of genres that leaves permanently unsettled the hierarchy between actual and unwritten plot. The affective logic of the novel's Gothic plots persistently subverts Walter's efforts at realist detection. The answer he fails to deduce, however, is composed precisely of the stuff of realism, forcing us to read past the legalistic content of the revelation if we are to find a resolution as well to the Gothic energies that have produced it.

Seen in this light, the Secret becomes far less of a disappointment. On one level—the level of story—it refers to the real fact of Sir Percival's illegitimate birth. On another—the level of plot—it is rather a point on which the novel's generic tension pivots, the nexus between the melodramatic promise of its unwritten plots and the domestic fulfillment of its actual one. The revelation consists of the material of the inheritance plots of Dickens or Trollope but is surrounded and formally enabled by the elements of the eighteenth-century Gothic—the ghostly encounter, the forbidding mansion, uncanny intuitions that override our rational faculties. It *tells* of a legal deception surrounding Sir Percival's identity, but it *suggests*, by virtue of its structural position within a previously dominant Gothic narrative, the answer to a central question about Anne's identity, one that has never been fully articulated: can Laura escape from the threat of Anne? For a time, the answer seems to be no. Even when it is discovered that Laura has survived and Anne been buried under her name, the Laura who emerges is indistinguishable from Anne: dressed in white, weakened both physically and mentally by her ordeal, she reveals herself from beside her own grave, as if in fulfillment of the vain supernatural promise of Anne's initial appearance.

Yet if a woman in white can be a ghost, she can also be a bride. The horror of Anne, of Marian, has never really been the feeble mind or the ugly face; the fear we ascribe to terror of the supernatural or the monstrous is really fear of the unnatural and the perverse. In the fairy tale or the allegory, the perverse must be transformed into legitimate desire, the acknowledged passion for the dangerous beauty converted into a wiser love of a better woman. In domestic fiction, the erotic is legitimized past the point of desire entirely. Walter's first meeting with Marian enacts a version of the archetypal stripping scene that annihilates, rather than redirects, desire: he confronts, not monstrous nether parts, but an ugly face that relieves him from the need to acknowledge the sexual possibility created by their meeting. Sir Percival's illegitimacy ultimately serves a similar function in the diffracted same-but-different plot that is Anne's gradual replacement with Laura. To allow that plot to play out on the level of story, to take on directly the implicit fear that Laura might be just as compromised as Anne appears to be, would require an acknowledgment precluded by the very genre such a plot strives to enable. Both the fantastic trappings of the Gothic and its erotic energy must be purged and displaced. Instead, the question of legitimacy is transferred from the erotic to the legalistic realm: in the proxy plot of the novel, as opposed to the phantom plots that continue to surround it, Sir Percival's identity, rather than Anne's or Laura's, comes into question, and the removal of his presence, rather than Anne's, is made the necessary precondition to the union of Laura and Walter. Not only Sir Percival's secret, but his entire role in the narrative has been on some level a mechanism for representing and attempting to resolve an otherwise unspeakable tension. Only by reading the actual revelation of his illegitimacy as, on some level, a proxy for the impossible, necessary revelation that would affirm Laura's total freedom from the Gothic taint can the realist marriage plot be saved.

In the wake of Sir Percival's death, the relationship between the living woman in white and the dead is stripped of its last vestige of the uncanny: Anne, we learn, was Laura's illegitimate half sister, the product of an affair between her father and a servant. The disclosure demystifies the likeness between them, but it also formalizes Anne's displacement and Laura's ascendancy; Laura, the trueborn and pure, need fear nothing from the pitiable, forlorn pretender who, in this version of their story, becomes clearly an ersatz rather than possible self. In either case, the children of Laura and Walter will be free from such shadows. The novel ends, not at the point of Laura and Walter's marriage, but some months after the birth of their son. In the final scene, Marian brings the child—named, naturally, Walter Jr.—to his father and asks him if he knows who the child is. For a moment, it seems that the old confusion over identity has resurfaced in another form, but Marian does not leave us in suspense for long: Mr. Fairlie, Laura's uncle, has died, and little Walter is now the rightful heir of Limmeridge. The uncanny normalized and the Gothic banished, the novel can conclude as a domestic drama governed by the salutary strictures of the marriage and inheritance plots.

The banality of Sir Percival's secret is not a failure; it is a sacrifice. A structural proxy for the melodramatic revelation Anne, and the novel itself, have taught us to anticipate, the secret exists within a Gothic world of charged sexuality, foreign menace, and radically unstable identities but deals in the realist language of wills and legacies. As a response to the novel's thematic energies, this substitution is on some level so inadequate as to promote, rather than cut off, the play of phantom possibilities. If Sir Percival is not, indeed, Sir Percival, then neither is Laura Lady Glyde, suggesting once again the deeper questions about her identity. Is she Anne or Laura, the otherworldly woman of lonely roads and nighttime meetings, or the virgin bride risen uncorrupted from the Gothic tomb to her marriage bed? The novel tells, and does not tell, leaving us, even in the midst of the fulfilling tableau out of sentimental romance, with the only half-resolved tensions of realist compromise. We will say that Laura is innocent, and her second husband's son the rightful heir, and only spare a passing thought for the clever aunt with the alluring body and the never-acknowledged one buried, for all we know, with another and a truer secret all her own.

But to the extent that even this uneasy peace is possible, it is by the replacement of Anne's Secret, whatever it was, or wasn't, or could have been, with Sir Percival's. By solving the latter, Collins has effectively neutralized the former, filling the space that might have been occupied by a fuller reckoning with the novel's Gothic plot with a realist proxy that enacts structurally what the Victorian novel cannot bring itself literally to address. We may be thrilled by the melodrama of the sensation novel and compelled by the psychologically evocative landscapes of the Gothic, but the domestic fulfillment toward which the text strives requires that these plots finally remain unwritten in the name of order and sentiment. "The way to the Secret," Walter reasons well before the revelation scene, "lay through the mystery . . . of the woman in white" (459). The reverse, however, is more accurate: the way to the woman in white—and, consequently, *The Woman in White*—leads through the Secret, for "woman in white" is itself a phrase that encodes the novel's pervading problem of reference, seeming, at first, clearly to refer to one woman but ultimately expressing the confusion between, not only two women, but the genres that contain them. We go to the church, where the fateful marriage record is kept, still uncertain. But the revelation that takes us in a moment from the Gothic to the domestic, from the graveyard to the probate court, settles it at last. Laura, and not Anne, or even Marian, is to be the heroine of the piece, the only woman who can successfully fulfill the promise of the revealed secret and complete the marriage plot.

The plots of the proxy narrative exist at the border of the actual and the unwritten. Written, they may exist only to be discounted as unworthy of the struggle that produced them; unwritten, they must be read back into the text that yearns for the very consummation from which it abstains. The sensation novel, which more than any other Victorian form resists the realism it finally affirms, is a natural home for the proxy plot because it effects a transformation that can be neither fully believed nor fully denied: we are told one Secret, but learn the lesson of another, one that no madwoman ever betrayed or marriage plot quite resolved. The next chapter continues the discussion of the proxy narrative with a turn to the novels of Henry James, which exist at another kind of border. The last Victorian or the first modernist, living in England but resolutely American, James found in the proxy narrative a fitting structure for a novelist who meant most when he said nothing at all.

3

"A Thing Quite Other than Itself"

Henry James and the Proxy Narrative

In 1904, *Life* magazine printed a brief parody of Henry James's *The Ambassadors*. Written in long, clause-strewn sentences ("The reader was, even then, although scarcely, as yet, consciously, arrived at that point"), "'The Ambassadors: A Question'" sees a frustrated reader of James contemplating throwing his book into the fire and wondering, in his own James-inflected fashion, "After all . . . why not, without periphrasis, lucidly, in English" (22)? Its author, the literary critic J. B. Kerfoot, had voiced similar complaints in his review of the novel the previous month, criticizing *The Ambassadors* for its dense writing, thin plot, and lack of "actual denouement." Yet Kerfoot's review was no hatchet job. Far from panning the novel, Kerfoot was ultimately enthusiastic, even effusive in his praise, ensuring his audience that for all its faults, *The Ambassadors* nonetheless "leaves [the reader] . . . aglow with the enthusiasm of a perfect art" (604).

Modern scholars, more likely to praise than to condemn both the prose and the plotlessness of James's works, have largely corroborated Kerfoot's final analysis of the novel while rejecting the preceding qualification. One element of the original criticism, however, still stands. In context, Kerfoot's claim that *The Ambassadors* has "no actual denouement" may be referring only to its failure to answer, except prospectively, the central question of whether Chad Newsome will return to his family business in Woollett, Massachusetts, or remain with his mistress in Paris. Yet the scene that does serve as the "actual denouement" of the novel, such as it is, has presented a far more enduring textual difficulty. Strether's refusal, on rather strained ethical grounds, of Maria Gostrey's tacit marriage proposal seems to represent a backsliding into the narrow New England moralism he has spent the novel learning to reject. At the same time, it seems narratively fitting that Strether should end the novel by asserting, even at great cost, a private moral code distinct from the values systems of both New England and Europe. We arrive, then, at a contradiction. The notion of a final renunciation is, to borrow Strether's own language, "right"; the precise form that renunciation takes is altogether wrong. It provides little enough resolution that Kerfoot can call it no ending at all, but satisfies so completely as to leave him radiant with joy at its perfection. It does what it needs to while doing the most incongruous thing possible. It is, in other words, the proxy narrative at its finest.

The Citizen of the World

Despite living in England for decades and publishing most of his works during the reign of Queen Victoria, Henry James is the obvious outlier in this book. No matter how long he lived in Europe, James could never be anything but an American abroad. It is not only that he writes so often *about* Americans abroad, constantly calling attention to the difficulties of assimilation. Rather, it is that he simply does not write like a Victorian novelist. His closest literary ancestor is Hawthorne, American romanticist par excellence. At his worst, he can be guilty of crude allegory (he names the hero of *The American* Christopher Newman); at his best, he still often trots out his characters as types and functions: Dickens had minor characters; James gives us *ficelles*.[1] He has scarcely any interest in contemporary political or social issues, *The Bostonians* and *The Princess Casamassima* being exceptions that prove the rule, and almost as little in the material details of realist fiction: as Mary McCarthy observes in *Ideas and the Novel*, James manages to write an entire novel (*The Spoils of Poynton*) about a dispute over antique furniture without bothering to describe the furniture in any detail (3–4).

Above all, he is not a plotter—or, to be consistent in my terminology, what I should call a "storyist." If we were to judge by summaries alone, James's narratives, full of subtle schemes and shifting allegiances, might seem byzantine, far more intricate than those of the Victorian novels he famously referred to as "loose baggy monsters" (*The Art of the Novel* 84). But for James, the story is rarely the point. Even in his more conventional early career, events are not themselves as important as the responses to them; his works are dramas of consciousness in which whatever scenario he engineers serves the purpose of forcing characters into a moral crisis or intellectual awakening. In *The Princess Casamassima*, the prompt is radical politics; in *What Maisie Knew*, it is a custody battle; in many others, it is some romantic complication or another, but in almost any case, the particulars are less important than the quest of an individual mind to achieve cognitive and ethical maturity. It is perhaps for this reason that James was a notoriously poor playwright, and why the play turned into the most successful film adaptation of a James novel, William Wyler's *The Heiress* (1949), had the good sense not to call itself *Washington Square*.

James nonetheless demands inclusion in any discussion about Victorian unwritten plots. On the most basic, thematic level, he is preoccupied with missed opportunities and paths not taken. His characters are haunted (on occasion, literally) by the thought of the lives they have not, but might once have, lived. Spencer Brydon and John Marcher, Ralph Touchett and Milly Theale—whether the chance is squandered in blindness or denied by death, their stories are suffused with the wistful melancholy of a sense of promise unfulfilled. To the extent that his novels do engage in conventional plotting, the outcomes of these plots often involve a struggle between competing narratives, each evocative of a recognizably novelistic paradigm. *Washington Square*'s Mrs. Penniman wants to turn plain, quiet Catherine Sloper's life into a melodrama; Catherine's father first denies that his daughter could have any narrative value at all, and then treats her relationship with fortune-hunting Morris Townshend as a species of romantic farce. Catherine herself behaves for a time as if she is the heroine of a marriage plot novel, but finally becomes a heroine at all only by rejecting such plots and plotters, refusing both the returned Morris and any other suitor who comes calling.

James's status as at once an American and an English writer heightens the sense of generic tension. One of the most resolutely American aspects of James's plotting is his virtual dismissal of the marriage plot; people don't get married very often in James's works, and when they do, it generally ends badly. Yet if James's heroes tend to wind up in a state of Leslie Fiedler-approved celibacy, the worlds they inhabit—even if only as visitors—seem constructed precisely for the drawing-room dramas of Victorian realism. Full of country estates, unexpected bequests, and plucky, attractive interlopers disrupting an established social order, James's works can be read as novels of manners, until the moment they veer off, like Catherine Sloper, on to a thoroughly unanticipated course.

But for protomodernist James, it is not just a particular generic paradigm—the Gothic, the sentimental, the picaresque—but the traditional plot itself that at times becomes the shadowy counterplot ever threatening, ever failing to emerge. Perhaps the prevailing sin in a Henry James work is attempting to force a person, whether oneself or another, into a fixed narrative role: Marcher wastes his life waiting for a conventionally dramatic destiny; Ralph Touchett wants Isabel Archer to play out a fantasy of independent American womanhood. Living in nineteenth-century worlds, these figures are representatives of a type that would become far more common in the twentieth. In the Victorian novel, the master plotter is, more often than not, a heroic figure, the benevolent old man who ties up all loose ends in the finale of a Dickens novel, the amateur detective who transforms evidence into narrative. The evil schemer is baffled by the good designer, who serves as an author-avatar capable of operating within the world of the story to bring a plot to fruition. By the rise of the modernist novel, however, asserting fixed meanings has become an increasingly futile, potentially perilous enterprise. Narrators are less omniscient and less confiding; the defining heroes of the age are wandering Jews whose journeys stall at Q with R just out of reach. In this world, the character who seeks to impose a sense of plottedness on his or her life must be either a tragic Quixote or a sinister puppeteer. The detective is reborn as a neurotic, if not an outright madman, and the grand designer becomes, at his worst, an egomaniacal monster bent on imposing a private will he mistakes for an externally validated master plot.

The uniqueness of James is that he adopts the sensibilities of modernism without abandoning the basic structure of the traditional novel. One of the hallmarks of the modernist novel is its relative de-emphasis of story. In place of a plot unfolding in time, it offers precisely what James so often does: extended portraits of consciousness that generate drama less from particular events than from crises of an embattled psyche. But James participates in this shift without appearing to do so. No reader could long mistake *Absalom, Absalom!* or *To the Lighthouse* or *Ulysses* for a traditionally plotted novel.[2] James, by contrast, leaves us with just enough of a consecutive story to provide the veneer of stable meaning. As conclusions go, "Verena and Basil elope" and "Strether returns to America" successfully complete their novels' respective plots in a way that "Molly Bloom has a spectacular orgasm" and "Ten years later, a supporting character paints a picture" do not. Modern readers of James, part of a highly self-selected group and with the benefit of over a century of received wisdom on his works, may see the essential strangeness of James's only superficially traditional plotting as self-evident. Yet it is telling that *The Turn of the Screw*, now considered a case study in modernist uncertainty, was read by a full generation of critics as a straightforward ghost story.[3] Like the works of sensation fiction discussed in the last chapter, it is nearly always possible to take a James novel at its word. As I began to suggest earlier, however, it is hard to escape a sense, in reading James, that the story is not enough, that the place toward which the text has directed our attention is perhaps the last in which we should be looking.

The proxy narrative is thus, to varying degrees, a consistent key to the riddles of Jamesian plotting. What I have been describing in James is precisely a disjunction between story and plot: it is not simply that there is an *additional*, subtextual meaning, but that there is an implied, nonstory realm of action for which the actual event or fact is, for one reason or another, a necessary proxy. In James, as in the sensation novel, the most obvious reason for the subterfuge is sometimes a socially imposed delicacy; *The Bostonians*, for instance, can scarcely be read rationally without attributing Olive's obsessive devotion to Verena to something rather more intense than political enthusiasm or platonic friendship. James's own presumed sexuality makes it especially tempting—and plausible—to read his works for signs of veiled homoerotic content, as Eve Kosofksy Sedgwick does in *Epistemology of the Closet*. Yet if there is a "queerness" to James's writing, it is perhaps the more pervasive one suggested by Kevin Ohi in *Henry James and the Queerness of Style*, a quality that, arising from a sense of doubleness and self-suppression, expresses itself in every elliptical phrase and representative dodge. Queer or not, this concealment is in any case undeniably strange, leaving the reader stranded, as James's own characters so frequently are, in a conversation whose frame of reference is but half-understood.

This chapter discusses two late James novels, *The Wings of the Dove* and *The Ambassadors*. Both novels have generated notably persistent critical problems. In *The Wings of the Dove*, it is the mystery of Milly's illness, and in *The Ambassadors*, the merits of Strether's sacrifice. These problems, I argue, can be addressed by proxy readings that identify in the very difficulty of these problems a potential key to their resolution. I begin with *The Wings of the Dove*, a text that, perhaps more than any other by James, suggests why in the world he can never quite, without periphrasis, play it straight.

The Matter with Milly

Milly Theale's illness in *The Wings of the Dove* is nonsensical as a real physical malady.[4] Its manifestations are plain enough to send Milly—whose subsequent behavior suggests she would have been content enough with denial, if denial had been possible—to a doctor, but not so severe as to require any prescription beyond "be[ing] happy" and making periodic doctor's visits that seem to double as social calls (428). Luke Strett, the eminent physician she consults, declines even to call her condition "a case" (427), but does not hesitate nonetheless in taking it. Her complaint is not, he tells Milly's companion Susan Stringham, the disease Milly had initially feared, but whatever it is, it is serious enough to leave Susan visibly shaken after he reveals it to her in an off-page visit. When the malady proves fatal, circumstances suggest a psychological, rather than medical, cause; Milly "turn[s] her face to the wall" after learning that Densher, who has passed himself off as her suitor, has been secretly engaged to Kate all along (581). Yet Milly begins visibly to decline before any obvious psychological trigger has presented itself, and it is in any case impossible to imagine James at the height of his talent doing anything so crude as having his heroine die of a broken heart.

The simplest course here would be for James to suggest that Milly is suffering from an actual illness that also reflects a psychological condition or, in what has become the prevailing critical reading of the novel, that her disease is a symbol of a more pervasive spiritual malaise. "Although the novel's very plot can be enacted only by virtue of the other characters' conviction that Milly does suffer from a fatal illness," writes Virginia C. Fowler, "equal importance is placed, in part through the mysterious and ambiguous treatment of her disease, on the spiritual deficiency that unfits Milly for life" ("Milly Theale's Malady of Self" 58). Thomas Mann had, a year earlier, done something similar in *Buddenbrooks*, in which the child Hanno's death is, like Milly's, a metaphorically resonant tragedy presented in the language of conscious surrender—but one that also has quite a lot to do with a severe case of typhoid fever. Even had James been loath to put something as vulgar as a name to Milly's illness—or to constrain his own representation by using a known disease with an established progression and prognosis—he could have suggested that Strett was simply humoring a dying woman with his cheerful assurance that there was nothing to prevent her from living a full and healthy life. Instead, James takes pains to exclude this possibility by having Susan repeat the doctor's bizarrely contradictory assurances to a third party while Milly is not present. James's purposes, then, evidently require specifically that Milly be physically ill with an ailment in which it is nonetheless impossible to believe.

This paradox reflects a larger tension in the novel. If Milly is suffering from cancer or tuberculosis, her death is the result of a grossly material cause, her body's undeniable betrayal the ultimate mockery of any attempt to assert a self beyond the physical. If she is not, then it is rather a confirmation of a refined spiritual sensibility that cannot long survive in a world of the vulgar real. But whatever the nature of her illness, the problem of Milly Theale's life has always been the gap between the material world she inhabits and the spiritual one to which she seems more properly to belong. For no immediately apparent reason, everyone adores Milly Theale. Susan Stringham wants to be her mother; Kate Croy her best friend, all of London, it would seem, her confessed and worshipful admirer. Yet one cannot help the suspicion that the source of this general fascination with Milly may be no more after all than the fact of her great wealth. Certainly, this proves true of Kate, who, secretly engaged to Densher but too poor to marry him, convinces Densher to woo the dying Milly so that she will leave him her money when she dies. Even as disinterested a party as Susan, however, who claims to see in Milly a "strangeness" that escapes the notice of less penetrating consciousnesses, must confess "the truth of truths that the girl couldn't get away from her wealth" (145). In the face of that admission, protestations to the contrary become hollow: "She had as beneath her feet a mine of something precious. She seemed to herself to stand near the mouth, not yet quite cleared. The mine but needed working and would certainly yield a treasure. She was not thinking, either, of Milly's gold" (150). Language undoes Susan's noblest intentions; while she has no desire to exploit Milly for personal gain, her conception of her is on some level inseparable from her awareness of her fortune. She need not think consciously of Milly's gold, for to think of Milly herself is at once to invoke that consciousness, to start dreaming in a vocabulary of mines and treasure. Milly is fascinating for her money and her beauty, for being an orphan and for being an

American, for her picturesque illness and approaching death, for anything but what transcends the bare facts of her material existence.

In this sense, death is the only possible solution for Milly, because it is only by ceasing to exist at all that she can overcome the burden of her own materiality; within the world of the realist novel, the spiritualized possibilities that she perceives herself and awakens in others are doomed to remain unwritten. Death is, as the writer Stephen Koch expresses it in an early critical study of the novel, "Transcendence in *The Wings of the Dove*," both apotheosis and betrayal, the single, self-annihilating means by which she can fulfill the symbolic potential that everyone ascribes to her, and in which she herself has come to believe (94). Long before she learns of Densher's treachery, Milly's fate is determined when she accepts Kate's image of her as a dove. Kate, who will prove herself to be the basest of the novel's major characters, gives her the name primarily to deflect an unintentionally revealing comment; in her mouth, the image is as empty as any of the vague words ("stupendous," "fascinating," "strange") that have already been used inadequately to describe Milly's appeal. Milly, however, embraces the title: "It was moreover, for the girl, like an inspiration: she found herself accepting as the right one, while she caught her breath with relief, the name so given her. She met it on the instant as she would have met the revealed truth; it lighted up the strange dusk in which she lately had walked. *That was what was the matter with her. She was a dove. Oh, wasn't she?*" (301).

"Truth" is a loaded word here, hearkening back to the "truth of truths" that is the undeniability of Milly's wealth. Potentially, this truth is an antidote to the other, a spiritual replacement for a rejected material identity. Yet if it is, it can only be a self-annihilating one. The crucial difference between "dove" and the other terms used to describe Milly is that it is a metaphor rather than an adjective. A "stupendous" Milly is, after all, still Milly; the word is so imprecise as to be almost tautological: Milly is stupendous, but the only meaningful reference point for what is meant by "stupendous" is Milly herself. Milly the dove, by contrast, is no longer Milly at all. Significantly, Milly instinctively identifies the image of the dove with her condition, her illness becoming synonymous with a self-conception that stands opposed to the physical.

The novel's title reinforces the untenability of Milly's identification with the dove by insisting on the bird's own physicality. Metaphors allow us to choose our point of comparison, which, in this case, seems more likely to refer to a symbolic dove than to a real one: Milly is a dove, it would seem from Kate's usage, in that she is gentle or innocent. The passage from Psalms that inspires the novel's title likewise uses the dove and its wings as a metaphor for a desired escape, one that encapsulates Milly's desire for spiritual transcendence of her reality: "[If] I had wings *like* a dove, [I would] fly away" (Psalms 55:6, emphasis added). "The wings of the dove" takes us from metaphor to metonym and in so doing shifts the image to a point of specificity at which the original comparison collapses: a dove is a symbol, a wing is a limb. Both Densher and Kate try, at different times, to expand the metaphor to accommodate the dove's wings, but their efforts are self-serving and revert to the material realities that Milly wishes to use the image to transcend. This is explicit in Densher's reflection on Milly's dovelike qualities, in which he half-acknowledges the inappropriateness of his extrapolation before succumbing to its lure:

> Milly was indeed a dove; this was the figure, though it most applied to her spirit. But he knew in a moment that Kate was just now, for reasons hidden from him, exceptionally under the impression of that element of wealth in her which was a power, which was a great power, and which was dove-like only so far as one remembered that doves have wings and wondrous flights, have them as well as tender tints and soft sounds. It even came to Densher dimly that such wings could in a given case—*had*, in fact, in the case in which he was concerned—spread themselves for protection. (533)

Densher's sensibilities are poetic as he imagines Milly's wondrous flying wings spreading themselves protectively over him. Yet he cannot resist the comparison of these wings to Milly's wealth nor—in a chapter that ends with Kate proposing her plan for obtaining Milly's money—the fact that the "protection" involves using a feigned attraction to Milly as a pretext for gaining access to Kate without arousing the suspicions of her disapproving aunt. Imagery thus becomes a form of self-justification; if Milly is Densher's benevolent, quasi-mystical protector, she is not then his dupe and victim.

Much later, after Milly has died and left an inheritance to Densher despite having learned of his scheme, Kate makes similar use of the metaphor, describing Milly "stretch[ing] out her wings . . . [to] cover us" (710). By now, however, the significance of the image has changed, for Densher, if not for Kate. Even Kate seems slightly chastened, whether by the reality of Milly's death, the magnanimity of her final gift, or Densher's obvious discomfort with his part in the affair. But, like Densher in the previous scene, it is also in Kate's best interest to see Milly in this romantic light, which enables her both to see herself as justified and, more practically, to justify accepting the money. In any case, her interpretation of Milly's gesture is mistaken. However it appears to Kate, or even Densher, Milly's bequest is in effect, less a token of magnanimity than a tool of vengeance. Milly knows too well how little her money has ever done for her. She is not bestowing a gift, but passing on a burden, as indeed the inheritance proves to be. In his false pursuit of Milly, Densher had confirmed for her, in the most brutal way possible, what had until then been only an inchoate suspicion: that actual life could offer nothing to live up to the romantic possibilities before her, that she herself might be in the end no more substantial than any other precious, beautiful thing, to be coveted but never loved. In turn, she repays him in kind. Densher has from the beginning been uneasy about the plot, which he could excuse only through his devotion to Kate. Indeed, he elevates it almost to an obligation: the only way he will consent to the deception is for Kate to prove her sincerity by agreeing to consummate their relationship, which he perhaps does less out of a desire to bind her to him than of a need to bind himself to her. If he "owes" her, he cannot help but carry out her design. By leaving Densher the money, Milly thus confirms, in the most brutal way possible, the transparent crassness of their actions, and of their relationship itself. Like his own treatment of Milly, Densher's relationship with Kate has been, in the end, all about the money.

The irony is that, at least as far as Densher's feelings toward Milly are concerned, this is not ultimately true. By the end of the novel, at which point there can be no hope of gain, he does love her. There is, finally, something stupendous in Milly, in her capacity for desire, in her refusal to compromise, in her metaphoric flights. On a wild promontory in Switzerland, she sees the world before her and resists the urge to jump: "It wouldn't be for her a question of a flying leap and thereby of a quick escape. It would be a question of taking full in the face the whole assault of life, to the general muster of which indeed her face might have been directly presented as she sat there on her rock" (150). Much later, she turns that same face despairingly to the wall, but not until she has given all her heart to the struggle; she is a dove, and will not heed that old nightingale's call, "to cease upon the midnight with no pain." The world must have its chance. She goes to the National Gallery to see Titians and Turners, but winds up among the lady-copyists, and knows even so that she will purchase no imitation. She is proposed to by a lord, and does not settle: there is one more plot yet to be tried. In Merton Densher, falling selflessly in love with a girl with no future, she sees the promise of a nobility that might have given her one after all. When he proves false, Milly has her final answer. She "fold[s] her wonderful wings" (664), we are told, and at last, the metaphor bears its weight.

Milly must die before Densher can love her. He protests to the end that he never loved Milly at all, but Kate is more perceptive than usual in her observation that while she believes that he did not love her while she lived, he has loved her since, as Milly herself perhaps knew that he would. At this moment, the gap between Milly and Kate appears most starkly before him: Milly has refused to accept a world too coarse for her, while Kate has been too coarse to accept a love that transcends calculated self-interest. It is this that leads him to propose an ultimatum very different from the one that demanded Kate's body in return for his promise. Either Kate will marry him at once and renounce all claims to Milly's legacy, or he will make the money over to her, ending their relationship. Kate refuses the proposal on these terms, presumably signaling her own acceptance of the money, although her words are ambiguous enough to suggest that her motives may not be entirely selfish: when Densher confirms that he will marry her "as [they] were," she responds, "we shall never be again as we were" (711), and leaves the room. Whether she means only that Densher has been irrevocably changed, or is acknowledging some change in herself, her act recognizes that Milly's death has altered the light in which her own relationship must be seen.

The reader, however, has had the means of understanding Milly almost from the start. Milly Theale must be physically ill because the story demands it. Even if James were willing to risk the aesthetic perils of any less literal malady, the logic of this particular story world simply cannot accommodate an imagined illness with earnest power to kill. This of course, has been precisely Milly's problem: she does not live in either a romantic landscape or a potentially more vital past, but in a disappointing present reality, a world of money and sex and actual doves with unpoetic wings. In this reality, young women die because they are ill, not because they have been disappointed in love or become disillusioned with life. But if the story requires us to take Dr. Strett at his ambiguous word, the plot requires us to do precisely the opposite. It is this dichotomy that accounts for the novel's impossible representation of Milly's disease: according to the story, she must be actually sick; according to the plot, she must decide herself spiritually unwilling to accept a hollow survival.

Again the question arises of why James cannot allow both to be true, creating a credible, rather than patently absurd, physical illness that the reader can be trusted to see also as symbolic. It is crucial, however, that we, like Milly, finally reject a tawdry physicality for a more authentic alternative, the difference being that the alternative we embrace does not require Milly's death to do her justice. In reading Milly's illness as a proxy for a painfully refined sensibility, we see something in the living Milly that, had Densher recognized it in time, might have given both of them the capacity to fulfill a desire that would not then have been cheap or empty. Of course, this does not happen; the plot in which Milly finds a world worth inhabiting remains necessarily unwritten. In the plot that does play out, Milly herself can only in death find genuine expression, shedding the material trappings that have proved so burdensome. But in the proxy reading that recognizes the source of her suffering, she has always been more than any apotheosis could make her. Witness to the courage and pathos of a spiritual struggle that could play out only in the novel's unwritten idealist plot, the reader is the first, and perhaps the only one, to give the living Milly her due. She dies for Densher as she has lived for us: she is a dove and stupendous; she is heartbreaking and loved.

Henry James was not a Victorian author. If the modernists did not invent the collision between reality and desire, they gave it a particular form, and James's characters are more closely related to Jay Gatsby than to Dorothea Brooke. Yet he is, finally, a realist author. Realism, as I have defined it, lies less in the exactitude of a text's portrayal of the actual than in its acknowledgment of limitation, that sense—shared by no one more than Henry James—of the gap between the world as it is and the world as it can't quite be, even for the space of a story. What becomes so prevalent in modernism is the conviction that not only reality but even the modes available for expressing our desires are themselves inadequate; we want the world, and wind up in a room full of shirts. It is why James's characters so often become heroic not in success but in renunciation, coming to possess a moral consciousness that is always more valuable than that which must be sacrificed to it. Crucially, for James, language itself becomes implicated in the general insufficiency: it is not just James's plots that are often impossible, but his conversations. No one speaks like a Henry James character, because to represent language as it is would betray James's sense of its inevitable failure. There are two modes of discourse available in James, one involving a specificity that reduces the most sacred into—in the metaphor of a different James—the crass vocabulary of "cash-value" (343),[5] the other involving a vagueness that represents nothing at all. The best James can do is, at crucial moments, to make not only his plots but the very words he gives us so transparently improbable that they require us to read past them to a significance for which they and their associated objects are only a proxy, to see what should be there but cannot be in what is there but should not be. Like all the best and most painful compromises, it will have to serve.

A Delightful Dissimulation

If *The Wings of the Dove* suggests the reason that Henry James can perhaps only plot by proxy, it is in *The Ambassadors* that the Jamesian proxy narrative finds its fullest expression. "Nothing," James writes in his preface to the New York edition of the novel, "is more easy than to state the subject of 'The Ambassadors'" (*The Art of the Novel* 312). Nothing more easy, he might have added, and nothing more deceptive. In the beginning of the novel, the fiancée of aging New Englander Lambert Strether sends him from their staid Massachusetts hometown to Paris to recover her wayward son from the clutches of a designing mistress. Strether finds, however, that Chad has been greatly improved, rather than debased, by his relationship and ultimately advises Chad of his obligation to stay with the woman who has done so much for him—a stricture that Chad seems likely to abandon as soon as the lure of a lucrative family business becomes stronger than his waning attachment to Madame de Vionnet. As Strether, in the final scene of the novel, prepares to return home, Maria Gostrey, an American expatriate who has guided Strether through the unfamiliar social world of Europe, essentially proposes marriage to him. Strether's engagement to Mrs. Newsome, never more than tacit, has by now been as tacitly ended by his betrayal of his original mission, theoretically freeing him to accept. Yet Strether declines Maria's offer, ostensibly on moral grounds: the only way he can be "right" is "not, out of the whole affair, to have got anything for myself" (512).

Critical opinion of the scene is mainly divided into two camps: those who see Strether's renunciation as genuine nobility, and those who regard it as a disappointing backslide into rigid New England morality. William Veeder, for instance, in "Strether and the Transcendence of Language" (1971), takes Strether's final act as the ideal synthesis between New England morality and European romanticism, while F. O. Matthiessen issued the rather devastating verdict that Strether's failure to fulfill his "wholly new sense of life" leaves readers ruing "his relative emptiness" (*Henry James* 39). Subjective preferences aside, the first option has considerable support within the text itself. Maria, who has the greatest reason to challenge Strether's logic, instead grudgingly accepts it: her half-hearted objection to his decision—"but why should you be so dreadfully right?"—is an implicit acknowledgment of the moral claim she suggests he overlook. More significantly, his acceptance of a more nuanced ethical code notwithstanding, Strether has been consistently unwilling to abandon his moral sensibilities. For much of the novel, his approval of Chad's relationship with Madame de Vionnet is predicated on his ability to maintain the illusion that theirs is a "virtuous attachment." Indeed, it takes Strether some two hundred pages to determine whether Chad is involved with Madame de Vionnet, who, aside from being an obviously experienced woman ten years Chad's senior, is also married, or her eligible, irreproachably innocent teenage daughter Jeanne. When a chance meeting with the couple leaves him unable to deny the nature of their relationship, he stops short of full endorsement of the affair. The relationship is complex, even beautiful, but all the force of Strether's considerable sensitivity cannot quite make it "right." He will counsel Chad of his continuing obligation to Madame de Vionnet; he will even assure Madame de Vionnet herself of his continued admiration and respect. Yet it is clear to both Strether and Madame de Vionnet that this is to be their final meeting: he has, as Maria Gostrey helpfully summarizes, "taken a final leave of her" (495). For his part, Chad, in his apparent willingness to leave Madame de Vionnet as soon as he grows bored with her, becomes a testament to the limitations of her training: "She had made him better, she had made him best, she had made him anything one would; but it came to our friend with supreme queerness that he was none the less only Chad" (482). If Chad's initial transformation suggests to Strether the narrowness of a moralism that would utterly reject the woman who effected it, his ultimate failure demonstrates the enduring relevance of a more nuanced ethical sense.

It is difficult to read the end of the novel, however, without feeling that if morality demands this of Strether, it is asking for too much. Nothing awaits Strether in Woollett. His engagement is off, and he would not have it back on if he could. His nominal job editing the town paper is tied to Mrs. Newsome and has presumably ended with the engagement. He has had experiences that alienate him from his previous life but lacks the youth or resources to meaningfully change his lot once he returns home. Even if his own happiness could be set aside—no small matter in a novel in which the phrase "live all you can" is invoked as a guiding principle—Maria's cannot. Strether is, after all, not the only man who ends the novel on the point of leaving a woman to return to Woollett, and if the disinterested nature of Strether's choice absolves him of the selfishness with which he charges Chad, it does not make his departure any less painful for the woman he leaves behind. In introducing Strether to the sophistication and subtlety of European society, Maria has performed a radically compressed version of Madame de Vionnet's "miracle" of transformation; if Chad owes a debt, so, too, does Strether. Weighing against these enticements to remain is a principle whose logic would be suspect even if its rigor were not so exacting. If Strether's sacrifice of his own and Maria's happiness is a moral victory, it is at best a Pyrrhic one. The most direct obligation Strether incurred in agreeing to act as Mrs. Newsome's agent in Europe was to attempt to persuade Chad to return home. He has instead done precisely the reverse. There might have been some argument for Strether's returning home before he had betrayed his original purpose so absolutely; there is only a tortured and tenuous one for a departure that cannot help Mrs. Newsome—who has by now broken with Strether in any case—and can only irreparably harm his own future prospects.

Ethics aside, the scene remains a puzzling endpoint for the novel. In the preface to the New York edition of *The Portrait of a Lady*, Henry James describes the *ficelle*, a secondary character with a strictly functional role in the narrative: "Not . . . true agent[s] . . . they may run beside the coach 'for all they are worth,' they may cling to it till they are out of breath . . . but neither, all the while, so much as gets her foot on the step, neither ceases for a moment to tread the dusty road" (*The Art of the Novel* 55). Not only does Maria fit the bill, she is, by James's own reckoning, the "most unmitigated and abandoned of *ficelles*" (*The Ambassadors* 322). Having filled, in the first several books of the novel, the *ficelle*-appropriate role of platonic guide and confidante, she, just as fittingly, becomes less prominent as the novel progresses and Strether is forced to put to the test the modes of analysis in which she has trained him. Yet after graciously ceding the stage to the legitimate actors, she boldly assumes pride of place in the final scene of the novel as no less a figure than that of the protagonist's acknowledged love interest. Several critics have suggested that Strether's moral justification for his return is nothing more than a tactful way of refusing an unwanted proposal, a solution that restores Maria to comparative insignificance while side-stepping altogether the validity of Strether's alleged scruples.[6] But if the assumption that Strether does not love Maria excuses Strether, it does not justify James, who has, in that case, chosen to end his novel with a scene of acknowledged unimportance.

The problem is by now a familiar one. It is right and fitting that Strether conclude the novel with a supreme moral act, drawing a clear line between nuance and relativism. Yet this particular act seems altogether wrong, combining needless self-denial with an object that is, on a narrative level, hardly worth the trouble of renouncing. James, however, is ready with an answer. James's preface to the novel, as Julie Rivkin has noted, is as much a conclusion as an addition to the novel, telling the untold story of the novel's own composition. But in so doing, she suggests, it calls attention as much to what is absent from the novel as to what is present; like Spencer Brydon in *The Jolly Corner*, the James of the prefaces is haunted by the unwritten plots that might have been: "[It] also inevitably hints at the intended novel that never got written.... As the process continues, the dropped blossoms become more important than those that remain; what the writer sees is not what is there but what was to have been there" (Rivkin, *False Positions* 60). And so, too, must the reader. The last scene, James tells us in the preface, is not properly a scene at all, but the representation of a scene: "Nowhere is it more of an artful expedient for mere consistency of form, to mention a case, than in the last 'scene' of the book, where its function is to give or to add nothing whatever, but only to express as vividly as possible certain things quite other than itself and that are of the already fixed and appointed measure. Since, however, all art is EXPRESSION, and is thereby vividness, one was to find the door open here to any amount of delightful dissimulation" (324). If Maria and Strether's relationship seems too minor a connection to sustain the burden of an ending, it is because it was never intended to do so. Adding nothing, giving nothing, it represents, not Strether's refusal, but "certain things quite other than itself." These things, James suggests, are already present in the narrative, and present they may be—but only, at this last and crucial moment, by proxy. The chosen story meeting the abandoned one, the unsatisfying facade standing in for the unwritten finale, the novel pauses on its jolly corner and lays a wistful ghost to rest.

Wistful, because there is another woman Strether leaves in Paris, a woman it would be both obligation and sacrifice to renounce. Maria is a friend and counselor, a stalwart Virgil to Strether's wandering Dante. But Madame de Vionnet is more than that. She is "beautiful" and "wonderful," rare and distinguished; she is a worker of miracles; she is Cleopatra on the Nile, in all her infinite, ageless variety. She is, "from the first, for [Strether], the most charming woman in the world" (493), and to the last as well. The sacrifice that is so senseless when it concerns Maria Gostrey becomes legible as a proxy for a phantom scene Strether cannot have with Madame de Vionnet. Accepting *her* offer would be indeed discreditable. Even setting aside the fact of her marriage—which Strether does not when he considers her relationship with Chad—for Strether not only deliberately to thwart his original mission but to become involved with Chad's mistress might legitimately be seen as a betrayal too far.

The final scene cannot, logically, take place between Strether and Madame de Vionnet. Morality aside, while it seems clear that Chad intends to leave her, he has not done so yet, and Madame de Vionnet's desperation over the thought of his desertion testifies to her continuing love of him. If there is no possibility of a relationship of any kind between Strether and Madame de Vionnet, there is, it would seem, nothing to sacrifice in the first place. Yet the final conversation between the two suggests that there is more at stake than either of them will consciously acknowledge; Maria Gostrey is not the only woman in the novel to make a proposal, of a sort, to Strether:

> "Why, if you're going, NEED you, after all? Is it impossible you should stay on—so that one mayn't lose you?"
>
> "Impossible I should live with you here instead of going home?"
>
> "Not 'with' us, if you object to that, but near enough to us, somewhere, for us to see you—well," she beautifully brought out, "when we feel we MUST. How shall we not sometimes feel it? I've wanted to see you often when I couldn't," she pursued, "all these last weeks.

How shan't I then miss you now, with the sense of your being gone forever?" (480)

To suggest that Madame de Vionnet intends or Strether interprets her offer as sexual would be to impute an uncharacteristic crassness to both. Yet the proposed arrangement would have the form, if not the substance, of a bizarre ménage à trois: Strether is to be the necessary third in Madame de Vionnet and Chad's relationship, almost a kept man, installed at a discreet distance from the couple and, given the comparative scantiness of his own resources, probably supported by them as well. There is a certain vagueness, too, to the nature of Madame de Vionnet's intense desire for Strether to remain. After Strether has confirmed his plans to leave, she reflects on what could have been: "We might, you and I, have been friends. That's it—that's it. You see how, as I say, I want everything. I've wanted you too" (485). Having struggled to define her own longing, she has now, in the language of friendship, found a vocabulary for it—"that's it," she says, hitting upon an explanation that satisfies her. But if all she is attempting to articulate is a desire for friendship, she has taken an unusually long time to do it, and, indeed, her next words preserve the very ambiguity she is trying to resolve. What she wants, most of all, is Chad; in saying she wants Strether "too," she is implicitly drawing an equivalence between the two men. For his part, Strether treats the hypothetical friendship as a temptation he must resist: when Maria, recounting her own conversation with Madame de Vionnet, repeats the other woman's belief that they might have been friends, Strether replies "That's just ... why I'm going" (495). Even granting that Strether sees sustained complicity in Madame de Vionnet's adulterous relationship with Chad as necessarily compromising, the resistance adds to our sense that what we are witnessing is a veiled seduction.

Of course, Madame de Vionnet is not, on any level, actually proposing an affair, nor is Strether renouncing it as a legitimate possibility. Rather, the potential for such a relationship between them exists as an unwritten phantom plot. At the beginning of the passage, James's characteristically ambiguous pronouns permit us for a moment to exclude Chad from the equation altogether. Madame de Vionnet asks if it is possible that "one" might not lose Strether; Strether asks if she is suggesting that he live with "you." Immediately afterward, Madame de Vionnet specifies that he need not live with "us," foreclosing the possibility that the previous lines had, however illogically, evoked. Yet the possibility remains manifestly in play for the rest of the novel, and indeed becomes more potent as we approach the final scene. By his closing conversation with Maria, Strether knows, as he did not before, that Chad is very likely to return home in the not terribly distant future; if Strether should stay, it will be with the promise that Madame de Vionnet's awkward threesome is to be reduced to a more congenial pair. While he sacrifices no immediately accessible chance at happiness, his renunciation is thus no empty gesture.

This is all the truer because of precisely what Maria is offering. Ostensibly, her question of why Strether should go home at all—asked immediately after she has confirmed that all is at an end between him and Mrs. Newsome—is an unspoken marriage proposal, and Strether seems to take it as such. Yet the most explicit offer she makes is framed, not in terms of mutual happiness, but of sacrifice on her own part: "There's nothing, you know, I wouldn't do for you. . . . Nothing . . . in all the world" (512). To understand her tone here, we must go back to the earlier conversation in which she and Strether discuss his belated realization about Chad and Madame de Vionnet's relationship. It is Maria who, in the course of that discussion, describes Madame de Vionnet as, for Strether, "the most charming woman in the world." As Strether continues to praise Madame de Vionnet, Maria remarks that she wishes the other woman could hear him, as Madame de Vionnet assumes that Strether must have lost any good opinion he once had of her. Indeed, not content with wishing, she asks Strether if he would like her to convey his message: "'If you'd like me to tell her that you do still so see her—!' Miss Gostrey, in short, offered herself for service to the end" (495). When Strether reiterates that, despite his continued admiration, he is "done with" Madame de Vionnet, Maria continues arguing her case, speaking "as if for conscience"; she recognizes this as an ethical act that is directly against her own self-interest. Only giving way when she has satisfied herself that she has "done her best for each," she concludes the scene by telling Strether she is sorry for "us all"; Strether's decision represents a loss for him and for Madame de Vionnet, but his assertions of undiminished admiration destroy Maria's hopes as well.

With this in mind, her proposal to Strether takes on a new dimension. Part of the richness of the proxy narrative in *The Ambassadors* is the capacity of James's own characters to recognize the dynamic at work. Obsessive interpreters of ambiguities and makers of meaning, James's characters are also the first readers of his plots, often considering many of the same possibilities that we ourselves do. In James, there is no clear boundary between the unwritten and the subtextual; the scene between Strether and Maria Gostrey is a proxy for a phantom one between Strether and Madame de Vionnet, but the actual scene hints that both parties to the proposal are tacitly aware of this. Fully aware of Strether's feelings for another woman, at best, Maria is offering to act as a consolation prize. Yet the air of sacrifice suggests that she goes even further than this. Doing "anything," in this case, means providing a pretext for Strether to stay in Europe with—or, as Madame de Vionnet herself had proposed, at least near enough to—a woman who provides more of an incentive than she does for him to remain. As in Madame de Vionnet's own proposal scene, the scenario envisioned is not one that is likely to lead to literal consummation between the two; it is difficult to imagine a scenario in which Strether could marry Maria and still have Madame de Vionnet in any physical sense. Yet what Maria's proposed arrangement does permit is precisely a relationship by proxy, a marriage between friends to enable a friendship between lovers, which is what Strether and Madame de Vionnet would be in all *but* the most literal sense.

If this is Maria's offer, then what, exactly, is Strether rejecting? On one level, his refusal is simply a more forceful reiteration of his earlier rejection of Madame de Vionnet's own proposal. Even now, knowing about Chad's likely departure and having been given a chance to do as he wishes without the appearance—or, perhaps, even conscious acknowledgment—of impropriety, he remains faithful to his principles. On another, he is acting out of consideration for Maria, who he will not simply use as a means to an end. In a larger sense, he is rejecting a particular kind of narrative or, indeed, two kinds of narratives, each associated with a distinct literary and cultural tradition. Both Richard Chase and Leslie Fiedler famously contrasted the American novel with its English and European counterparts. The English novel has its marriage plot, the European its doomed adulterers, but the American novel is comparatively sexless, trading domesticated David Copperfields and cuckolding Julian Sorrels for Huck Finn and his endless, unreconstructed boyhood. The American-born, European-educated, naturalized Englishman Henry James leaves Strether poised among the three options. To choose Maria as Maria is to embrace, belatedly, the marriage plot, in which virtue is rewarded with an equally virtuous romance. To choose Madame de Vionnet, or Maria as a proxy for her, is to abandon scruples to the dangerous passion of adultery. And to choose, as Strether does, to leave both women behind is to resign oneself to the essential loneliness of the American wanderer, who must pay so heavy a price for his forbidden seas and barbarous coasts. Strether's conscience returns him to a world of social entrapment, while Huck's leads him away from it, but both man and boy are damned by the very consciousness that, morally, has saved them.

Yet more than a nation, or a narrative, or a woman, what Strether rejects is the representational system that permits Maria to offer herself to him as a surrogate for another. This is a novel, as Julie Rivkin has detailed at length, about various forms of representative relationships.[7] Strether, of course, is an ambassador, sent to Paris as Mrs. Newsome's proxy, but so too are most of the rest of the characters, to a greater or lesser extent. People are agents of Chad or agents of his mother, representatives of free-wheeling Europe or decorous New England. As a *ficelle*, Maria Gostrey theoretically exists outside this system: she is not an agent, but a function with pretensions. Her final, repudiated offer to act as a proxy for Madame de Vionnet would have given her a belated place among the novel's ambassadors; indeed, it would have rendered her the perfect ambassador, her selfhood utterly effaced by her principal. Her attempt to establish such a connection, however, is less of a departure than it may initially appear to be. In the beginning of the novel, Maria seems poised for a place as one of the novel's many representative national types; she is the Europeanized American, just as Strether's friend Waymarsh is the stubbornly provincial expatriate. She quickly, however, becomes subsumed by a host of other characters—Little Bilham, Miss Barrace, Chad himself—who will assume, in more significant ways, the same, quasi-allegorical function.

Rather than a representative agent, Maria consistently serves as an intermediary in events in which she otherwise bears no cognizable part. Even before Maria has been formally supplanted, James emphasizes the insubstantial nature of her connections to the various people with whom she is associated. Maria has met Waymarsh, the pretext for her initial conversation with Strether, through mutual friends and recollects him clearly, but she acknowledges that their encounter was so insignificant that he may not remember her at all, as indeed he will not, when the two later meet. Her other potential link to Strether proves similarly tentative: he recalls seeing her at a previous hotel, where she had been meeting some of his fellow passengers, but he does not know the family in question well enough "to give the case much of a lift," and her own dealings with them were, in any event, no more than a "brief engagement" (57). Lacking a discernible life of her own, she drifts from hotel to hotel and casual friend to casual friend; connected to a seemingly inexhaustible number of people, she never finds a fixed place with any of them.

The most important of these vague connections is to Madame de Vionnet, who will, more than any other character, usurp her potential narrative space. The relationship between the two women, like so many of Maria's ties, refuses quite to bear its narrative weight: Maria says that she and Madame de Vionnet—whose given name, not incidentally, is Marie—are old friends, but their acquaintance for the past twenty years has been intermittent, "and above all with a long recent drop" (222). Mostly, the link serves as a mere convenience, allowing Maria to brief Strether on Madame de Vionnet's history. Yet long before the novel's final scene, there are hints of a deeper significance. Almost the first words that Madame de Vionnet says to Strether are about her old friend: "Hasn't Miss Gostrey . . . said a good word for me? . . . I'm so glad you're in relation with her" (211). Even before the identity of Chad's mistress is known, Maria draws an unconscious semantic link between them: "I'm talking," says Strether, of the woman presumed to be keeping Chad in Paris, "of some person who in his present situation may have held her own, may really have counted." "That's exactly what *I* am," returns Maria (179). Superficially, she is merely corroborating Strether: "That exactly what *I* am [talking about]." But she is also unwittingly preparing us for a deeper parallel between herself and the woman who turns out to be Madame de Vionnet. Even more suggestive is a much later instance of verbal confusion between the two. After Chad tells Strether he has needed no one's help to be improved by Europe, Strether objects that he has, like Chad, been made better by "women—too" (503). Chad, however, misunderstands him ("Two?"), prefiguring the final conflation of the women in Maria's offer to Strether.

Madame de Vionnet's entry into the novel signals the end of Miss Gostrey's period of prominence. Indeed, she for a time literally leaves the novel, ostensibly because she is unwilling to betray either Madame de Vionnet or Strether by becoming too closely allied with one camp or the other, but also, possibly, because she is pained by her recognition of Strether's attraction toward the other woman. Whether or not Maria yet sees it, however, as soon as Strether meets Madame de Vionnet, Maria's own narrative role is sharply diminished. Until this point, the prospect of a marriage plot in which Strether chooses to stay in Europe with Maria has been a legitimate possibility; based solely on the evidence of the first seventy-five pages of the novel, there would be nothing at all discordant about such an ending. But Madame de Vionnet emerges so clearly as the novel's dominant woman that, by the time we arrive at that concluding scene, what would once have seemed natural now reads as disappointingly anticlimactic.

Maria's relationship with Madame de Vionnet—again excluding, for the moment, the final scene—is not quite representative, in the sense of the novel's other ambassadorships. Indeed, in refusing to collude with either Strether or Madame de Vionnet, she explicitly declines such a role. If the novel's minor cast, its Waymarshes and Miss Barraces and Pococks, *stand in* for another, Maria, until that final scene, is rather *associated with* these other women. Yet this association in itself involves, at its extremes, a kind of substitution, an interchangeability in which a reference to one woman may be a reference to two, or perhaps to all three. It is the difference, not between representation and free agency, but between metaphor and metonymy.

On one level, the looseness of Maria's associative, rather than strictly representative, ties, her capacity to change allegiances, affiliated first with one woman, then with another, and never, definitively, with any of the novel's partisans, is a model for escaping the rigid scheme of alliances that constrains so many others. It is a model that Strether will, in part, follow. His progress in the novel requires that he emerge as a moral, rather than representative, agent, transcending the narrow sensibility that would confine him to Mrs. Newsome's strictures. Yet this freedom carries its own kind of moral peril. If Maria's narrative position allows her to escape one kind of representative trap, it ensnares her just as surely in another. Even as it criticizes the rigidity of the one-to-one surrogate relationship of the ambassador and his principal, *The Ambassadors* repeatedly suggests the opposing problem of the lack of direct correspondence between language and the thing signified by it. Early in the novel, the difficulty is evoked comically: Strether refuses, absurdly, to tell Maria the name of the trivial item whose production is the source of the Newsome family fortune, as if concealing the name could change the fact of the object's existence.

But the unwillingness to attach meaningful signs to objects of actual significance has more serious implications as well. When Chad's friend Little Bilham tells Strether that Chad and Marie's affair is a "virtuous attachment," he is deliberately separating the term from the conventional meaning he knows that Strether will attach to it. Of course, Strether himself will later distance himself from the puritanical social codes that would require a "virtuous attachment" between two unmarried people, one of them unable to divorce the husband from whom she has long been separated, to be necessarily chaste. Yet Bilham's phrase is also a deliberate act of obfuscation that, beyond hoodwinking Strether, encourages a laissez-faire morality that Strether will never fully endorse and in which the real ethical stakes of the couple's behavior may be glibly obscured. Ultimately, there are actual consequences that cannot be eliminated through verbal subterfuge: from the possibility that Jeanne may be married off in part to facilitate her mother's affair to the position of vulnerability in which Madame de Vionnet is left by Chad's ability to casually break their informal tie, there are costs to violating arbitrary codes that have nonetheless acquired legitimate force.

The social language in which Strether becomes so adept compounds this moral danger, consistently liable to collapse into a set of allusive games in which words need have no meaningful relationship to the world they claim to describe. People and situations are described as "magnificent" or "wonderful" or "horrible," placeholder words that, like "stupendous" in *The Wings of the Dove*, become a substitute for an attempt at greater specificity. Ambiguous pronouns that could logically be attached to multiple referents rob discourse of fixed meaning. Deictic phrases, like Strether's frequent "there we are," appear out of context. This kind of vagueness facilitates the looseness that would use the same language to describe platonic friendship and adultery: if there is no precise relationship between words and their meaning, then an affair might as well be a "virtuous attachment." Maria, as Strether's guide to fashionable society, is particularly implicated in this type of language, with all the moral peril it implies. When Waymarsh becomes noticeably irritated with Strether's and Maria's jaunts to London shops and theaters, Strether reflects on his friend's attitude in a manner that reveals Miss Gostrey's influence: "'He thinks us sophisticated, he thinks us worldly, he thinks us wicked, he thinks us all sorts of queer things' . . . for wondrous were the vague quantities our friend had within a couple of short days acquired the habit of conveniently and conclusively lumping together" (82). When Strether suggests there might be something "base" about his willingness to join a new acquaintance in mocking an old friend, Maria declares their sudden intimacy at Waymarsh's expense "magnificent" and thus "[makes] an end of it" (83).

It is appropriate, then, that Maria, in her inability to attach herself meaningfully to any single place or person, is both ultimate figure and ultimate victim of the imperfectly representational aesthetic. The *ficelle* is precisely a figure of apparent representational value that in the end lacks correspondence between form (what she is) and function (what she does). If she is not constrained by the representative model that contains Waymarsh or Sarah Pocock, she is bound no less rigidly by her position as *ficelle*, dramatized in her role as volunteer tour guide for countless travelers who never, in any sense, repay her. She acts, but never manages to attach herself meaningfully—with that one, significant exception of the novel's ending—either to the people she helps or the plot within which she finds herself.

In declining Maria's proposal, Strether escapes, to the extent that it is possible, both of the novel's representational traps. Refusing the possibility of any kind of future with Madame de Vionnet, he affirms a private moral code that he acknowledges as binding. No verbal sleight of hand, including Maria's own substitution of herself for the forbidden other, can dissuade him from a resolve that is all the more valid for being self-imposed. But Maria herself must also, at long last, be taken into account. In making her offer, she attempts to trade the lonely freedom of association for the self-effacing union of representation. Never more than a *ficelle*, she cannot, like Strether, emerge as a stable self; the best she can hope for is to graduate from metonym to proxy. Or, rather, she could not have so emerged, had Strether not saved her. In rejecting Maria, he rejects Madame de Vionnet. But he also rejects the logic that would permit such a substitution: Maria must be refused as Maria, too. It is his supreme moral act.

Crucially, understanding the full effect of Strether's choice requires that we preserve both readings of the scene. To ignore the proxy relationship between Maria and Madame de Vionnet forces us to regard what should be genuine nobility as false morality; Strether's declared notion of what being "right" requires bears no more reference to any recognized ethical standard than Little Bilham's definition of "virtuous attachment." Yet to treat

Maria, for the purposes of the scene, merely as a surrogate for a phantom Madame de Vionnet is to replicate the ambassadorial system Strether has so thoroughly rejected. Dissimulation, no matter how delightful, must end somewhere, allowing even Maria to become, at last, a character in her own right. "There we are," concludes Strether, and for perhaps the first time, the phrase is not empty. There we are, he is saying, you, and I, and Madame de Vionnet as well, all present, all recognized, all significant.

Costs and Gains

For all its hinting, its winks and gestures, the proxy narrative ultimately suppresses a text's most radical possibilities. The "what if?" that is explicit in *Villette* or *The Old Curiosity Shop* can in these texts never be articulated and need never be considered: the story that we read, imperfect, illogical, disappointing, will nonetheless serve. Indeed, it can save. Sometimes, the rescue does no more than preserve a novel from the censor's pen, or for the young lady's leisure hours. In other cases, the gain is more profound. When the substitute is all that is left, we do well to make the best of her, and the marriage plot is no heavy ransom to one trapped in a world of Gothic horror. Yet even the best trade involves a sacrifice. The logic that exorcizes Anne denies Marian; the text that cannot peek under Lady Audley's robes will not, in the end, look far into her mind either before it moves on to a safer heroine.

Of the proxy narratives I discuss in the past two chapters, none includes a sacrifice greater than that of Strether, who denies himself so much for so little return. Gaining nothing, he also has the pain of knowing, as Walter Hartright and Robert Audley do not, precisely what he loses. After trying, for so long, to "suppose nothing," Strether, after the meeting that leaves him in no doubt of Madame de Vionnet and Chad's relationship, finds himself "supposing innumerable and wonderful things" (468). This supposition is distinct from the knowledge Strether has just acquired. There is no need, any longer, to suppose anything about Madame de Vionnet and Chad, the nature of whose "virtuous attachment" has at last been placed beyond the need for conjecture. The price of that knowledge will come, as it always does, with pain, and exile, and a fig leaf to conceal his shame. It will come, but not yet. Before the rigor of law catches up to him, he has a brief space of freedom to entertain the full range of possibilities awakened by his new awareness. For a moment, the unwritten plot will not be denied, or suppressed, or superseded. In the new, more generous moral universe in which even this relationship can be beautiful and justified, what gifts might not be lying in wait? Yet Strether is not, after all, in a new world, but an old one. One need not be Mrs. Newsome's ambassador to be bound by an ethical sense that limits possibilities even as they unfold. The wildest of Strether's suppositions could, in all likelihood, never have materialized. But sacrificing those that do is sacrifice enough. The universe, in the form of two women, offers its gifts to Strether, and Strether politely, nobly declines.

Strether, in knowing what he sacrifices, loses more than his counterparts in other novels. But he also loses less. When Strether tells Maria that the only way for him to be "right" is "not, out of the whole affair, to have got anything for myself," she points out the great flaw in his logic: "With your wonderful impressions you'll have got a great deal" (512). It is nothing that can be seen or touched, nothing Mrs. Newsome would think to reproach him for. It will often be, even to Strether, a burden, the reminder of all that might have been, all that he has lost. It is inescapable, and precious. There are possibilities that must be rejected, and those that cannot even be spoken; those that do not materialize, and those that never directly make it to the page at all. But to have contemplated them is to have been enriched, imperceptibly, by the wonder of our own supposing.

4

Fancying the Delight

Hypothetical Realism in The Woodlanders *and* Mary Barton

Early in *Mary Barton,* Elizabeth Gaskell describes a tea hosted by an elderly Manchester washerwoman for two young neighbors. For the most part, the description is the standard stuff of nineteenth-century realism, full of rich detail (Alice uses half a pound of tea and a quarter of a pound of butter) and psychological insight (Mary wears a new gown to impress the other young woman, even though there is no need for her to make any particular impression at all). Suddenly, however, the narrator interrupts the scene with a direct address to readers: "Can you fancy the bustle of Alice to make the tea, to pour it out, and sweeten it to their liking, to help and help again to clap-bread and bread-and-butter? Can you fancy the delight with which she watched her piled-up clap-bread disappear before the hungry girls, and listened to the praises of her home-remembered dainty?" (44) The questions are clearly rhetorical: of course we can fancy it; Gaskell is creating the image for us even as she writes. They are also quite literal. Are we *really* picturing old Alice at her kettle, anxious to please her guests with offerings of sweet tea and buttered bread? Can we feel her pride when these gifts are praised, or imagine a life so stark that they would constitute a rare indulgence? If we cannot, then the dream of empathy on which the novel's vision will rely is compromised from the outset.

Thus far, I have focused on how unwritten plots affect the world of the novel. While readers must collaborate in the construction of alternative narrative possibilities, the options we consider will refer to that world, rather than our own; having given ourselves over to a text's immersive will, we can absorb ourselves in thoughts of what Pip might have been or whom

Strether should have married. In the case of the realist novel, however, our assessment of these possibilities is inevitably connected to our sense of the actual world. If a novel appears to be set in a reality that more or less obeys the rules of our own, we will not consider hypothetical scenarios that presume the existence of time travel or teleportation. If a novelistic world seems, in addition to this baseline level of relationship to the actual world, to feature convincingly drawn characters whose lives and struggles likewise resemble those of similarly situated humans, we will further and more subtly narrow our range of possibilities. A socially conscious novel about a desperately poor family of miners can end hopefully, but a sophisticated reader will not expect—and a sophisticated author will not, ordinarily, write—a late-novel turn in which they win the lottery and fulfill their dream of owning a professional sports franchise. Similarly, while a character with a serious illness might or might not survive in the ordinary course of realist narrative, we would not anticipate a miraculous recovery for a character who has received a terminal diagnosis.

These expectations arise from an understanding of generic convention. But they also depend on our understanding of reality—or, at least, our ability to assess the *text's* understanding of reality. If I am reading a novel infused with a deeply religious sensibility, a miraculous recovery might not be out of the bounds of plausibility, even in an otherwise realistic narrative universe. Shakespeare's mental model of Europe evidently contained Bohemian coasts; the solution to the Sherlock Holmes story "The Speckled Band" relies on an adder's ability to respond to a whistle, as Arthur Conan-Doyle was unaware that snakes are deaf (Hodgson, "The Recoil of 'The Speckled Band'"). More to the point, within the range of the theoretically possible, the difference between a credible realist outcome and romantic wish fulfillment will depend in part on an individual author's or reader's worldview. Horatio Alger's rags-to-riches narratives of street boys made good reflect Alger's sincere belief in the availability of opportunity to the deserving poor, but are more likely to be read today as representatives of a simplistic faith in the promise of the American Dream.

Similarly, the status of a plot may shift as a result of actual societal changes. In the 1967 film *Guess Who's Coming to Dinner*, Sidney Poitier's character responds to his white prospective father-in-law's concerns about the prejudice his children would be likely to face by noting that "[your daughter] feels that every single one of our children will be President of the United

States . . . frankly, I think [she] is a bit optimistic. I'd settle for Secretary of State." In context, the comment is both an earnest statement of faith—the film, which completed production in an America in which interracial marriage was still illegal in many states, plainly believes that racial progress is possible—and a credibility-saving check on such optimism.[1] Joanna's hyperbolically represented belief that *all* her children will grow up to be president is a nod to her by now well-established naivety, while her more realistic fiancé's joking deflation of her dream suggests that he regards even a Black secretary of state as a too-sanguine prospect. But of course, the son of a Black father and a white mother born several years before the hypothetical children of John and Joanna Prentiss would indeed go on to be president; what was excluded by the rules of 1967 realism is now part of our established reality. On the other hand, a work of fiction produced in the immediate wake of Barack Obama's 2008 election, when pundits were proclaiming the dawn of a "post-racial" America, might have been impossible only months later, by which time reminders that one biracial man's success was wildly unrepresentative of the lives of most Black Americans had reasserted themselves.

The changing nature of the possible and the realistic in a given society was a subject of deep interest to Victorian authors. The realist novel and the novel of reform are not entirely overlapping genres; though it would be difficult to find a realist novel without some investment in principles of social change, not all are dominated by such concerns, and certainly there are reform novels that are not realistic. The two genres, however, are inextricably linked. Embrace of certain broad principles of realism—namely, its emphasis on faithful representation of the lives of ordinary people—was a necessary precondition for the rise of the novel of reform. In turn, a growing belief in the capacity of literature to effect social change made realism a matter of urgency. Amanda Claybaugh has resurrected the nineteenth-century term "the novel of purpose" to reflect the prevalent Victorian notion that a novel could "act on its readers—and, through its readers, the world." Both reformist and non-reformist novels of the era were thus "written, published, read, and reviewed according to expectations learned from social reform" (*The Novel of Purpose* 7). The sympathies inculcated by the realist novel would be wasted if they could not be translated into action; a reader who can pity the Alice of the novel, but not the one in the streets, has missed the point.

As a result, the most potent unwritten plots in realist novels of purpose are, in a significant subset of texts, not those that represent active narrative possibilities, but those that suggest a hypothetical future for the world outside the boundaries of the novel. We have already seen one example of this phenomenon in the ending of *Hard Times*, in which plots rejected as impossible within the realm of the novel ("such a thing was never to be") are reactivated as hypothetical potentialities for the reader: "It rests with you and me, whether, in our two fields of action, similar things shall be or not" (399). This chapter reads Hardy's *The Woodlanders* and Gaskell's *Mary Barton* as instances of what I call *hypothetical realism*, the imagining of a *currently* unwritten plot that may be realized within the realist novels of a transformed future. The two novels are tonally disparate, one almost unrelentingly grim, the other nearly utopian in its final vision. They are united, however, by a shared ethical commitment to examining, not the might-have-been, but the might-yet-be. In honoring this commitment, they extend the role of the unwritten plot in defining and testing the borders of narrative possibility into a practical challenge to the reader, whose capacity to envision social alternatives becomes fundamental to the project of the novel.

Unwriting Plot

Thomas Hardy's pessimism ended his career as a novelist. Readers had endured the execution of Tess and Eustacia Vye's suicide, but their patience ended somewhere around the moment that an eight-year-old known only as Father Time took it into his allegorical head to kill his younger siblings and himself to relieve their parents of the burden of supporting them. Margaret Oliphant, writing in *Blackwood's*, said that "nothing so coarsely indecent . . . [had] ever been put in English print" (in Cox, *Thomas Hardy* 270). The Bishop of Wakefield publicly declared that he had burned the book, and he was not alone: one reader sent Hardy a packet of ashes that had once been his copy of the novel (xxx).[2] Many of these attacks focused on the novel's immorality, particularly its critique of the institution of marriage. For others, however, *Jude's* grimness was enough to condemn it. The *Morning Post* reviewer declared that "even Euripides . . . might well have faltered" before the work's "gloomy atmosphere of hopeless pessimism" ("Books of the Day" 6), while the preacher Thomas Selby accused Hardy both of peddling smut and dealing in "the most lachrymose and intractable types of pessimism that a morbid ingenuity can devise" (Yevish, "The Attack on Jude the Obscure" 242). Hardy may or may not have been exaggerating when he claimed that these reviews "completely cure[d] me of further interest in novel writing." But exaggeration or not, in the thirty-three remaining years of his life, he turned exclusively to poetry, hoping that he could "express more fully in verse ideas and emotions which run counter to the inert crystallized opinion—hard as a rock—which the vast body of men have vested interests in supporting" (F. Hardy, *The Later Years* 57).

Inspiring one's very own bonfire of the vanities might well be enough to turn a far sunnier author than Thomas Hardy cynical. His comment reflects, however, not only bitterness but disappointment. Hardy had hoped that his prose would *do* something, only to realize that he had delivered his prophecy to a stiff-necked and obdurate people. At least in this account of the decision, Hardy's move from prose to poetry signifies his resignation: he does not believe that his ideas will be more effective in verse, but that the formal shift will render them toothless enough to escape censure. "If Galileo had said in verse that the world moved," he concludes, "the Inquisition might have let him alone" (58). His beliefs will still be available to those who care to recognize them, but the freedom of his expression depends on the assumption that most of his readers will decline the offer.

The relationship between the world of Hardy's novels and the world outside of them had always been complicated. Hardy once described Wessex, the location of most of his novels, as "a merely realistic dream-country" that combined the detail of realism with the freedom of imagination (Gatrell, "Wessex" 30). Mimetic realism, he believed, was inherently inartistic; the artist should not strive to reflect too nearly the conditions or probabilities of the actual world: "Art is a disproportioning... of realities, to show more clearly the features that matter in those realities, which, if merely copied or reported inventorially, might possibly be observed, but would more probably be overlooked. Hence 'realism' is not Art" (F. Hardy, *The Early Years* 299). Hardy deals in extremes of human passion; people rarely love wisely in a Hardy novel, and when things end poorly, as they almost invariably do, they do so in the most horrific manner possible. For Hardy, characters' experiences need not be representative, but evocative. But as Simon Gatrell has found, over time, Hardy's Wessex became progressively less dreamy, more an alternative reality than a liminal space of possibility. The editions of Hardy's early novels that we now read have been revised significantly from their original published form; among other changes, Hardy retroactively added local detail to make the settings of these novels conform with his more developed vision of Wessex. Hardy accompanied his increasing attention to the history and geography of his fictional world with a turn toward greater focus on social issues (Gatrell, "Wessex" 25). Having first introduced genteel characters into his fiction under pressure from editors to give middle-class readers figures with whom they could identify (20), Hardy had by the mid-1880s become far more invested in class conflict and the particulars of labor.[3] *Jude's* specific criticisms of the educational system and divorce law reflect this shift, highlighting issues whose reach could not be plausibly contained within the borders of Wessex.

As in the case of most of the novels in this study, then—as, indeed, in the case of most realist novels—Hardy's works, while now a staple of the accepted realist canon, have complex, competing generic affiliations. Containing heavy elements of melodrama, allegory, and pastoralism, his novels as easily invite comparisons to Greek tragedy as to George Eliot. Most strikingly, they are shaped by an apparent determinism that conflicts sharply with the logic of realist plotting, grounded so heavily in the multiplicity of active possibilities. The very grimness of Hardy's novels provides a fertile source of unwritten plots, making readers long for pleasanter alternatives that lie just out of reach. If Angel Clare had forgiven Tess, Michael Henchard held his liquor better, and Grace Melbury been less of a social climber, all might have turned out right after all. The novels point, as well, to reparative social alternatives: the world would be a better and a kinder place, Hardy evidently believes, were divorce laws liberalized, educational opportunities expanded, and ruined dairymaids no longer subject to execution for murdering their rapists.[4] Yet while characters' circumstances might suggest alternatives, these possibilities are ultimately more taunts than active potentialities, the confluence of fatal forces militating against serious hope of escape. Beset by Job-like accumulations of catastrophe, many of Hardy's characters, though situated within an identifiably realist world, enact parables of suffering rather than believably human-sized stories of opportunities denied and missed. Tess and her fellow sufferers are doomed by the designs of both the President of the Immortals and the manifest will of their human creator; a well-timed tear, it seems, could never have saved her at all.

On closer examination, however, this impression of fixed design breaks down and complicates the impression of inexorable narrative order. Time and again, Hardy undermines the significance of his own plots. Sometimes, he raises what seems to be a counterfactual possibility—if Jude and Sue had been able legally to marry, their miserable lot would have been relieved—only to enact and then sabotage it: when Jude and Sue do win their divorces, an improbable development that seemed already to have been excluded by the narrative, it changes nothing, as the couple obstinately refuse to formalize their union. What had seemed determinative proves merely incidental. In other cases, events that should by rights prove devastating wind up having comparatively little effect, while those that seem inconsequential produce horrific ends. The twenty-one-year term limit on Henchard's vow of temperance—conveniently made approximately twenty years before the main events of the novel begin—is a prop gun destined to go off, but when Henchard returns to the bottle after the pledge expires, it has virtually no effect on his story. In *The Return of the Native*, Mrs. Yeobright seems to have lost her best chance of repairing her relationship with her son Clym when her messenger gambles away the money she has sent as a peace offering; Diggory Venn wins it back with a second throw of the dice, and it all ends poorly thanks to an entirely different mistake. By contrast, Sue's routine complaint about the pressures of supporting a family leads to the murder-suicide of the Fawley children when one of them decides that the best way to help his foster mother is to relieve her of three mouths to feed. In this world of attenuated and unpredictable consequences, determining what might have been, let alone how that outcome could practically have been achieved, is as dicey a proposition as Diggory's game of chance.

Hardy's novels do not, then, represent a simple case of plots of allegorical determinism overcoming plots of social realism. Rather, however intricately, even painstakingly plotted they may seem, Hardy's novels, in the final analysis, wind up undermining the notion of traditional plot itself. The blind chance that seems so often to govern the lives of Hardy's characters undercuts the impression that they are prey to the predictable machinations of a force of deliberate malignancy. Chance also, however, opposes the gentler workings of realist design, which depends on principles of causal and narrative coherence disrupted by Hardy's frequent severing of actions from their expected and seemingly plot-ordained consequences. Implicated with realist plotting is, necessarily, the logic of reform. Gillian Beer and George Levine are among the scholars who have connected Hardy's pessimism to a grim reading of the Darwinian universe, in which the replacement of manifest design with unpredictable biological selection leads to an undermining of both providential promise and meaningful human agency. Despite this, Hardy is obviously invested in reform, his novels containing explicit, extended social critiques that seem to urge, like so many realist novels, the possibility of extra-novelistic action. Yet a world governed by chance is not one that can be reliably responsive to individual or collective reparative effort. In Hardy, the social crusader would seem to have met his or her match: between cruel fate and indifferent chance, action of any kind would seem almost beside the point.

Reformist potential in Hardy, rather, seems to reside in a character scheme that reinforces his suspicion of conventional realist order, redistributing attention to favor those who lie outside the usual boundaries of narratability. Social change appears more achievable in Dickens's London than Hardy's Wessex. Yet Hardy retains and even extends the realist novel's commitment to inculcating sympathy for those normally forgotten by society. If Hardy did not fully subscribe to the positivism of Herbert Spencer or Augustus Comte, who coined the term "altruism" in 1851, his works nonetheless reflect his close reading of late nineteenth-century theories that presented inspiring affective response to suffering as a means of fostering social progress (Keen, "Empathetic Hardy" 358–64). Favoring not just the ordinary, but the obscure, his shepherds and reddlemen are a humbler sort than the minor country gentlemen and rising urban professionals that populate so many Victorian domestic novels. Indeed, Elisha Cohn and Suzanne Keen have separately traced the extent to which Hardy, as part of his late-career "ethical turn" (Cohn, "'No Insignificant Creature'"), extended more widespread Victorian concerns for the marginal and oppressed to animal as well as human figures. Even among Hardy's array of unfortunates, the characters on whom he chooses to focus are often those who would seem least worthy of his narrative attention. George Eliot, known for her generous dispersals of consciousness among her characters, famously has the narrator of *Middlemarch* wonder "why always Dorothea?" (264). But if it need not be *always* Dorothea, there is reason enough why it usually should be. Our recognition of Casaubon's "equivalent centre of self" warrants only a detour into the sad old pedant's consciousness before returning to the struggles of his more prepossessing young wife (201).

Hardy's protagonists, by contrast, are at times not only flawed, but almost relentlessly unsympathetic, given to fits of perversely selfish and self-defeating behavior. Michael Henchard begins *The Mayor of Casterbridge* by drunkenly selling off his wife and daughter; this is not, arguably, the worst act he commits in the novel. Even so, Hardy encourages the reader to care more for him than for his ignorant, coarse wife or, more strikingly, his (presumed) daughter Elizabeth-Jane. Elizabeth-Jane is sweet, and innocent, and undoubtedly the wronged party in her relationship with Henchard. In the course of the novel, she experiences dramatic changes in fortune, learns the secret of her paternity, and falls in love. Despite this promisingly novelistic trajectory, Elizabeth-Jane does not, finally, claim our attention as her bitter, petty, self-destructive father does. Elizabeth-Jane is wise, no doubt, to remain relatively unruffled by the vicissitudes of fate, to welcome back her false suitor without reproach and move seamlessly from one father figure to another. It is right and proper that she should bound her "deep and sharp" regret for her tardy forgiveness of Henchard within appropriate limits, and that she should respect his final request to leave him without mourning rites or Christian burial, rather than assuage her guilt with theatrical demonstrations of grief (322). Yet the very traits that confirm her worthiness and good sense give her an air of shallowness; Henchard's torment is self-inflicted, but it invests him with a moral weight that demands more struggle and depth of feeling than the novel ever allows Elizabeth-Jane to display. Hardy has chosen Casaubon, and not Dorothea.

As Elizabeth-Jane's story shows, it isn't that conventional plots are entirely unavailable to Hardy's characters. Yet Hardy's *protagonists*—already distinguished by their less than conventionally novelistic qualities—are, in contravention of usual narrative practice, precisely those likeliest to see a thwarting of their most logical plot trajectories. Elizabeth-Jane lives out, if only in the margins, a satisfying realist plot; Henchard, finally, is all but excluded from a narrative order that has superseded its ostensible hero. His plot is, literally, unwritten: the fates that narrative logic would dictate have been undone by the workings of an arbitrary force that subverts both the determinism of romantic plots and the probabilistic calculations of realist design. Unable to accommodate reform, Hardy's novels take as their key ethical act the shifting of narrative attention to characters whose stories finally fail to conform to the typical expectations of realist narratability. Instead, in a gesture that will finally lead Hardy away from the novel entirely, he calls for a redistribution of narrative focus to traditionally neglected and perhaps even unnarratable lives, the ones unchosen and betrayed by the forces of traditional plotting. His are the heroes of the most reliably unwritten plots, not only of his own novels, but of Victorian fiction.

This is both a narrative and a social gesture. For Hardy, the conventional realist order is one that reflects and replicates a communal order in which certain people have become superfluous. This is perhaps most strikingly evident in the scene that, more than any other, ended Hardy's novelistic career: the death of Jude Fawley's children. Before killing himself and his siblings, Father Time pauses to write a suicide note: "Done," it explains, "because we are too menny" (286). In a world that resists easy attributions of causality, the note offers a clear statement of motives: Father Time has acted as he has because of a sense of himself and his siblings as superfluous, mouths to feed and nothing more. An indictment of the society that has caused his family's plight, the child's declaration also has narrative implications. Little Father Time was not born a symbol: named after his own father, he too is an obscure Jude who might have been elevated to prominence by grace of authorial will. The change in his name suggests a flattening of his potential narrative role. Father Time's siblings—who go entirely unnamed—belong unambiguously to that class of minor characters that Alex Woloch calls "worker" characters, defined as "flat character[s] . . . reduced to a single functional use within the narrative" (*The One vs. the Many* 25). They exist to be burdensome and then dead. The second Jude Fawley, with his ageless gloom and preternatural morbidity, has the capacity to be more than this; if he has not been selected as *the* Jude of the novel's title, he is at least granted a measure of individuating characterization. The allegorical name "Father Time," however, underscores his narrative function at the expense of his independent identity. We sympathize with Jude and Sue, recognize Philotson and Arabella, but Father Time is not a real boy to be pitied or loved. Father Time's act takes his and his siblings depersonalized narrative roles to their logical conclusion: living, the children are no more than structural excess, loose ends to be tied up; dead, they serve their purpose. Father Time must wield his scythe at last. But if the act itself is an affirmation of his role, the note he leaves behind is a challenge to it.[5]

The manner of the children's death is so aggressively melodramatic as to risk bathos. What saves it is one word: "menny." The childish misspelling for the first time humanizes the boy—Pinocchio gets his blue fairy; Little Father Time makes do with a phonetic suicide note. While we have focused Jude's suffering at the hands of an unfeeling world, there has been still a humbler victim languishing forgotten.

In society, Hardy suggests, as in the novel, someone is always left out. One of the obvious questions raised by Hardy's use of chance is why a theoretically neutral force nonetheless leads to such reliably disastrous results. In one hundred coin tosses, it would actually be unusual if the split were precisely fifty-fifty, whatever the mathematical probabilities of each individual wager. If, however, the coin always comes up tails, more than chance should be presumed to be at work. This cannot, in Hardy, be either supernatural malignancy or plot contrivance; the subversive logic of his disrupted causal sequences militates against belief in any such principle of design. Rather, if Hardy's characters cannot outrun their fates, it seems a commentary on a social reality that is finally inescapable. Tess could have *not* killed Alec, and Jude might have married Sue. Yet they are not, ultimately, the victims of a particular plot, law, or decision, but of conditions that prove systemic.

Hardy's melodramatic extremities, to be sure, exaggerate the hopelessness of the picture, both in scale and in sheer impossibility of escape. And even in Hardy, not every character, as we have seen, is subject to such an inexorable set of inevitably fatal options; there are, Hardy acknowledges, *some* brighter endings to be found. His choice to center the stories of those for whom no potentially saving plot twist is coming, however, acts as a corrective against a realist system in which such characters are excluded. Conventional realism, in theory, works toward the inculcation of both narrative and social sympathy by highlighting the struggles of ordinary individuals. Yet ultimately, the fundamentally unnatural devices of conventional plot leave unwritten the most probable of outcomes: that the character and experiences of a given individual will lie outside the scope of the narratable. The character system Woloch identifies in the realist novel has room for these anonymous many; in brief vignettes and narratorial exhortations, in street scenes and panoramic descriptions, we glimpse their faces. But in the necessary economy of realist plotting, they cede their space to those more favored in the game of narrative selection. The limits of conventional narrative are most obvious in the case of the especially overdetermined plots of romance, which in Hardy at times appear in the form of near self-parody. Ultimately, however, any traditional plot works against recognition of the decidedly unnarratable lives we see around us every day. It is sympathy for Little Jude—too many for even Hardy's more generous narrative order—even more than for his father, that most reflects the need for a reformist impulse not dependent on the lure of plotted and plottable literary lives.

Yet if Father Time, consigned to his minor character space, is designed to act as a reproach, several of Hardy's protagonists—enmeshed in conventionally narratable *events*, but themselves barred brutally from the causal trajectories of conventional plot—locate a possible solution, suggesting the potential viability of a different and more accommodating realist and social vision. This is true, perhaps most significantly, of *The Woodlanders*'s Marty South. Rendered narratively marginal by her exclusion from meaningful participation in the key events of the novel's plot, Marty is structurally less prominent than several other characters, most notably Grace Melbury, Marty's more successful rival for both love and character space. Yet in asking us, all the same, to extend the majority of our narrative sympathies to Marty, who conspicuously fails ever to fully enter into conventionally narratable existence, Hardy makes an ethical move toward a radically more egalitarian vision. In our willingness to follow him in choosing Marty—heroine of only the novel's unwritten plots and never its actual plots—as our focus resides in the chance of overcoming the most socially and narratively determined of forces, pointing forward, perhaps, to world in which more Marty Souths might be recognized within the confines of realist narrative.

Paths in the Woods

Unlike Father Time, whose problem is reflected in the rigidity of his narrative role, Marty's presence in the plot of *The Woodlanders* is stubbornly diffuse. Indeed, the events of *The Woodlanders* can be easily summarized without reference to her at all, as is reflected in some contemporary reviews of the novel that ignore her almost completely. Ostensibly, the heroine of *The Woodlanders* is Grace Melbury, whose fickle affections drive most of the action of the novel. Engaged almost since childhood to the simple, incorruptibly noble woodsman Giles Winterbourne, Grace, newly returned from a ladies' seminary, is persuaded to break the engagement by her father, who encourages her to marry the charming doctor Fitzpiers. He promptly cheats on her; when she discovers his adultery, she renews her relationship with Giles (now in severe financial straits), but, unable to secure a divorce, is forced to return to her father's home. When Grace shows up at Giles's cabin during a storm, his insistence on preserving her reputation induces him to spend the night outdoors, where he contracts a fatal illness. As her loyal admirer languishes and dies, Grace forgives a penitent Fitzpiers, whose lover is also now dead, and rather quickly dispenses with her vow to remain true to Giles's memory.

Marty South precedes and outlasts the romantic quadrangle that provides the novel's main plot. Before we have heard of Giles or Grace, we meet Marty, a young woman who immediately earns our sympathies by selling her hair to provide for her ailing father. After events have played themselves out, Marty, truer-hearted than Grace, keeps vigil over the grave of Giles, whom she has long loved in vain. In between, however, she is ruthlessly sidelined. Unusually for a Hardy novel, with their byzantine and abruptly changing romantic entanglements, Marty plays no factor in the erotic arithmetic of the novel; neither Giles nor anyone else seems aware of, let alone concerned with, her obvious attachment to him. She remains near at hand, but not at center stage, relegated to the less dramatic roles of silent witness or sympathetic confessor.

Yet both socially and narratively, Marty's role is not negligible, but only unrecognized. We first find Marty making spars in place of her invalid father, a task she conceals lest potential buyers suspect the quality of her work. This furtive labor amounts to a doubling of the inherent anonymity of the producer in an economic exchange, who tacitly consents to the effacement of his original role in production—and resignation of his de facto, original title to the created object—for monetary compensation. The appropriation of Marty's hair as another object to be bartered further dramatizes the exploitative potential of any transaction. It also, however, suggests a parallel between Marty as a hidden economic producer and Marty as a covert narrative engineer. The woman to whom Marty sells her hair is Felice Charmond, Fitzpiers's lover. By enhancing Felice's attractions, Marty unknowingly contributes to the chain of events that shape the novel, allowing the other woman to maintain the sexual power that will draw Fitzpiers away from Grace and, consequently, drive Grace back toward Giles, to tragic effect. Similarly, not only does her labor prematurely age her, detracting from her own romantic appeal, but it enriches her rival Grace: the buyer of Marty's spars is Grace's timber-merchant father, whose money has made Grace "as valuable as [it] could" by providing her with the education that so refines her (19).

At times, Marty resists her narrative sidelining. Denied an active part in events, she parlays her position as unobserved observer into a quasi-authorial role. When Giles's declining fortune threatens his match with Grace, Marty writes a verse on the wall of his house in a bizarre act of prophecy: "Oh, Giles, you've lost your dwelling-place, / And therefore, Giles, you'll lose your Grace" (107). Her most direct attempt to influence events again comes in the form of text: Marty writes a letter to Fitzpiers telling him of Felice's borrowed hair, hoping that this will lead him to return to Grace and again separate Grace from Giles. In doing so, she tries to reverse her initial exploitation as a doubly unacknowledged producer. Breaking the terms of her economic exchange, which had included an expectation of secrecy, she also attempts to arrest the chain of events that sale may have initiated. One of these events is, at least symbolically, her own narrative usurpation: if Marty had retained her own sexual power—and, more practically, if Grace had remained irrevocably lost to Giles—she might have been indeed the protagonist she appeared to be until the moment of the other woman's return.

In this context, the novel's final turn back to Marty seems to offer grim reparation. To the labor system, she is an exploitable tool; on the marriage market, she is a bad bargain, but in the novel, her worth can be recognized. Yet while it might be tempting to identify Marty throughout as an unrecognized heroine denied her rightful place, her moral claim on us is finally detached from her role in even the narrative order. Our task is not to value Marty's role in driving a plot, but to value her despite her peripheral status. Indeed, Marty's most significant role in the text is finally to undermine the primacy of plot altogether. *The Woodlanders* is at times, even more than in most Hardy novels, almost overwhelmed by melodramatic plots requiring exaggerated narrative contrivance. Hardy adds bizarre complications to situations that would already seem sufficiently involved: Fitzpiers has already left Felice, so why must she also be murdered (off-page) by an ex-lover? What moves Hardy to add yet more sides to his crowded romantic polygon with the introduction of Fitzpiers's one-night stand, Suke Damson, and the vengeful husband who *fails* to exact revenge against him? What are we to make of the disastrous death of Marty's already ailing father—who has secured the claims to his own and Giles's cottage by virtue of an old life right that will expire with his death—being a result of, not the ordinary course of nature, but an unaccountable fixation on a tree to which he ascribes semi-mystical properties?

Yet as we have seen, Hardy simultaneously takes great pains to undermine the causal chain that would seem logically to connect the events of his novels. Despite ample suggestions that Marty is an unacknowledged cause driving the events of *The Woodlanders,* the consequences of her actions are at best unknowable and at worst entirely ineffective; in the final analysis, she is, as Dale Kramer has written, "as nearly irrelevant to the plot as a major character can conceivably be" (*Thomas Hardy* 104). The sale of her hair appears to be fraught with significance, but the later revelation that Fitzpiers and Felice had been lovers years earlier casts its role in their affair into doubt: the attraction between them had existed long before Felice's unnatural enrichment. Marty's letter to Fitzpiers, if it has any influence at all, succeeds only in an unexpected manner that has precisely the opposite effect from the one she intended. While Marty believes that Fitzpiers's knowledge of the transaction will cause him to end his affair in disgust, when he finally reads the letter, his attitude is rather one of cynical amusement; the relationship ends because his words have wounded Felice's pride, not because Fitzpiers has any qualms about loving a woman despite her revealed artifice. Instead of freeing Giles from Grace's influence, as Marty had hoped, Fitzpiers's subsequent return to his wife sends her running desperately to Giles's protection, which may in turn lead to his death. Yet it is again unclear that Marty's intervention has had any such power. Fitzpiers's mockery of Felice's borrowed hair is so bitter and her reaction so extreme only, we are told, because their affair had already soured; the final break seems to have been forthcoming with or without this particular incident. The cause of Giles's death remains equally uncertain: to Grace's great relief, Fitzpiers the doctor maintains that typhoid fever might well have killed him eventually whether or not he had exposed himself to the elements to protect Grace's honor. Marty's other attempted intervention is similarly fruitless. If Marty's prophecy is intended in part to reclaim Giles as a romantic possibility for her, it is completely futile, while as a predictive statement, it is at the very least misleading. Giles does lose Grace, but not simply because he has lost his home, and not, at that point of the novel, irrevocably: Grace herself subverts Marty's message by altering it to read that Giles will "keep" his Grace in a moment of affection toward her old sweetheart.

Nonetheless, the failed plotter is the one who endures. Patricia Ingham, in her introduction to the novel, distinguishes between native woodlanders Marty and Giles, who are defined most prominently as "readers" of the natural signs around them, and the city-bred or educated Grace and Fitzpiers, who are rather characterized by their participation in conspicuously theatrical dialogues and encounters. While the latter couple proves more successful in the traditional calculus of the marriage plot, it is the former—never even a couple at all—that command our sympathies and attention. The fellow readers, and not the actors themselves, are the rightful heroes of this novel, particularly Marty, who avoids, against her will, enmeshment in the novel's web of contrivance. We open with loving, dutiful Marty at work, and end with loving, dutiful Marty in grief. The victory of Marty over Grace—as Giles's truest lover, as the worthiest subject of our regard—stands in opposition to the story that has intervened. The progress from Marty longing for Giles to Marty mourning for him requires some linking action; the events of the novel account for how Giles has died and how, precisely, his relationship with Marty has developed in the period between the sale of her hair and the vigil at the grave. Yet in not only decisively transferring our sympathies to Marty, but retroactively withholding them from Grace, Hardy renders moot many of the events that have transpired. If Grace is the novel's designated leading lady, it should by rights be she that we finally leave at Giles's grave, having learned his value too late. Instead, she compromises her own worth by returning—happily enough, it seems—to Fitzpiers over the obvious displeasure of even her indulgent father, whose regret over encouraging his daughter to aim higher than Giles Winterbourne is more enduring. If *Marty* is our heroine, however, the attention lavished on *Grace* becomes excessive. In a story that centers on Giles and Grace, Marty's role is oddly unaccountable, while significant attention to not only Grace but also Fitzpiers and Felice is manifestly warranted. Recentering the narrative around Giles and Marty removes all these other characters a degree farther from its structural core, leaving them to occupy a disproportionate amount of space.

The alternative to Grace's story, however, is not Marty's story, but no story at all. Marty's attempts to assert a place in the plot are not misguided simply because they prove ineffective. For all its tragedy, the novel's plot teeters on the edge of both melodrama and farce. Nothing can be more absurd, for instance, than the "man-trap" that Suke Damson's husband Tom sets for Fitzpiers. Were we permitted to believe that the silly revenge plot actually led to Grace and Fitzpiers's reunion, the conceit might seem merely contrived, but as usual, Hardy undermines his putative assertion of a causal chain: Grace had already held conciliatory meetings with her husband before he rescued her from the trap, and indeed, she had been on her way to meet him when she met with her accident. The intense emotions both profess are, in context, nearly parodic. Fitzpiers makes a passionate declaration of grief when he believes Grace to be dead—only to be quickly interrupted when she appears before him not much the worse for wear, as Hardy reveals with an air of mock mystery: "[There] a female figure glided, whose appearance even in the gloom was, though graceful in outline, noticeably strange. She was in white up to the waist, and figured above. She was, in short, Grace, his wife, lacking the portion of her dress which the gin retained" (356). Fitzpiers's overwrought declarations effectively punctured, Grace answers his hyperbole with the claim that "there has been an Eye watching over us to-night" (357), a faith that, in light of Giles's recent death, is both painfully naive and outrageously egocentric. Perhaps an oddly selective eye has chosen to turn its lazy gaze to the restoration of Grace and Fitzpiers's marriage—but Fate has an assist, as well, from the new business prospect that leads Grace to look at her estranged husband "much interested" (358).

To become involved in the plot of *The Woodlanders* is to be implicated in this absurdity. Giles himself, though undoubtedly, as Marty says "a good man [who] did good things" (367), cannot entirely escape the taint: when Grace reveals herself unworthy, Giles's own adoration is exposed as a species of folly. The novel's woodland setting, though technically a part of Hardy's greater Wessex, itself evokes the enchanted space of Shakespearean comedy, complete with lost and baffled lovers. If Marty cannot be one of the bewitched mortals, then she will enter the plot—or try to—in the role of fairy schemer: she brings couples together and drives them apart, gifts Felice with a disguise and then reveals the deception. Her most eccentric act of the novel, the writing of the poem on Giles's barn, is indeed explicable only if we regard her as a kind of elfin figure, to be granted oddities and freaks that might seem cruel in the hands of lesser mortals. Her father's belief in his dryad-like attachment to an old tree reinforces the impression that Marty—at least as she appears between Grace Melbury's return to town and her final departure from it—may be something other than an ordinary human woman.

Theoretically a sign of power, this identification of Marty with a woodland sprite or trickster becomes another form of marginalization, an assignation of a fixed role in a narrative economy that replicates, rather than resists, its mercantile counterpart. Again, Marty's father underscores his daughter's position. Old South's life may not literally be bound to a tree, but it is associated with the quirk of property law that makes the ownership of several cottages dependent on his survival. Giles, who has known the old man for years and really does care for his well-being, recognizes nonetheless that the arrangement inevitably corrupts human concern into material self-interest: it is impossible for him to register his concern for the man without turning him into a metonym for the home he will lose with the other man's death. Narratively, the same logic applies. South may be a very good sort of man, one that Marty loves and Giles respects. But in the brutal commerce of the novel, he is a mere adjunct to Giles and Marty, a cog fixed in place to permit the operation of a narrative that does not require him to be more than his function has made him. Though a far more significant figure than her father, Marty—short of indeed winning Giles's heart and becoming the protagonist of a sustained marriage plot, an option the text never seriously considers—can resist a similar process only to the extent that she transcends plot entirely.

In 1903, Hardy, by then a poet and not a novelist, returned to Marty in "The Pine Planters," a mournful lament for unrequited love, which, in some editions, was published with the subtitle "Marty South's Reverie."[6] That it would be Marty, and not another character, who followed Hardy in his transition from prose to poetry, seems entirely fitting. If any Hardy novel presages the author's formal transition, it is perhaps not *Jude*, but *The Woodlanders*, where the logic of Hardy's always chaotic plotting is strained to its limit and exposed as hollow. Simon Gatrell attributes Hardy's turn away from the novel primarily to his creation of a more realistic—and therefore less imaginatively liberating—setting: "His losses [in creating 'New Wessex'] included the desire to write more novels.... He was no longer content with the requirements the realistic novel imposed on him.... The sense he had of the closure of Wessex as a living culture was central to his slow decision to end his career as a creator of fiction" ("Wessex" 32). But lyric offers a respite from plot as well as setting. Plot, in Hardy, is less an elegant design than a field of quicksand bordered by a mirage: there seems to be a way out, if only one could reach it, but when the illusion fades, one path is as treacherous as another. Part of the problem, no doubt, is a general pessimism toward the possibility of social or individual progress. Beyond that, however, Hardy seems suspicious of plot as a type of system that can, at its worst, be as reductive and dehumanizing as any market transaction. Marty South gets it wrong: the ultimate metric of worth, in Hardy, is not defined by any action—the good man who does good things—but by a quality of authenticity that makes suffering unromantic and transforms melodrama into tragedy. The novel attempts to create an alternative order in which characters abused and cast aside in life can receive at last their due, where Henchard will be remembered by us when Elizabeth-Jane has dutifully forgotten him and been herself forgotten. Yet this egalitarianism becomes its own form of exclusion; someone must always be sacrificed to the hierarchy. The protagonist wins narratability with an excess that obscures the human; the minor character becomes an allegory or a function, left to move us only in stolen moments of legitimate pathos.

Again, the antidote here is not precisely an unwritten *plot*. Apart from any ethical considerations, grand narratives, as we have seen, end poorly in Hardy. The person who seeks fame or fortune is humiliated or humbled or forced home to a world that no longer satisfies him. By contrast, the few (sympathetic) couples whose stories end happily escape the general devastation by essentially reverting to an arrangement that existed prior to plot. The traditional novel may, as D. A. Miller suggests, always move toward the exhaustion of its own narrativity. Yet Hardy's successful marriage plots do not simply resolve complications, ending the need for discourse; they cancel, so far as it is possible, everything that has intervened. Both Diggory Venn and Thomasin Yeobright and Gabriel Oak and Bathsheba Everdene are couples that should have been together from the first, that in fact share an early romantic history disrupted by the foolish ambitions of one or other of the potential partners.

The Woodlanders does these novels one better. The happiness of the Venns and the Oaks represents a pastoral promise that cannot always, or perhaps ever, be fulfilled; for good or, more often, for ill, Hardy's Wessex is not a real English county. The possibility that Marty will win a living Giles after all, as other unrequited lovers have done before her, is one unwritten plot lying at the margins of *The Woodlanders*. Yet to make the strongest ethical claim, Marty must win the reader's sympathies while avoiding, not only farce and melodrama, but the realist marriage plot as well. The proliferation of plots of romantic contrivance only underscores the danger of all conventional plots, which grant their readers the pleasure of narrative sensation without demanding the self-reproach of recognition. It is in isolated scenes and fugitive moments that Hardy's characters move us most, and in these moments that their claims are least dependent on assessments of social or narrative utility. In Little Father Time's six-word-story ("Done," he writes, "Because we are too menny"), in Marty South's bookended love and grief, we see briefly the potential of a more generous narrative order.

For Hardy himself, this more generous order would not come in the shape of long-form narrative at all. The hypothetically realist world, in which Marty's non-plot could indeed become central, can come about only through an audience responsive to her claims—and, more vitally, to the claims of the Martys that live outside the pages of *The Woodlanders*. Absent such an extraliterary response, Hardy resigns himself to the intractability of a world in which the unwritten plots of Marty South must always be secondary. The move to poetry is a logical extension of the alternative to normative realist order Hardy the novelist toys with most explicitly in *The Woodlanders*: the character who cannot find a home in the plots of the novel seeks her mayfly moment in the images of poetry. There, Hardy hoped, she might yet have an influence on the obdurate hearts of his book-burning countrymen.

Yet Hardy's sense of the limits of novelistic form does not, of course, inevitably require that form's destruction. Hardy's revolt against plot anticipates a narrative revolution in which he himself, by turning away from the novel entirely, would not participate. *Jude the Obscure* was published in 1895. By the time Hardy died in 1928, the Marty Souths of the world were no longer confined to verse or bookends: Joyce and Woolf and Proust had brought the plotless wanderer, whose life was witnessed in moments and measured out in coffee spoons, to the forefront of narrative discourse. This change did not, perhaps, transform the conditions of the world, except in the incalculably diffusive ways that the Eliot of an earlier era had so honored. But in expanding the scope of the narratable beyond the bounds of conventional realism, these authors at least transformed, as Hardy had hoped, the possibilities available to the novel.

Utopian Realists

The desire to influence his readers led Hardy away from the rigid plotting of the Victorian novel. In Elizabeth Gaskell's much earlier *Mary Barton*, by contrast, we find a confident endorsement of the power of traditional plot to bring about practical social change. Many critics have commented on the formal oddities of *Mary Barton*, generally classified as one of the major midcentury industrial novels.[7] Yet while the text reflects that realist subgenre's commitment to unflinching description of the desperate conditions of England's working poor, its second half hinges on a murder plot notably more melodramatic than anything in *Hard Times*, *Shirley*, or Gaskell's own *North and South*, while its final pages are nearly utopian in their vision. Gaskell offers her requisite sacrifices to the gods of realism; we open on a death in childbirth and will see the deaths of starving children and broken-down fathers before we are done. Yet for our main characters, the final disposition of fates plays out according to the dictates of a seemingly providential justice. Mary marries honest Jem, who has been freed from an unjust murder charge. Her friend Margaret is engaged to Alice's nephew Will; having gradually gone blind over the course of the novel, her sight is restored by its end. Not everyone, of course, can be saved; Mary's aunt and father die before they can be incorporated in the happy final tableau. But this, too, we can gather, is justice—justice, and mercy. Aunt Esther, having completed a Hogarthian descent from vanity to vice, seals her journey with her death. John Barton, the union radical, has murdered his master's son and almost let Jem die for his crime. Both deaths, too, offer a reassuring sense of redemption. Barton dies in the arms of John Carson, the father of the man he has killed, the two men finally, briefly united in a perfect moment of mutual understanding and forgiveness. Afterward, we are told, Carson becomes an exemplary employer—vigilante murder, it seems, has its uses after all—while Barton shares a grave with Esther, whose fall he had helped precipitate through his uncompromising severity. The inscription on their stone bears a message from psalms, promising divine forgiveness for all sinners.

God may indeed forgive all, in time, and in another world. Precisely what kind of a world *this* one is, however, is, as it is in *The Woodlanders*, a question of real anxiety for the novel. In offering such a jarringly ideal conclusion, Gaskell in effect enacts what should have been a romantic shadow-plot, the kind of perfect dispensation of justice toward which the realist novel gestures but ultimately rejects in favor of an often satisfying yet still compromised alternative. The world in which the last become first, where the blind can see, and all wrongs are made right is one that, in even the most generous of realist novels, is not to be. The utopian tradition with which the novel finally associates itself, however, plays out in a liminal space somewhere between a necessarily alternative world and a possible one. On one hand, unlike the fantasies and romances they only superficially resemble, utopian novels, no matter how implausible, are acutely aware of the world as it is. Romance requires suspension of disbelief; if we are to enjoy, say, *Lorna Doone*, we must arrive at the point at which nothing seems more natural than finding out that the little girl one encountered by chance on the moors is actually a long-lost heiress kidnapped in infancy by a clan of brigands. Utopian writing, by contrast, demands that readers maintain awareness of the reality against which the fiction has defined itself: social criticism, rather than immersion, is the order of the day, and that requires, not forgetfulness, but recognition of the actual world.

Yet the relationship of the utopian world to the actual one is often uncertain—here, too, only some unwritten plots emerge as active, as opposed to nominal, possibilities. Fredric Jameson defends the continued political value of utopian thinking with the claim that even if the utopian world is almost by definition void of practical content, its virtual existence provides an aspirational context in which social change may be fostered: "Even if we succeed in reviving utopia itself, the outlines of a new and effective practical politics for the era of globalization will [not] at once become visible; but . . . we will never come to one without it" ("The Politics of Utopia" 36). But many literary utopias seem so detached from any kind of accessible reality that their relationship to our world can be better characterized as cynically critical than productively reformative. In many of those works most commonly identified as utopian—those that, like More's *Utopia*, create elaborate models of an alternative society—the worlds constructed exist at considerable geographic remove from our own; the word "utopia" does, after all, mean no place. In the language of modal logic, they have fewer points of accessibility with our own than the world of a realist novel does. Many of the socialist and feminist utopian novels of the late nineteenth century take place in the future; some take place in different worlds. Though these novels occasionally locate the origins of their enlightened societies in a specific, contemporary moment—in Florence Dixie's *Gloriana*, a woman disguised as a man gets elected to Parliament and ushers in a matriarchal golden age—the utopias serve more often as instructive comparisons than as attainable possibilities. Indeed, they do not necessarily even represent desirable futures. There is an obvious element of sly wish fulfillment in the imagining of feminist utopias characterized by matriarchal or exclusively female, as opposed to gender-egalitarian, societies. The primary function of such models, however, is not to advocate for the subjugation or elimination of men, but to trace male domination to social practice rather than natural law. This understanding would, ideally, lend itself to immediate social reforms; it is no coincidence that these novels proliferated during the period at which the campaign for women's suffrage had begun to gain traction in Britain. The potential worlds themselves, however, were even at best more rhetorical than real. It is telling that with remarkable consistency, the most reliable way of getting to utopia seems to be, not active labor for a better society, but a magical vision that transports the sleeper to a realm only a dreamer could think possible.

Mary Barton does not fit neatly into this paradigm. Unlike the fabulous journeys of the classical utopian novel, the events of *Mary Barton* are at least technically possible, occupying a recognizable, immediately accessible reality. The open question is that of precisely how possible they are. Even the starkest work of social realism takes place in a world distinct from our own; were *we* to be transported in a dream vision to Manchester in the early 1840s, we would look in vain for Mary Barton and Jem Wilson and Carson's Mill. A novel's realism rests on the extent to which its world can be seen as representative: is the Manchester that includes Mary and Jem a Manchester that could be real, but simply happens not to be, or one that can merely *seem* real for as long as we consent to inhabit the fiction? The novel's structure frustrates attempts at a consistent answer. Its first half reads like a cross between a Manchester *Middlemarch* and *Mary Barton's Apprenticeship*, shifting between a panoramic social gaze and more focused concern for the progress of an individual. The plot consists mainly of a love triangle between working-class Mary, her childhood sweetheart Jem, and

Harry Carson, son of the richest man in town, with the scenes of poverty and rumblings of political unrest serving as a grim backdrop to the developing romance plot. In any event, these elements add up to seventeen chapters tilting heavily toward the realist end of the spectrum of possibility. If there was never really a family named Wilson who lost twin sons named Joe and Will to a slum-borne fever exacerbated by hunger and lack of medical care, we can be pretty sure that there were families of some other name losing children in parallel circumstances. As for Mary, Harry, and Jem, the most incredible part of that little triangle is that Harry hasn't marshaled the persuasive powers of his wealth and looks to secure more than a kiss from Mary before she has had time to reevaluate her choice.

Barton's murder of Harry is, in this context, more than a shocking turn of events. It vitiates our previous understanding of the nature of the novel. The events of the first half of the text may produce the crime whose consequences dominate its second, but the murder plot cannot simply be folded into our long-sustained sense of the novel as a portrait of urban poverty given narrative interest through a sympathetic protagonist and her fairly run-of-the-mill love story. Any initial classification of the story in terms of its love triangle proves not just incomplete, but incorrect: the rivalry between the two men turns out to have a comparatively slight functional role in the plot, while the central conflict of the novel proves to be the one between Mary's love for Jem and her love for her father. More than that, the second half of the novel seems to take place on a different plane of reality from the first. If the latter prefigures Eliot, the former rather recalls Scott's *Heart of Midlothian*, whose plot contains significant parallels with that of *Mary Barton*.[8] Without offering any absolute impossibilities, the novel has slipped into unlikelihood and severely strained its mimetic claims; Mary's experiences are no longer representative, but exceptional. To Marxist critics, in particular, the second half of the novel has been regarded as a disappointing retreat from the serious social criticism of its opening. Raymond Williams, in perhaps the best-known of these critiques, argues that the novel's sentimental turn is not only frivolous but reactionary: by turning union man John Barton into a killer, Gaskell plays into middle-class fears of mob violence. The shift in tone intensifies the betrayal: "Mrs. Gaskell was under no obligation to write a representative novel; she might legitimately have taken a special case. But the tone elsewhere is deliberately representative, and she is even, as she says, modelling John Barton on 'a poor man I know.'"

For Williams, the generic change is evidence of representative failure, the victory of Gaskell's instinctive fear over her "deep imaginative sympathy" (*Culture and Society* 97).

Only in a world of such special cases, perhaps, does the novel's final vision of happiness become possible. Industrial novels as a group are notable for what social critics have identified as an excessively rosy attitude to the possibilities of reform, often prescribing, as Gaskell does both in *Mary Barton* and *North and South*, the development of interclass understanding as a viable alternative to practical political action. Yet again, *Mary Barton's* conclusion surpasses the far more measured gains of its counterparts. The utopia that social realism could never have produced, romantic melodrama, with an assist from Christian parable, wistfully enacts. Even as she actualizes this romantic plot, however, Gaskell signals that it is, on some level, properly unwritten within a world of conventional social realism. The novel's idyllic ending can be sustained only through a geographical as well as a generic dislocation, one that removes it from the realist world of embedded material realities. Carson's reformation offers some modest hope of change in Manchester, one that is relatively consistent with the measured successes of other industrial novels. Jem and Mary, however, wind up in Canada, where they are, even more implausibly, expecting a visit from two of their working-class neighbors from home. Canada itself is depicted as less a physical space than the (nominally) realist analogue of the utopian novel's remote lands:

> "Thou knowest where Canada is, Mary?"
>
> "Not rightly—not now, at any rate;—but with thee, Jem," her voice sunk to a soft, low whisper, "anywhere—"
>
> What was the use of a geographical description? (519)

Far less fully realized than the similarly inaccessible reformist utopias of Bellamy or Charlotte Perkins Gilman, Gaskell's Canada is not a world to be created, but a paradise to be inherited. Rather than a plausible alternative to a sociopolitical status quo, what Gaskell offers is an escape from it, a Celestial City to requite the worldly travails of our good pilgrims.

It is not so clear, however, that the attenuated realism of the novel's conclusion is for Gaskell incompatible with an earnest, achievable social vision. Over the course of the novel, Gaskell occasionally ventures into political specifics, objecting, for instance, to child labor laws that deprive poor families of desperately needed income without offering them any other means of support. Yet overwhelmingly, her preferred corrective to the abuses she catalogs, as I suggest, is nothing more or less than the development of a heightened sense of empathy. In Gaskell's social vision, urban misery is primarily a function, not of bad policy or unchecked capitalism, but of a tragic lack of understanding between the classes. During a period of particular privation, Gaskell tells us, the suffering of the poor was so great that not even a Dante could adequately describe it. Even so, "the most deplorable and enduring evil" of the crisis is "[the] feeling of alienation between the different classes of society" (121). Gaskell's explanation for this feeling—which she will articulate at greater length in *North and South*—is less reminiscent of Dante than of Sophocles; in Gaskell's account, social distrust is the result of a series of mistakes made by blind but fundamentally decent men who simply fail adequately to communicate to one another their competing claims.

At first glance, Gaskell's proposed solution of harmony through Christian love and forgiveness seems hopelessly naive. Barton repents fully of his crime after connecting Carson's pain at losing Harry to his own grief for a long-dead son; as the other man mourns, the two become not employer and worker, but "brothers in the deep suffering of the heart" (525). Carson is at first less yielding, vowing vengeance even as his enemy begs for mercy on his deathbed. But his sympathies, too, are awakened in time to embrace Barton as he dies, pitying the desperation that impelled a good man to murder. Later, he will be responsible for "many of the improvements now in practice in the system of employment in Manchester" (558); although we do not learn what any of these improvements are, we are assured that they proceed from his acknowledgment of "the Spirit of Christ as the regulating law between both parties" (557).

But if Gaskell leaves much to be desired as a political reformer, she is more astute as an affective theorist. Well before he resorts to murder, John Barton goes to London as part of a union delegation to Parliament. Before he leaves, his neighbors suggest particular measures for relief, some reasonable (a shorter workday and a reduction of protective tariffs), and some less so (the destruction of all machines and a mandate that wealthy gentlemen purchase calico shirts). Barton, however, is not concerned with their proposals, convinced that simply telling the government of their sufferings will be enough to bring about relief: "When they hear o' children born on wet flags, without a rag t'cover 'em, or a bit o' food for th' mother; when they hear of folk lying down to die i' th' streets, or hiding their want i' some hole o' a cellar till death come to set 'em free . . . they'll surely do somewhat wiser for us than we can guess at now" (127). Barton's logic here is Gaskell's, and the manner of his failure affirms his and Gaskell's shared faith in the power of empathy. The rejection of the Charter deprives Barton of even the chance to bear witness to the plight of the laboring classes; had he been able to do so, he might have succeeded.

More specifically, the incident validates the necessarily *affective* nature of the politically *effective* understanding that Gaskell promotes as a general solution to social ills. Although Barton curses "them as so cruelly refused to hear us" (146), the petition, as Gaskell's readers would have recalled, was not rejected entirely without a hearing. Nine years before the publication of *Mary Barton*, Thomas Attwood, the MP for Birmingham, introduced the People's Charter before the House of Commons, and on July 12, 1839—presumably the day of John Barton's crushing disappointment—he brought forth a formal request for its consideration. For Attwood, "consideration" meant more than debate on the five proposals included in the Charter. While Attwood, unlike Gaskell and Barton, is also concerned with particular reforms,[9] he, too, believes that it is essential that the petitioners themselves be given the opportunity to speak; had his motion passed, deliberations were to include the testimony of working-class representatives:

> Many petitions had been presented to that House from Birmingham, complaining of the state of suffering in which the people were, but their petitions had been altogether disregarded, and that hon. House had refused, in several instances, not only to grant the prayers, but even to receive the petitions of the industrious classes, and relied on the representations of lawyers and gentlemen and the public press. . . . That House had chosen to legislate in the dark—not, he believed, intentionally, because it was composed of noblemen and gentlemen of the highest honour and virtue, but because they had not a clear view respecting the matters they were dealing with.[10] (HC Deb 12 July 1839 vol 49 cc220-74)

If Attwood's fellow MPs are blind, it is not because they lack knowledge. Certainly, they are well aware of the Charter's five principles, and Attwood himself has represented to them, if only in abstract terms, the suffering that has inspired the appeal. The problem is rather that their knowledge is of the wrong kind; they may be aware that prices are high and wages low, but without any more direct encounter with the victims of their policies, they remain effectively in the dark.

To the extent that Gaskell's final vision of empathy and forgiveness is a fantasy, then, it is one created, like so many utopian visions, to address specific features of a disappointing social reality, ones that the author sees, not as inevitable elements of the human condition, but as potentially changeable contingencies. In the proxy narrative, the inexorability of realist logic forces the psychologically essential phantom plot to hide behind a more palatable substitute. In the hypothetically realist *Mary Barton*, the romantic plot can, unexpectedly, emerge as the actual, rather than unwritten, plot because of Gaskell's anticipatory invocation of a world in which its idealism will be possible. In his final moments, Barton realizes his dream of effectively representing the sufferings of his class. He does so, however, not as a union delegate, but as an allegorical martyr-penitent; Gaskell softens the historical fact of the Charter's rejection by rewriting Barton's mission in the context of Christian parable. Departing from the realm of immediate social reality allows her to rehabilitate as an active political possibility the affective logic that has failed: when circumstances conspire to bring John Carson to a dying worker's door, his response is exactly the one that Attwood had anticipated—had the people been allowed to plead their own desperate case. One might have imagined that John Barton, having lost a son of his own, would have had sufficient theory of mind to perceive that John Carson might be similarly affected by Harry's death, but in ironic fulfillment of his own belief in the power of direct encounter, it takes the sight of the grieving father for him to feel remorse for what he has done. Even more to the point, Christian forbearance and charity are not themselves sufficient to prompt Carson's forgiveness of Barton, or to induce him to become a more compassionate employer. Rather, he can only do these things once he has been moved by seeing the other man's home: "In the days of his childhood and youth, Mr. Carson had been accustomed to poverty; but it was honest, decent poverty; not the grinding squalid misery he had remarked in every part of John Barton's house" (531). It is a diffracted version of Barton's mistake: if Barton fails to perceive the similarity between Carson's loss and his own, Carson assumes his own recalled experience of poverty must be universally and indefinitely applicable. Once he is confronted with the stark reality of current conditions, he is able to understand and forgive even his son's murderer.

The Reader's Choice

In *Mary Barton,* what appears to be a romantic, utopian plot is actualized, while the realist plots go unwritten. As good readers of Victorian realism, we might have, at the novel's halfway point, imagined a number of non-tragic outcomes for Mary and Jem and the rest, but they would not have included a Canadian paradise, miraculous restorations of vision, and a murder that effects healing and sustained, if small-scale, social reform. Gaskell is not, however, writing a wistful throwback to the generically stable romances of a prior generation. Rather, she knowingly reverses the conventional plot hierarchies of realist fiction to express her earnest belief in the possibility of a better world that is not, but may soon become, a reality. The world she envisions is not a fictional realm, but a possible future; by moving her readers to productive action, Gaskell can in turn help bring about what is now only a hypothetically realist social and narrative order.

In this sense, Gaskell's emphasis on direct experience poses a potential problem. Amanda Anderson has written of Gaskell's anxiety over the ability of necessarily aestheticized fictional depictions, specifically, to mobilize readerly sympathy into productive reform; a novel inevitably mediates experience. Gaskell, to borrow Attwood's categories, is more equivalent to the inadequate outside advocate than to the rightful representative of the masses. Yet strangely, the text contains a number of conspicuously anti-immersive elements that exaggerate, rather than ameliorate, this distance. At times, Gaskell's narrative "I" is, as Robyn Warhol suggests, an "engaging" figure whose presence in the text fosters readerly investment. Yet Gaskell's narrator is often a more intrusive presence than she need be, from merely superfluous self-insertions ("the friend . . . was more handsome and less sensible-looking than the man I have just described") to more substantive reminders of her presence ("what I wish to impress is what the workman feels and thinks," where the reference to an outside narrator risks negating the illusion of intimacy she claims to cultivate) (10, 34). While she positions herself as one well-acquainted with the city and people of whom she writes, she also maintains an obvious and sometimes even exaggerated distance; she *knows* them but is not *of* them.

This is never more apparent than in the ethnographic tendencies of her narration. When Margaret sings a regional folk ballad, Gaskell doesn't simply transcribe the lyrics; she tells us that it *is* a regional folk ballad, and that she is therefore going to copy it for us so that we as outsiders may learn the local tune. Descriptions often focus on collective experiences; we are given characteristics of the laboring men or the factory girls as a class—members of the manufacturing population, for instance, can be identified as a rule by "an acuteness and intelligence of countenance" (8). Above all, there are the footnotes, most of which provide definitions of dialect words such as "nesh" and "farrantly." Critics have generally regarded the presence of these footnotes, unusual for the genre, as an authenticating gesture by an author eager both to confirm her personal knowledge of the class of which she writes and to force her readers to acknowledge the reality of the conditions she describes. Yet even Terry Wyke, a Manchester historian who was among the first to devote extended (and admiring) critical attention to Gaskell's footnotes, observes inconsistencies that call into question the reason for their inclusion.[11] Gaskell annotates a reference to one real historical figure mentioned in the text but lets another pass without comment. Her decisions about which dialect words require translation, to which Wyke refers only in passing, are similarly irregular. We get the definition of "getten" but not "whatten" (for *got* and *what*, respectively), of "pobbies" (porridge) but not "brosten" (bursting), and of "sin'" for "since" but not "mun" for "must."

Whatever other purposes they serve, then, the footnotes do not seem to be important to Gaskell primarily for the information they convey. This would be consistent with the conventional reading of them as an authenticating device; Gaskell needs to demonstrate only enough knowledge of Manchester and its actual history to make her rhetorical point, which will not be served more forcefully by defining *every* unfamiliar term. Yet I would suggest that the pattern of Gaskell's footnote use is not random, and like her narrative intrusions, the footnotes rather have the counterproductive effect of impairing our capacity to fully engage in the world of the novel. Wyke, the historian, writes approvingly that the footnotes "[break] the rhythm of the text" ("Authenticating the Text" 121), granting the reader direct access to an extra-narrative authorial voice with lived experience of the people and places behind the fiction. The price of this break, however, is the disruption of our immersion in the fictional narrative, a quality that we generally regard as much more vital to the inculcation of sympathy in a reader than overt reminders of any real-world basis for the fiction. We may derive some marginal advantage from knowing that a "ritling" is a child with rickets, and, perhaps more to the point, from knowing that Gaskell herself knows it and the people who use such language. But this cannot compensate for the damage done to our illusion of intimacy; were we really there with the Bartons and Wilsons, we would not have the benefit of a glossary.

These troublesome footnotes—which Gaskell does not include in any of her other novels—represent more than an instance of an author's reportorial zeal overcoming her stylistic instincts. Indeed, it is hard to escape the impression that Gaskell is, for some obscure purpose, *deliberately* interfering with her readers' capacity to engage with the world of the text and, worse, to be affected by it. Some of the most questionable glosses occur at precisely those moments that should by rights be the most moving. In one early scene, Barton and his friend Wilson go on a mission of charity to the Davenports, a family of five living in what even the two workingmen, no strangers to poverty themselves, consider to be desperate conditions. The father, dying of untreated typhus fever, has long been unable to work. Having pawned nearly all their possessions, they live in a nearly bare cellar; an old sewer line running through their street leaves their home, such as it is, suffused with the stink of excrement. Wilson sees with surprise that the mother is nursing a three- or four-year-old child and asks if the boy has been weaned, prompting the following dialogue:

> "Going on two year," she faintly answered. "But, oh! it keeps him quiet when I've nought else to gi' him, and he'll get a bit of sleep lying there, if he's getten nought beside. We han done our best to gi' the childer food, howe'er we pinched ourselves."
>
> "Han ye had no money fra' th' town?"
>
> "No; my master is Buckinghamshire born; and he's feared the town would send him back to his parish, if he went to th' board; so we've just borne on in hope o' better times. But I think they'll never come in my day," and the poor woman began her weak high-pitched cry again.
>
> "Here, sup this drop o' gruel, and then try and get a bit o' sleep."
> (91–92)

The first ten chapters of *Mary Barton* have an average of just under four footnotes per chapter. This brief passage alone has three, on the words "childer," "han," and "sup." All are easily understandable in context, if indeed they require context at all. In fact, in all three cases, Gaskell does not even bother to provide a definition to justify the intrusion, simply referring us to lines from classic texts—by Wycliffe, Spencer, and Mandeville, respectively—in which the words appear. Her decision, at such a moment, to put a gloss on "han" is particularly puzzling given that she had used it without comment during a far less sensitive scene six pages earlier. The pattern is repeated in other scenes; when one of Wilson's own young sons is dying, Gaskell feels the need to tell us that "poor lile fellow" means poor *little* child (109), and Barton's vow to "not speak of [the petition's rejection] no more," at the end of a bitter, despairing account of his trip to London, is punctuated with the observation that Chaucer, too, often uses double negatives (146).

Interrupting those passages most likely to elicit sympathy, the footnotes undercut the very emotional responsiveness Gaskell is ostensibly trying to inculcate. This contradiction, however, may be precisely the point. In simultaneously presenting and disrupting scenes of human misery, Gaskell dramatizes—in the body of the text and in the footnotes—two possible modes of reading her only provisionally realist text. For all her belief in the persuasive and affective value of personal testimony, Gaskell is not, like John Barton, naively convinced that the opportunity to bear witness automatically solves middle- and upper-class indifference. Barton is not crushed only by Parliament's refusal to hear his appeal, but by the callousness of those along the way who did. As they make their way toward Parliament, the delegates are stopped and abused by policemen who try to turn them back, claiming that they are disturbing the ladies and gentlemen taking the same route to a ball. Here, Barton does get the chance to speak, passionately, about working-class suffering, only to be met with laughter from the listening officer. When he says a moment later that he will "curse them as so cruelly refused to hear us" for the rest of his days (146), he is referring to the rejection not only by Parliament but also by the ordinary Londoners who remained impassive even after a direct encounter with the desperate men. The officer has heard Barton, but it isn't the right *kind* of hearing; given the chance to respond compassionately to the suffering of another, he elects to remain unmoved by the appeal.

Gaskell's depictions of individuals who are either affected by or detached from scenes of suffering has direct implications for the experience of the reader, for whom a text can be immersive or merely informative, a light diversion or a serious call to reflection and action. The policeman's laughter does not simply dismiss Barton's appeal, but treats it as an object of amusement. It has entertained, rather than moved him. The parallel is even sharper in an earlier scene in which Mary and Margaret go to see a fire at Carson's Mill because, as Mary says "they say a burning mill is such a grand sight" (70). Her desire is grounded in love of spectacle and a longing for distraction; Margaret has just told her of her incipient blindness, and Mary hopes that the fire will provide a diversion to occupy both of their troubled thoughts. When she arrives at the mill, however, Mary is horrified to realize that there are people trapped in the building, and more who are risking their lives to save them; she had wanted to see the fire only because she "had no idea any lives were in danger" (74). Indeed, even before she learns there are men in the mill, the sight of the flames alone is enough to "almost [wish] herself away" (72). Other members of the "deeply interested" crowd are less affected. While they, too, are caught up in the emotion of Jem Wilson's perilous attempt to save the trapped men, their response suggests the pleasurable terror of the sublime rather than empathetic anguish for their endangered fellows. Their anxiety arises from "suspense"; their sobs are "excited."

While Mary tries to leave the scene and then, unable to push through the crowd, hopes to faint as her only remaining means of escape, the masses can't pull their eyes from the building until Jem appears about to fall to his death, when "many," but not all, finally shut them. Their emotion is, in any case, short-lived: when all are safe, "the multitude in the street absolutely danced with triumph . . . and then with all the fickleness of interest characteristic of a large body of people, pressed and stumbled . . . in the hurry to get out of Dunham Street, and back to the immediate scene of the fire" (78). The fact that many in the crowd might have answered the call for help themselves only makes their comparatively distant "interest" all the more culpable; even after Jem and his father have gone in, the trapped workers continue "praying the great multitude below for help" to no avail (73). Sensation is not sympathy, and tears no pledge of action.

Mary's response to the plight of the endangered men—which, Gaskell takes care to clarify, manifests itself before she realizes that her old friend Jem Wilson is among them—is thus a model for the desired reaction to Gaskell's own text. I began this chapter by considering the first of many questions Gaskell asks of her readers: "Can you fancy the bustle of Alice ... can you fancy [her] delight?" (44). Most of these questions are more directly exhortative and thus easier to write off as evidence of a somewhat wearying moralism. But for Gaskell, all are legitimate questions with the power to transform not only the experience of reading but the nature of the text itself. They, in other words, create two active possibilities, ones whose actualization—in the world outside, more than even the world within the novel—depends in this case on the reader's answer to Gaskell's appeal. During the fire at Carson's Mill, the area in which the men are trapped is, by the time Mary arrives, no longer actively burning; rather, the men are in a smoke-filled fourth-story room with no means of escape, the staircase having collapsed. As a result, the crowd has to turn *away* from the fire to watch their rescue because, as Gaskell says, "what were magnificent terrible flames, what were falling timbers or tottering walls, in comparison with human life?" (73). But as we have seen, the question is not at all rhetorical: really, what are they? Do those below turn because of their sense of the value of human life or, as Gaskell suggests, at least in part because they have found a more compelling drama to replace the last sensation? Like John Barton's own question to the policeman—"'Which business is of most consequence i' the sight o' God, think yo, our'n or them gran ladies and gentlemen as yo think so much on?'" (145)—it is a question that *ought* to be rhetorical but is proved in the response not to be so.

The answers are as uncertain in the case of the reader. For Gaskell, *any* exhortation is implicitly a question because command or not, it remains in the power of the listener to either accept or refuse the charge. True even in the case of ordinary requests, this doubt over outcome is magnified in the case of the questions asked by a text of its readers. One could hardly miss the moral in Gaskell's "'Sick, and in prison, and ye visited me.' Shall you, or I, receive such blessing?" (227). Yet her use of the biblical source text reveals the capacity of countless readers to do precisely that—or, at least, to fail to act up to it. The reader who appreciates the wisdom and power of the Gospels without taking up their charge reduces instruction to mere rhetoric; the Bible becomes a good book, rather than a guide for virtuous living, the word admired, and not the word made flesh through the incarnating power of action. "Does [the parable of Dives and Lazarus] haunt the minds of the rich as it does those of the poor?" (142), asks Gaskell. "To whom shall the outcast prostitute tell her tale? Who will give her help in her day of need?" (228). Would we not, like John Barton, who turns to opium in his depression, "be glad to forget life, and its burdens" (244)? These are questions that interrogate both the nature of the reader and the nature of his or her reading. Does our engagement with the parable, whether of Dives and Lazarus or John Barton and John Carson, outlast the brief space of its telling? Are we moved by the prostitute's tale, and if so, will we help as well as pity her? Is our immersion in the novel itself an escape from our own lives, or an encounter with the lives we neglect? For Gaskell, the ideal reader is the one who, having picked up the novel as entertainment, reaches with Mary the moment of horrified recognition that real human lives are at stake.

If lives are at stake, so too, finally, is the status of the novelistic world itself. The novel's structure, with its inconsistent generic affiliation, prepares readers for and then subjects them to a test of their capacity for right reading—which is to say, a reading that is both emotionally responsive and generative of action. Both Gaskell's footnotes and her questions to readers are disproportionately located in the novel's first, realist half, underscoring the possibility for two contrasting modes of reception. Readers who can continue dutifully consulting the footnotes as the Wilson boys lie dying have gotten it wrong. They are *interested* rather than touched, entertained rather than transformed. They may answer Gaskell's questions in a catechistic call and response—*I* will help the prostitute, *I* will receive the blessing of the righteous—but then be as easily distracted by a return to Mary's love life (is it to be handsome Harry or loyal Jem?) as by the definition of "donnot." When the novel's realism is co-opted by the melodramatic murder plot, they can thus be carried away with a new sensation, feeling all the pleasurable anxiety of watching, from a distance, the fight for Jem Wilson's life. It is, as Mary's callous acquaintance Sally says, like something "at the theatre" (515).

The experience of the other readers is radically different. At first, perhaps they, too, appreciate their guide to unfamiliar Manchester life, the soothing mediation of the narrator who can both define "nesh" and "farrantly" and furnish a quotation from Chaucer. But as they are pulled deeper into the world of the characters, of their modest joys and desperate privations, of their hopes and struggles and suffering, such readers outgrow their pedantic conductress; what, after all, is an unfamiliar word, in comparison with human life? If they miss the meaning, they have absorbed the sense of the novel's expressions of grief and pathos. For these readers, Gaskell's questions merit serious and sustained contemplation, consideration of whether they have, in fact, done enough to lighten the burden of their neighbors. When the novel turns to more conventionally romantic subjects, then, their attention is only half diverted. Not only are they more intimately invested in Jem's trial and Mary's conflict than the other readers, but they maintain their awareness of the everyday tragedies that have, in this case, given birth to the sensational one, and the obligations they themselves have incurred through that awareness. The melodramatic murder plot is the final test of these readers' awakened sensibilities. Having surpassed the emotional limits of informative text, they must now resist the affective excess of an entertainment that would excite their emotions past the point of productive engagement with ordinary human experience, instead allowing for what Thomas Recchio has called the "affective knowledge" that the novel's melodrama, properly directed, works to produce.[12]

The possibility of such disparate reactions destabilizes the new world created at the end of the novel. As Jameson suggests, the utopian vision comes to us "from a future that may never come into being" ("Politics of Utopia" 54)—but also one that could, hypothetically, be realized. In most of the other novels I discuss, generically opposing actual and unwritten plots exist alongside one another; the two begin together and then diverge into parallel paths. In *Mary Barton*, they are rather consecutive. The first fifteen and a half chapters create a realist narrative world that suggests a fairly muted set of possibilities. Historical fact alone tells us that Barton's appeal to Parliament will fail, and there is little in the prevailing grimness of Gaskell's Manchester to give us hope that smaller-scale union activity will be rewarded with productive change. We do not know precisely what will happen to Barton—imprisoned for labor agitation? Death by suicide or fever? Spared for a bearable, if not entirely comfortable, old age cared for by a loving daughter?—but we can make some educated guesses. As for Mary, the possibilities seem equally stark. In the image of her aunt Esther, we see one clear alternative before her: if she, like her once-pretty and thoughtless aunt, is swayed by the blandishments of a rich suitor whose intentions are not likely to include marriage to a seamstress, her end will be shame and degradation. If she instead recognizes the worth of Jem Wilson, she can look forward, at best, to the comparatively cheerful poverty attainable with a loving family, steady factory work, and lucky avoidance of grave illness or death in childbirth. At the very end of chapter 15, however, we get a radical revision of these possibilities when Gaskell abruptly introduces a union plot to assassinate some still unnamed member of the employer class. At this point, all bets are off; if the novel is willing to deal in such extremes, almost anything might happen. And indeed, Barton killing Harry Carson with Jem Wilson's gun, thereby implicating him in the crime, immediately after Mary has recognized her love for Jem, is about as sensational a scenario as we might have imagined.

If we respond as the first readers do, the final outcome, with Barton and Carson reconciled, Carson becoming a benevolent employer, and Mary and Jem prospering in Canada, can be possible only because of the novel's sharp anti-realist turn. Only in a world of murder plots in which a father is *coincidentally* tasked with assassinating his daughter's ex-lover, thereby implicating the dead man's successful rival for her affections, can we plausibly believe that the killing will finally lead to reconciliation, reform, and a general outbreak of increased goodwill and happiness among men, or at least among all of our surviving characters. This is escapist fantasy, and nothing more.

Yet if the first half of the novel successfully awakens our sympathies, the world of the novel's conclusion, if not the road by which we traveled there, is perhaps no longer so inaccessible. Our empathy cannot make the Barton-Carson-Wilson affair and its associated complications any less theatrical. Strictly speaking, however, the final disposition of fates is not dependent on these contrivances. There are, as Gaskell demonstrates in *North and South*, easier paths to productive and mutually beneficial class understanding than murdering a recalcitrant employer's son, and the seeds of Mary and Jem's Canadian retreat are laid early in the novel, when Jem's master gives him increased responsibilities for a project based in Halifax. Even more importantly, Gaskell's belief in social change through empathy is established in the midst of the novel's darkest scenes. The world such empathy would create has not yet been achieved, as the failure of the People's Charter has too plainly shown, so a literary realm that enacts Gaskell's vision can only exist as the willful, wistful enactment of a plot that should by rights have remained unwritten. But the assumption that it is therefore anti-realist does not follow; the presently impossible remains potentially achievable. If the middle-class reader, who has come to be entertained, who does not understand the speech of the laboring man, let alone his plight, who has heard sermons all his life, and listened and wept and yet walked away unchanged, who knows Chaucer and Spencer, but not the mind or heart of his neighbor, can be gradually converted to true empathy by Gaskell's text, then why not Carson, or anyone?

The realist novel is grounded in the conditions of our world. But those conditions are not static, and neither are the boundaries of narrative realism. Fittingly, one of the agents capable of changing the actual world is precisely the realist novel. The structure of *Mary Barton* is hypothetically realist, asking that readers perform the change that will render possible its own outcome. In the ultimate collaboration between an author and her reader, we are asked both to imaginatively recover lost possibilities and to actively create new ones. Accepting Gaskell's charge, we extend the possibilities of our own world. In turn, we extend the possibilities of the novel, which will not always be about Dorothea after all, though we love her no less for having widened the scope of our concern.

The last rhetorical question in *Mary Barton* is asked, not by the narrator, but by Mary. Having just been told that her lost aunt Esther has been seen walking the streets as a prostitute, she declares that she and Jem must find her. Jem wonders what they could do if they did, to which Mary returns, "Do! Why, what could we *not* do, if we could but find her?" Roused to action by Mary's faith, Jem agrees: they will take the fallen woman to Canada, and their love will make her good. But Gaskell, like Dickens, decrees differently: "it was not to be" (561). Mary's faith could never have been enough: like Nell, like Strether, like Marty, Mary must confront the limits of a narrative world that can only be so much better than the world and time that produced it. The road is rough, for all that we are wise and kind and faithful; even Mary and Jem can find their happiness only in a Canada invested with all the reality of Shakespeare's Bohemia and its stormy coasts. But it is no coincidence, perhaps, that the novel ends with the news of the miraculous restoration of Margaret's vision. Like any unwritten plot, the event is both present in and absent from the text: we hear about it only thirdhand, through a letter from across the seas. Like the crucial scene in a proxy narrative, it is almost impossible to accept; the novel can only manage it at all by slipping, again, into vagueness—"they" have done "something to ... give her back her sight" (576). Yet what is at stake here is finally not Margaret's vision, but our own. At the end, we return to the old question: Can you see them? Can you really? And, at least for a moment, we do see, and hear, and love, and hope that that will be enough to make new worlds in their image.

EPILOGUE

Returning Dickens to the Map

In Paul Beatty's *The Sellout*, an African American urban farmer winds up in front of the Supreme Court after instituting a short-lived but successful attempt to reinstitute segregation in his de-incorporated ghetto community. Supporting characters include Hominy Jenkins, an elderly former child actor turned voluntary slave campaigning for the release of a series of grossly racially offensive episodes of *The Little Rascals*, and Foy Cheshire, a prominent Black intellectual known for such revisions of the classics as *The Point Guard in the Rye*, *The Old Man and the Inflatable Winnie the Pooh Swimming Pool*, and *The Pejorative-Free Adventures and Intellectual and Spiritual Journeys of African-American Jim and His Young Protégé, White Brother Huckleberry Finn, as they Go in Search of the Lost Black Family Unit*. Several real-life figures make cameos as well. During the trial, "the black Justice," a paper-thinly disguised Clarence Thomas, can't resist breaking his usual silence to shout out, "Why you bitch-made motherfucker, I know goddamn well your parents raised you better than that!" (24). Later in the novel, the Black diplomats "C _ _ _n _ _ w _ _ _" and "_ o n d _ _ _ _ z z _ _ _ _ e" learn to Crip Walk from the local gangbanger at a meeting of the neighborhood intelligentsia known as the Dum Dum Donuts intellectuals.

Plainly, we're not in London anymore. Beatty's fictional corner of Los Angeles (modeled after Compton) is as far removed narratively as it is spatially and temporally from Victorian England, existing within a text marked by digression and self-conscious absurdity. If the Victorian realist novel is immersive, *The Sellout*, like many postmodern novels, is expulsive, foreclosing sustained affective alliance with its characters in its sheer outrageousness. George Eliot gave us *Middlemarch*, a novel whose very title suggests the restrained tenor of her English home epic; Eliot is concerned with the mass of ordinary human experience and not those living, for good or for ill, at its fantastic extremes. Her ides of March come with no dagger or sword. Paul Beatty gives us, courtesy of Foy Cheshire, *Middlemarch Middle of April, I'll Have Your Money—I Swear*, a broad joke that undercuts both the reality of his narrative world and the inherent pathos in Foy's vision of what a blackwashed version of the canon would necessarily be.

But objects in a mirror—even a dark one—may be closer than they appear. Beatty's diffracted Compton is called Dickens, California; when the narrator draws a boundary line between the right and wrong side of the tracks in a mock-up of his reimagined city, he labels them "the best of times" and "the worst of times" (99). In *Reaping Something New*, a study of the often unrecognized connections between Victorian and African American literature, Daniel Hack further notes that Cheshire's revision of *Middlemarch* is the only text in his series based on a novel that is not a staple of American middle and high school curricula, suggesting the more than casual nature of its inclusion (211).

The links between *The Sellout* and the Victorian novel are structural and affective as well as allusive. After the absurdist prologue set—near the chronological endpoint of the story—at the Supreme Court, the novel proper begins with an account of the narrator's abusive, motherless childhood, which ends with the death of his father. If the details are frankly bizarre (the narrator's social scientist father tries to condition racial pride in his son through electroshock-based aversion therapy and allows him to be savagely beaten in an attempt to test his theories on Bystander Effect), the basic form of the plot is familiar, a bildungsroman shaped by parental loss and sealed in a painful coming-of-age. For a novel blurbed by bawdy comedian Sarah Silverman, *The Sellout* can also be surprisingly sentimental, from the narrator's lyrical reminiscence about the birth of his ex-girlfriend's first child by her abusive partner to his Quixotic quest to reinstate Dickens as an officially recognized community.

Resisting resolution on one plane of narrative, *The Sellout* satisfies it on another in a weaving together of plot threads that is nothing if not—pun certainly intended—Dickensian. We never learn the outcome of the narrator's case, and the "closure" of the title of the novel's final, unnumbered chapter, set on the eve of Barack Obama's inauguration, is clearly meant ironically. Yet two chapters earlier, many of the novel's other elements had already come to a far more satisfying conclusion. After winning a civil suit against the nearly bankrupt Foy Cheshire, the narrator collects his settlement in the form of the Hominy-centric, lost *Little Rascals* shorts that Cheshire has, as rumored, been hiding all along. At first, the narrator cannot understand why Foy has gone to such lengths to suppress the shorts: while offensive, they are scarcely more racist than many of the aired episodes. As the narrator, Hominy, several neighborhood drug dealers, and the narrator's now, and perhaps permanently, on-again girlfriend Marpessa watch, however, the motivation becomes clear. Foy Cheshire, darling of the Black intellectual class, had himself featured in these demeaning shorts as a very young boy.

Perhaps it is this revelation, or perhaps a more general sense of catharsis that inspires Hominy to emancipate himself from his self-imposed slavery. As the viewing party—which will retroactively be revealed to its guests, if not to readers, as either a welcome home or going-away party for the narrator, depending on the court's decision—winds down, Marpessa flips the television to the news, where the weatherwoman is announcing the current temperatures in a number of local cities: Thousand Oaks, Santa Monica, Van Nuys, and, finally, Dickens. "I can't stop crying," the narrator admits. "Dickens is back on the map" (284).

In the nineteenth century, realist plots became predominant over their romantic predecessors. The triumphant journey gave way to the winding road; the compromised peace replaced virtue rewarded as the guiding paradigm of fictional narrative. The models they supplanted, however, were not eliminated. Rather, they lingered on in the form of unwritten plots, doomed, maybe, but still vital. The ghosts of the eighteenth century, if not banished, moved inward, haunting us as evocative suggestions and half-invisible intimations rather than as literal spirits. From this process came what we, largely retrospectively, call the Victorian realist novel.

By the first decades of the twentieth century, conventional plotting was on its way out, at least as far as canonical literature was concerned. Joyce and Woolf, Faulkner and Hemingway, Beckett and Stein—the authors who most defined the prevailing aesthetic of their day—abandoned or radically revised Victorian-received notions of plot. They ignored the demands of "narratability" and disrupted sequential time, systematically unwinding the connective threads their predecessors had so painstakingly tied. The line between modernism and postmodernism—let alone between postmodernism and what has sometimes been called "post-postmodernism"—are as vague as those between realism and romance. Yet one discernible difference is the latter's relative return to more traditional plotting. This is not, of course, to say that the novels of the late twentieth and early twenty-first centuries abandon the experiments of the modernist era; if anything, they intensify some of the period's prevailing trends. Amid metafiction and parody, however, at least a subset of postmodern novels betray a yearning for the traditional plots in which they can no longer quite believe. What results is a reversal of the pattern I identify in the nineteenth-century novel: in these later texts, the realist plot returns, not as the victorious active plot, but as the unwritten alternative resisting its generic rivals.

Sometimes, the realist underplots in postmodern novels reflect a wistful longing for a past unavailable in the modern age. In David Foster Wallace's *Infinite Jest*, the multi-plot structure sets the hyperintellectualized, upper-middle-class world of the Incandenzas and the students at their family-run tennis academy against the throwback earnestness of the Ennet House Drug and Alcohol Recovery House. The late Incandenza patriarch was an avant-garde filmmaker of the "post-post-structuralist" school whose final work, the unreleased and almost unseen *Infinite Jest*, is rumored to be so entertaining that its viewer cannot stop watching, the ultimate symbol of the novel's thoroughly commercialized world. While the Incandenzas—including "lexical prodigy" Hal, whose college application essay is entitled "The Implications of Post-Fourier Transformations for a Holographically Mimetic Cinema" (7), and his mother Avril, a militant prescriptive grammarian—are associated with a world of gamesmanship, irony, and self-conscious manipulations of established structures and ideologies, Don Gately, ex-thief and recovering addict, rather subscribes to the koans of his Narcotics Anonymous program: "Ask for Help"; "Turn it Over"; "Just Keep Coming" (273).

We might expect these trite slogans to become the subject of Wallace's own satirical sensibilities, part of his larger cultural critique of technological dependency and self-help culture, among other aspects of modern American life. Instead, Wallace takes Gately's journey to recovery seriously, treating his struggles with a gravity he rarely brings to the Incandenza family narrative, let alone to the novel's overarching plotline, which involves the attempt of a group of wheelchair-using Quebecois separatists to get their hands on James Incandenza's *Infinite Jest*, often referred to simply as "the entertainment." The text does not ask us to care very much about how this political intrigue ends; intricately plotted, it is also paradoxically contentless, a postmodern void that militates against any real meaning or feeling. Rather, much of the pathos of novel comes from the efforts of Gately and the other Ennet House residents to rebuild their lives, and much of its tension comes, not just from our concern over their fate, but from the implicit question of whether it is Gately's largely realist tale or the postmodern pastiche of the Incandenza and geopolitical plotlines that will carry the day.

That we find ourselves rooting for Gately is perhaps in itself a kind of victory for the realist plot. If so, however, it is a grim and equivocal one, as the novel in the end refuses our desires. In the first chapter of the novel, Hal recalls an incident in which junior tennis champion and probable Canadian spy John N. R. (for "no relation") Wayne "[stands] watch in a mask as Donald Gately and I dig up my father's head" (16–17). The line hangs proleptically over the rest of the novel, whose second chapter is set chronologically before both the events of the first chapter and the remembered disinterring of James Incandenza's corpse. In the normal course of narrative, we would expect the novel ultimately to circle back to where it began, using its long middle to fill in the gaps between the beginning of chapter 2 and the end of chapter 1, including that fateful graveyard scene. For nearly a thousand pages, we wait for it: when will Don and Hal meet? When will they become aware of the international conspiracy that, for different reasons, will envelop both? But the expected convergence never occurs. Wallace offers us enough clues that a careful reader could make some educated guesses on the geopolitics of the situation; indeed, while we never see the conclusion, the labyrinthine plotting that weaves together *Infinite Jest*'s three narrative threads rivals that of any Victorian novel. Yet to spend too much time solving the puzzle of what precisely the Quebecois wheelchair assassins are up to is to have missed the point. What we are denied is precisely what matters: we want to know whether Don Gately stays sober, whether he and Joelle van Dyne—formerly James Incandenza's muse, and the star of his *Infinite Jest*—make a life together, whether the influence of Don, however the two meet up, can save Hal from the aphasic breakdown that is the ultimate indictment of the world of cheap intellectual gamesmanship in which he has been raised.

The dominant plot, with its high-concept satire and formal detours, was only ever an entertainment. What we postmodern readers long for in the novel is finally precisely what our ancestors might have: to follow two recognizably human lives playing out in parallel, intersecting, and coming to some at least provisional closure. Maybe Don Gately will make it after all, and even bring Hal along with him. Yet the final defeat of traditional narrative in *Infinite Jest* represents the destruction of the values Don represents. To end a novel, whether hopefully or painfully, is to make a claim about life and its possibilities: who, as some unknown psalmist wondered, long before any novelist, shall live and who must die, who merits riches and who is consigned to poverty, who attains peace and who remains in torment, who by fire and who by water. It is to assert that something is worth saying at all. Its message is older than any support group slogan, and no less true: Just Keep Reading, the author tells us, just keep reading, and fiction will bring you at last to the real. Instead, Wallace—knowingly, sadly, brutally—offers only an endless deferral of meaning, the last bitter joke in an infinite jest.

For Wallace, the longing expressed in his unwritten traditional plot seems associated with a pre-postmodern cultural and intellectual moment, an age in which what could today only read as irony was still available for unselfconscious articulation. Other novels in this vein include Nabokov's *Pale Fire*, which sets the interpretive distortions and wild fabrications of the mad editor/narrator Charles Kinbote against the sentimental, moving, personal drama of the poem he tries to co-opt, and Italo Calvino's *Invisible Cities*, in which the tales of fantastic cities that Calvino's Marco Polo spins out at the court of Kublai Khan act as a nostalgic reflection on both Polo's distant Venice and Calvino's own prewar Italy.

This attempt of traditional plot to reassert itself in a postmodern world is complicated in *The Sellout* by the problem of the historical exclusion of African American stories from traditional narrative forms. Beatty's hero is frequently troubled by the enforced self-consciousness that inhibits Black America from living out more conventional trajectories of success or embracing normative cultural models. The narrator's father is incensed when his young son chooses Barbie and Ken dolls over Harriet Tubman,

Martin Luther King, and Malcom X action figures, the child explaining that he prefers Barbie and Ken's accessories—including a dune buggy and speedboat—to the lanterns and walking canes of the civil rights heroes. Ordinary childish preferences become, in the highly politicized world the narrator inhabits, the mark of the race traitor; later, the narrator will first earn the title "sellout" from Foy Cheshire for apparently no offense worse than choosing a stereotype-breaking farming career over following his father into a more politically conscious line of work.

The narrator's relationship to traditional narrative is the cultural analogue to this political commentary. Foy Cheshire's blackwashed versions of the classics treat the originals of these texts as necessarily irrelevant and even hostile to the Black experience; notably, the narrator's ally in attempts to improve the local school system, who embraces a pragmatic willingness to adopt any tactic that seems likely to help the students succeed, has refused to distribute Cheshire's revisions in favor of a more conventional curriculum. At a lower register, the neighborhood children's enjoyment of *The Little Rascals*, as well as Hominy's continuing pride over his role in the series, is rendered illicit by the show's racism. This is not to say that Beatty denies the potentially troubling elements of these cultural artifacts; the described episodes of *The Little Rascals*, in particular, feature blatantly racist material. The fraught nature of Black engagement with white culture, however, is not limited to such obviously compromised examples. The narrator recalls a childhood incident in which he declared to his father that there was no longer any racism in America. In response, his father takes him on a two-thousand-mile trip to Mississippi, stops him in front of a group of slur-spouting rednecks outside a filling station, and loudly orders him to whistle at a white woman. Evidently unaware of the history his father is invoking, the confused child starts whistling what the rednecks unexpectedly recognize as Ravel's *Boléro*. Instead of garnering praise, however, the narrator's precocity earns him racist incredulity from the white men and anger from his father, whose staged racial performance has been destroyed by his son's inability to follow his assigned role.

These instances of Black engagement with white culture underscore the bind in which the narrator and his community find themselves. The *Boléro* scene recalls social psychologist Claude Steele's famous *Whistling Vivaldi*, the title of which comes from an anecdote about a Black graduate student who had adopted the (apparently successful) habit of whistling music by Vivaldi to defuse white perceptions of him as a threat. The anecdote, most directly, criticizes the stereotype-laden society that requires the student to employ this tactic. Yet, it also underscores the inevitable tension underlying the student's relationship with Vivaldi. As he transforms what would normally be a spontaneous, perhaps unconscious act of appreciation for high art into a deliberate utilitarian strategy, the pressures of racial identity turn art for art's sake into a signifier of cultural identification. A Black man whistling Vivaldi is safe to the extent that the act deracinates him. Black men are dangerous, but Black men also don't know Vivaldi; a Black man whistling Vivaldi may thus, in a sense, be reclassified—perhaps by himself and his own community, as well as by the nervous white passersby—as hardly Black at all.

A similar dynamic pervades *The Sellout*. Still living in a world dominated by white values and norms, those who would embrace aspects of it, from the material aspirations represented by Barbie's yacht to the cultural capital represented by the literary canon to the reassuringly sanitized urban childhoods of *The Little Rascals*, cannot do so innocently. In a narrative sense, what could, for a different kind of Dickensian character, be a predominantly personal narrative of *bildung* becomes for Beatty's Dickensians an inevitable referendum on racial identity and development. For the earlier narrator's "I called myself Pip, and came to be called Pip," Beatty's nameless one must begin his story with the defensive "This may be hard to believe, coming from a black man, but I've never stolen anything" (3).

In this context, the narrator's attempt to revive Dickens the city becomes a symbolic resistance against the Black protagonist's exclusion from traditional realist narrative. Several generations of African American writers have embraced postmodern genres of the absurd and the fantastic as the expressive mode most capable of reflecting the distorted realities of minority experience (Dubey, *Speculative Fictions of Slavery*). Beatty's work situates itself within this tradition. At the same time, *The Sellout* suggests a yearning for realist narrative. Unlike Wallace in *Infinite Jest*, Beatty cannot look back nostalgically to a premodern Eden; if the West ever enjoyed an age of unironic authenticity, the ancestors of the urban Dickensians could not have shared in its bounties. Now permitted, to a much greater extent, to take part in prevailing cultural narratives, the intense pressures to perform a different type of authenticity inhibit the self-assertion at the heart of this tradition. The price of achievement for the most successful of Beatty's characters is the suppression of racial identity: this version of Condoleezza Rice, we learn, loves to Crip Walk when given the chance, while a provoked Clarence Thomas breaks his long silence at the Supreme Court in a burst of enraged Ebonics. The inverse of this commonplace, however, is that the most extreme (and, often, necessarily stereotypical) manifestations of that identity can come at the cost, not only of stagnation, but of the denial of an individual selfhood that might gravitate toward white-coded tastes as well as Black ones, for whom whistling Vivaldi should indeed be a choice and neither a defensive posture nor a mark of racial treachery.

The narrator's ambiguous name reflects the competing narratives in which he finds himself. The character is repeatedly called Bonbon, after the word he spelled correctly to win a childhood spelling bee, and his Supreme Court appeal is filed in the name of *Me vs. United States*. Yet Bonbon, aside from plainly not being the character's real name, is complicated by its mocking undercutting of an ostensible academic achievement (the girl the narrator defeated in the spelling bee was given a much more difficult word), while it is unclear whether "Me" is to be taken as an actual surname or as an anonymizing placeholder. Reviewers and critics of the novel have chosen, alternately, to refer to the narrator as Bonbon Me or to keep him nameless, as I have done until now. But these choices are not value neutral. The otherwise nameless narrator with the winkingly reflexive "surname" is a figure of postmodernism, where the particularity characteristic of the traditional novel need no longer apply. Bonbon Me is rather a Dickensian figure, a colorfully individualized character fit to join the ranks of the Nicklebys and Twists and Copperfields that came before him.

Yet a Bonbon Me confronts a danger that no tongue-twisting Nicholas Nickleby ever did. In his preface to the 1922 *Book of American Negro Poetry*, James Weldon Johnson argues that dialect poetry has outlived its usefulness in representing the scope and subtleties of African American life. This is not because of any inherent limitation of "this quaint and musical folkspeech," but because it has become so compromised by its association with the white minstrel tradition as to be left like "an instrument with but two full stops, humor and pathos" (41). Similarly, Bonbon Me, Hominy Jenkins, and the lawyer Hampton Fiske (named, presumably, after the historically

Black colleges by those names), cannot serve as benign, comic absurdities because their genealogy will be traced inevitably, not to Dickens, but to Buckwheat and Uncle Remus and Jim Crow.

It is a problem that, in a sense, proves intractable. The novel does not end with the triumphant resurrection of Dickens, but with what is clearly intended to be a more equivocal victory: the inauguration of the "black dude" as president of the United States. Foy Cheshire, for the first time in his life, waves an American flag around the neighborhood, but the narrator doesn't join in the general merriment: if America has expunged its original sin against one race, what about its abuses of many others? Foy shakes his head despairingly at his continued treachery, and the narrator concedes that he will never understand what it is that Foy and the other Black intellectuals grasp that he seems to miss. The "closure" that the chapter's title ironically promises, the traditional endpoint of narrative, is as illusory as the closure supposed to be provided by the historic election itself, hailed as the advent of a post-racial future.

The Sellout is not quite a bildungsroman, much as it sometimes wishes it could be. Early in the novel, the narrator, in the wake of the loss of his father and his community, can't answer the most basic questions about his identity: "Who am I? And how may I become myself?" (39). Chapters later, he is still asking. Dickens is saved, but perhaps not for him, and maybe not for anyone: his unorthodox school reform plan fails, and the conditions that made the city of Los Angeles so reluctant to claim the neighborhood as its own persist. There is no promised land to find, and he no Moses.

But, as in so many nineteenth-century novels, taking their Quixotic arms against a sea of realist troubles, we—and Me—have nonetheless perhaps gained something from what could only ever be an unwritten plot, at least in this world and this time. As a child, the narrator tries to formulate a motto (preferably in Latin) for Black America: "Other ethnicities have mottos. 'Unconquered and unconquerable' is the calling card of the Chickasaw nation . . . *Allahu Akbar. Shkata ga nai. Never again. Harvard Class of '96. To Protect and Serve.* These are more than just greetings and trite sayings. They are reenergizing codes. Linguistic chi that strengthens our life force and bonds us to other like-minded, like-skinned, like-shoe-wearing human beings" (10). His attempts, however, all end in what even a ten-year-old recognizes as either crass stereotype (*Black America: Veni, Vidi, Vici—Fried Chicken*) or anodyne fluff ("One body, one mind, one heart, one love") (11).

If he hasn't found such a motto, however, by the end of *The Sellout*, he has at least learned to stop searching for it. In the penultimate scene of the novel, the narrator recalls a performance in which a Black comedian, appearing at a nearly all-Black venue, angrily tells the single white couple in the room, who have been visibly enjoying the show so far, to leave: "this shit ain't for you," he shouts. "This is our thing" (287). The narrator had done nothing at the time, but in retrospect, he observes, he wishes that he had had the courage to respond to the comedian: "So what exactly is *our thing?*" (288) he would have asked.

What the narrator wants, ultimately, is not to locate Black America's defining motto, but to resist the constriction inherent in such definitions. This isn't for you, generations of white cultural guardians have told the narrator and his community. This isn't for you, say Foy Cheshire and the narrator's own father and the forces of racial unity. But who are you, responds *The Sellout*, and who is Me? An urban farmer who grows weed alongside his satsumas, versed in Latin as well as hip-hop, and Dickens as well as Douglass. In whose own off-center version of America, gangsta rap was invented by a hallucinating hip-hop artist shouting out a remixed version of "The Charge of the Light Brigade," and the single-mother bus driver reads Kafka and Tolstoy. Where Mississippi rednecks know Ravel's *Boléro*, and Condoleezza Rice knows how to Crip Walk. Where an internet search for the name of your blighted urban city turns up only the name of a Victorian author. Where saving Dickens, perhaps, doesn't mean anything more or less than loving its people, with their heartbreakingly limited possibilities, more authentically than the Foy Cheshires of the world ever will.

Because Dickens, of course, was never really gone; he was simply unrecognized. Replaced formally with an absurdist fantasy, still the realist plot lives on: in a barely there love story, in the whispers of a missing mother, waiting to be found, in its social critique, in its overwhelming sympathy for the compromised, complicated lives it contains. That plot doesn't win in *The Sellout*, but then, even in the nineteenth century, it didn't always. Its antagonist has transformed from the cloying improbabilities of romanticism to the unfeeling excesses of the postmodern. But, born itself from the pressures of competing worlds and modes, it knows better than to despise the power of the unwritten. Bonbon Me can't overcome the constraints of either his society or the genre in which he finds himself: any closure, on both levels, will only be an illusion. His story, however, forces us, in the manner of the best Victorian unwritten plots, to virtually contemplate what could have been, and what, perhaps, could still be. When we do, we may find we are less sophisticated, and more sentimental than we had believed ourselves to be, and are the better for it. With none of traditional narrative's closure, we must imagine what comes next, which discarded possibilities of today or yesterday will become the ur-plots of tomorrow. It is up to you and me, reader, if such things are to be, in our lives and in our stories.

NOTES

INTRODUCTION

1. The *Saturday Review* concurred. Wondering at George Eliot's apparent affection for Ladislaw, the reviewer complains, "The chance of his choosing the right woman to worship . . . saves him from the consequences of idleness and mere self-pleasing; while poor Lydgate—ten times the better man—suffers not only in happiness but in his noblest ambitions . . . because he marries and is faithful to the vain selfish creature whom Ladislaw merely flirts with" (D. Carroll, *George Eliot* 318–19).
2. Samuel Johnson indeed complained about "mixed" characters in the novel, fearing that readers would emulate the bad behavior of heroes and heroines. Yet Patricia Meyer Spacks's account of the mid-eighteenth-century novel suggests how comparatively limited this mixing was in most works of the era, as even novels with erring heroes and heroines coded negative behaviors as such and made characters' ultimate successes contingent on reform (*Novel Beginnings*).
3. From "Review of *Jane Eyre*," 481–87.
4. The most recognized one may be Susan Fraiman's critique in *Unbecoming Women*, which reads Jane's social rise as a betrayal of the more marginal class allegiances that inform her identity earlier in the novel ("Jane Eyre's Fall from Grace," *Unbecoming Women* 88–120).
5. The Many-Worlds Interpretation was first proposed in 1957 by Hugh Everett, although Everett did not himself use the term, and the extent to which he accepted what later came to be called Many Worlds as a valid extrapolation of his quantum theory is not entirely clear. See Simon Saunders et al., *Many Worlds?*
6. This debate traces itself most prominently, in the modern era, to the early twentieth-century work of Bertrand Russell and Gottlob Frege.

7. For a general overview of modal logic, see Patrick Blackburn, Maarten de Rijke, and Yde Venema, *Modal Logic*.
8. This is true, for instance, of Gerald Prince's "The Disnarrated," an influential forerunner to discussions of literary "counterfactuals."
9. For a summary of the controversy, see Gordon Haight, "Dickens and Lewes on Spontaneous Combustion."
10. Both Michael Tondre's and Adam Grener's accounts of the history and philosophy of probabilistic thinking follow the earlier work of the philosopher Ian Hacking, whose 1975 *The Emergence of Probability* traces the origins of the concept of probability itself to broader sixteenth- and seventeenth-century intellectual developments.
11. For an in-depth study of the bigamy plot and its relationship to Victorian cultural and aesthetic values, see Maia McAleavey's *The Bigamy Plot*.
12. In addition to the reviews cited above, *The Spectator* called Will "altogether uninteresting... without any wholeness and largeness" (D. Carroll, *George Eliot* 311).
13. In *Unbecoming Women*, Susan Fraiman reads even *Pride and Prejudice*, possibly the closest the nineteenth-century novel comes to an ideal marriage plot, as "the humiliation of Elizabeth Bennet" (59). D. A. Miller is similarly dissatisfied with the fate of Austen's heroines, observing that "the realism of her works allows no one like Jane Austen to appear in them"; the "style" of Austen the narrator must be sacrificed if her heroines are to become proper subjects of narration (*Jane Austen, or the Secret of Style* 28).
14. Talia Schaffer's *Romance's Rival* suggests that this ambivalence toward the marriage plot was far more widespread than most critics have recognized. In her account, the primary alternative to this paradigm was, not more radical possibilities, but the more conservative model of "familiar" (as opposed to romantic) marriage.
15. This, of course, is central to Sandra Gilbert and Susan Gubar's seminal reading of the novel in *The Madwoman in the Attic*, which treats Bertha Mason as a psychic proxy for those elements of Jane's character that are incompatible with the values of English domestic realism. Their analysis of *Villette*, correspondingly, reads M. Paul's death approvingly as a deconstruction of the marriage plot that allows Lucy to preserve her autonomy. While largely following this reading, I believe they go too far in trying to soften the essential tragedy of the novel; Lucy preserves her autonomy, but this cannot in context be seen as anything but a deeply pyrrhic victory.

1. SEEING SHADOWS

1. *Frankenstein* is one of the key texts in George Levine's realist tradition (which runs, according to the subtitle of his *The Realistic Imagination*, from *Frankenstein* to D. H. Lawrence's *Lady Chatterley's Lover*), while Scott figures heavily in Harry Shaw's work. Levine also wrote a separate monograph titled *"Frankenstein" and the Tradition of Realism*.
2. A standard account of the origins of the English novel—including extended consideration of its relationship to romance—is Michael McKeon's *The Origins of the English Novel*. A recent examination that centers romance, rather than the novel, is Scott Black's *Without the Novel*.
3. See, for instance, Henry Knight Miller's *Henry Fielding's "Tom Jones" and the Romance Tradition*, which counters Watt's view of *Tom Jones* and other eighteenth-century texts as essentially realist.
4. See also Northrop Frye's account of romance—as distinguished from the "low mimetic" mode of realism—in *Anatomy of Criticism*.
5. Monica Correa Fryckstedt's study of the reviews of Geraldine Jewsbury in *The Athenaeum*—which she uses as a metric of Victorian middle-class culture—observes Jewsbury's habit of applying markedly different standards to works she considered "novels" and mere "romances," which she exempted from her ordinary expectations of plausibility of character and event.
6. For an account of late-Victorian and Edwardian Romances and their complex formal affiliations, see Nicholas Daly's *Modernism, Romance and the Fin de Siècle*.
7. The definitions of "plot" and "story," of course, have a long critical history that is further elaborated in the next chapter.
8. Indeed, Gerald Prince notes that there are in theory as many genres as there are texts, although he finally contents himself with calling for classifications that are deductive and descriptive rather than inductive and prescriptive ("On Narrative Studies," 278).
9. This is despite the fact that it is almost certainly apocryphal; see my own analysis of the subject in Carra Glatt, "When Found Make a Note Of."
10. Leavis only tacitly acknowledges his own reversal, arguing against previous critics who have dismissed Dickens without including himself in their number. Well before Leavis had made his conversion, Humphrey House's *The Dickens World* was the text perhaps most responsible for turning the critical tide in favor of Dickens.
11. Often this has resulted in diminished critical attention to the earlier works; Stephen Marcus's 1986 *Dickens from "Pickwick" to "Dombey"* is written in part to counteract that trend.

12. See also Robyn Warhol's essay "What Might Have Been Is Not What Is," which focuses on the prevalence of moments of narrative refusal (in which characters decline to speak of an event as it actually occurred) in the author's later works.
13. For a reading of the novel that emphasizes Nell's gender, see Laurie Langbauer, "Dickens's Streetwalkers."
14. See also John Kucich's discussion of the communally restorative properties of Nell's death in *Repression in Victorian Fiction*.
15. Citing Gissing, Laurie Langbauer calls *The Arabian Nights* the "most important romantic influence on Dickens' writing" ("Dickens's Streetwalkers," 416).
16. The most comprehensive argument in favor of the original ending—in addition to the most thorough overview of critical approaches to the two conclusions—is Edgar Rosenberg's "Putting an End to *Great Expectations.*" See Jerome Meckier's "Charles Dickens's *Great Expectations*" for a similarly vigorous argument for the altered conclusion.
17. Edwin Eigner notes that even readers who have appreciated the revised ending have tended to be suspicious of the motives behind it in part because of Bulwer-Lytton's role; he quotes Sylvère Monod's suggestion that we try to forget "that Bulwer originated the change" ("Bulwer-Lytton," 105). The decline in Bulwer-Lytton's own reputation has not helped the second ending's case; although he was a respected member of the literary establishment in his own day, he is now perhaps best known for inspiring the annual Bulwer-Lytton Fiction Contest for the worst sentence written in the English language.
18. Edgar Rosenberg's swipe at Meckier caricatures the latter's position but bears repeating for its comic value: "Because the composition of Pip's story coincides with Dickens's, Meckier would have you believe that Estella must have been dead by 1861 or she would have collapsed of shock at reading her shaming story in the pages of *All the Year Round*. I can't be the only biped in creation who finds the very notion of Estella's reading any issue of *All the Year Round* deeply distressing" ("Putting an End to *Great Expectations*," 503).
19. Hilary Dannenberg suggests that this is more broadly characteristic of nineteenth-century counterfactuals, which mediate between the rigid causality of realist texts and the radical instability of many postmodern ones (*Coincidence and Counterfactuality*, 193).
20. One such comparison can be found in David Lodge's "Ambiguously Ever After." Lodge prefers the second ending to *Great Expectations* on the

grounds that it more closely approaches the openness of modernism than do most traditional novels.

21. Rachel DuPlessis, in *Writing beyond the Ending*, focuses her argument on twentieth-century female writers. Fraiman, in *Unbecoming Women*, without framing her discussion explicitly as one of resistance to closure, writes rather about the struggles of eighteenth- and nineteenth-century female authors to reinvent the traditionally male narrative of the novel of development. Dannenberg's reference to writing "around the ending" is a more explicit attempt to apply DuPlessis's framework to the nineteenth-century novel.
22. Edmund Wilson was not the first to propose this theory, which suggests that Jasper was influenced by the Kali-worshiping Thugee cult that had been active in Britain in the 1830s and 1840s, but his "Dickens" provides the most thorough elaboration of it.
23. See, most notably, Gerhard Joseph's 1996 "Who Cares Who Killed Edwin Drood?" in *Nineteenth-Century Literature*. Despite the title, Joseph spends some time laying out a convincing case for Jasper as murderer; for Joseph, the novel is not really intended as a mystery at all, and there is thus no compelling reason to search for an ingenious, but invariably unconvincing, solution to the case.

2. RAISING THE VEIL

1. See especially Lyn Pykett's *The Sensation Novel*.
2. Gerald Prince's unnarratable also includes events that can be presumed to occur in a text but that cannot be represented for other reasons, for instance, because of social taboo. By contrast, the disnarrated, which refers to considerations of counterfactual alternatives, comprises those events that are represented despite not actually taking place in the actual world of the text, for instance, a character's imagining of a possible future event that will not occur.
3. A related effect in visual processing is "serial dependence," which explains, among other phenomena, why most people do not catch minor continuity errors in movies (i.e., the color of a character's shirt changing within a single scene). Essentially, because our minds are accustomed to a visually stable "continuity field," the automatic expectation of such logical sequence leads us to overlook rare disruptions to this usual order. See Jason Fischer and David Whitney, "Serial Dependence in Visual Perception."
4. Kingsley Amis, in his aptly titled 1957 essay "What Became of Jane Austen?," called Fanny a "monster of complacency and pride" and observed that she and her clergyman husband would be unwelcome dinner guests (439–40). Other critics have treated Fanny's apparent weakness and

conservativism as, alternatively, an instance of Austen's irony (Trilling, "Mansfield Park"), an intentional commentary on Fanny's emotionally abusive upbringing (Shields, *Jane Austen*, 152–56), and a mask for hidden strength (Tomalin, *Jane Austen*)—but generally acknowledge that these explanations will not satisfy most modern readers.

5. Adaptations include a 2003 BBC radio drama featuring David Tennant and Benedict Cumberbatch, a 2007 miniseries starring Billie Piper, and a 2012 Theatre Royal stage version.

6. Austen was by no means opposed to theater and in fact wrote of her acute disappointment on missing the chance to see Sarah Siddons perform. Her family had even staged private theatricals during her childhood. Her objection to the *Mansfield Park* performance seems to come rather from the moral danger posed by staging that particular play among a group of young people liable to become overinvested in roles that reflect their own desires—as indeed happens in the case of Maria Bertram, who uses the license provided by the play to begin her disastrous flirtation with Henry Crawford. See Judith W. Fisher's "'Don't Put Your Daughter on the Stage Lady B,'" and David Lodge, "A Question of Judgment."

7. *Gone with the Wind*, to use one prominent example, remains a perennial favorite of readers and viewers, despite widespread criticism of its racial politics, especially its depiction of the Ku Klux Klan as noble defenders of white womanhood. For several recent critical attempts at grappling with the novel's legacy and enduring popularity, see James Crank, *New Approaches to "Gone with the Wind."*

8. The foundational reading of the novel's gender politics is Elaine Showalter's in *Literature of Their Own*. For a reading of Robert's masculinity that does not primarily focus on his potential queerness, see Rachel Heinrichs, "Critical Masculinities in *Lady Audley's Secret*."

9. To the extent that insanity could have been accepted by contemporary readers as a logical extension of the novel's themes, it would have been by evoking what was essentially a cultural proxy narrative that associated female insanity with sexual immorality. For more on this relationship, see Elaine Showalter's *The Female Malady*.

10. See A. L. French's "A Note on Middlemarch" for an extended (if sometimes excessively literal) close reading of the passage as a metaphor for the consummation of Dorothea and Casaubon's marriage.

11. For Eliot and for Maggie, the crime seems to be the betrayal of Lucy and Philip rather than sexual impropriety, but the effect is the same; in either case, the relevant distinction is between a completed and perhaps

irrevocable lapse, and one that seems ambiguous and mild enough to admit of some degree of narrative forgiveness.
12. It is worth noting here that *The Mill on the Floss* is the first of Eliot's novels published after her identity—and the scandal of her affair with George Lewes—had become known, so Eliot and Blackwood may have felt the need to tread particularly carefully; as Tillotson observes, Eliot's relationship with Lewes risked compromising her publisher's reputation as well as her own ("The George Eliot Letters" 67).
13. Dinah Mulock, for instance, writing in *Macmillan's Magazine*, summarizes the relevant portion of the "very simple story" as one of Maggie being "tempted to treachery and [sinking] into a great error, her extrication out of which . . . is simply an impossibility" ("Review" 155–56). Ruskin's imperfect knowledge of the novel's plot in *Fiction, Fair and Foul* similarly suggests the easy conflation of the boat ride with a more complete fall: "Rashly inquiring the other day the plot of a modern story from a female friend, I elicited, after some hesitation, that it hinged mainly on the young people's 'forgetting themselves in a boat'" (166). The friend's tactful hesitation, combined with the scare quotes around the description itself, suggests euphemism, but the summary is in fact almost literally true.
14. The term "legless angel" is George Orwell's and was originally applied to Dickens's Agnes Wickfield, who he called the "real legless angel of Victorian romance" (459).
15. Collins was involved for years in a bigamous relationship with two women, neither of whom he ever legally married.
16. See also D. A. Miller's "*Cage aux folles*," which sets the novel's investment in the literal "sensation" awakened by the sensation novel against its ultimately inadequate, legalistic structure.

3. "A THING QUITE OTHER THAN ITSELF"

1. A *ficelle* is, in James's definition, a character who exists for purely functional purposes; see complete explanation later in the chapter.
2. In *Reading for the Plot*, Peter Brooks sees the puzzle of reading *Absalom, Absalom!*, and by extension many other twentieth-century novels, as the problem of finding any plot at all; in Brooks's reading, *Absalom, Absalom!* contains an overabundance of story and narration but suppresses the plot that would render them intelligible. In James, by contrast, there is if anything too much plot—his novels work at the level of narrative meaning, but the events of story often seem unable to bear the weight their role in this plot suggests they should carry.

3. Edna Kenton is credited with having been the first critic to deny the reality of the ghosts in "Henry James to the Ruminant Reader," published in 1924, but the reading only began to gain currency a decade later when Edmund Wilson published "The Ambiguity of Henry James." Sidney Lind's *"The Turn of the Screw"* provides a useful survey of the novella's early reception.
4. Not that this has prevented people, including some medical professionals, from attempting to diagnose her. Caroline Mercer and Sarah Wangensteen, in "Consumption, Heart Disease, or Whatever," suggest that she has chlorosis, a popular diagnosis for "hysterical" women in the late nineteenth century, while Adeline R. Tintner and Henry D. Janowitz argue instead for cancer in "Inoperable Cancer."
5. The phrase is used by William James in *The Varieties of Religious Experience* to suggest that the validity of a belief is tied to its utility.
6. See, for instance, Marco Portales's *Strether and Women*, which discusses both Strether's lack of romantic interest in Maria Gostrey and his unrequited love of Madame de Vionnet.
7. My argument has several similarities to Julie Rivkin's argument on representation in *The Ambassadors*, which also accounts for the novel's final scene as a rejection of a representative system. Rather than suggesting that the novel ultimately rejects representative systems, Rivkin, however, argues that in a world without stable authority—either verbal or of any other kind—there are finally *only* ambassadors, albeit ones characterized, not by Mrs. Newsome's rigidity, but by "a freely disseminated selfhood." See Rivkin, *False Positions*, 57–81.

4. FANCYING THE DELIGHT

1. *Loving v. Virginia*, the case that declared anti-miscegenation statutes forbidding people of different races from marrying unconstitutional, was decided on June 12, 1967. Spencer Tracy, who had starred in the film, had died the previous day, shortly after completing filming on the movie.
2. Reviews of *Jude* were actually mixed, rather than wholly negative; see, for instance, William Dean Howells's defense of the novel, first printed in *Harper's Weekly* (in Cox, *Thomas Hardy*, 265–68).
3. True of novels of the period such as *The Mayor of Casterbridge*, this tendency is also reflected in Hardy's 1883 essay "The Dorsetshire Laborer" (Gatrell, "Wessex," 25).
4. By the time of the novel's publication in 1895, divorce had been accessible to the mass of the English public for over thirty years, since the Matrimonial

Causes Act of 1857 had removed the requirement that couples seeking to divorce obtain a private act of Parliament. That act would not, however, technically have permitted either of the divorces in *Jude the Obscure;* Jude and Sue ultimately obtain their divorces by the common practice of "colluding" with their ex-spouses to claim facts that satisfied the demands of the Act. See Amanda Claybaugh, "*Jude the Obscure.*"

5. To again borrow Woloch's language, Father Time is essentially recovering himself as, no longer a worker but an "eccentric character," whose "disruptive, oppositional role" demands that he be excised from the narrative (*The One vs. the Many*, 25).

6. See Laurence Estanove, "'[A]s though / I Were Not By,'" for a fuller discussion of Marty's status as a liminal figure mediating between the worlds of Hardy's poetry and of his prose.

7. For a study of the industrial novel as a whole that includes an extended discussion of form in *Mary Barton*, see Catherine Gallagher, *The Industrial Reformation of English Fiction.*

8. Like *Mary Barton*, *Heart of Midlothian*'s Jeannie Deans circumvents an ethical crisis over her testimony in a loved one's trial by finding an alternative means of saving the defendant.

9. Despite his advocacy, Attwood was ambivalent about several of the particulars of the Chartist platform. For more background on Attwood and the People's Charter, see David Moss's biography *Thomas Attwood*, especially chapters 8 and 9.

10. The text is taken from *Hansard*, the official edited report of proceedings of the English Parliament. The citation indicates that this is a House of Commons debate of July 12, 1839, recorded in volume 49, although I have used the online version maintained by the UK Parliament at https://hansard.millbanksystems.com/.

11. See also Robert Poole's "'A Poor Man I Know'" for an account of the working-class poet Bamford's role in the construction of the footnotes. Poole and Wyke both remark as well on uncertainty over whether the footnotes were added by Gaskell or by her husband William, who was an expert on dialect. It is clear, however, that Elizabeth Gaskell played at least an active role in decisions over the use of dialect and accompanying annotations.

12. Catherine Gallagher has written on a corresponding *political* motivation for rejecting elements of the novel's melodrama plot. While John Carson initially interprets his son's death as the result of a love triangle, the root cause of the tragedy has been the far more prosaic suffering of his own workers; his mistake is in reading the event as melodrama rather than urban realism.

WORKS CITED

Ackroyd, Peter. *Dickens*. London: Vintage, 1990.
Allan, Janice M. "Sensationalism Made Real: The Role of Realism in the Production of Sensational Affect." *Victorian Literature and Culture* 43, no. 1 (2015): 97–112.
Amis, Kingsley. "What Became of Jane Austen?" *The Spectator*, October 4, 1957, 439–40.
Anderson, Amanda. "Melodrama, Morbidity, and Unthinking Sympathy: Gaskell's *Mary Barton* and *Ruth*." In *Tainted Souls and Painted Faces: The Rhetoric of Fallenness in Victorian Culture*, 108–40. Ithaca, NY: Cornell University Press, 1993.
Armour-Garb, Bradley, and Frederick Kroon, eds. *Fictionalism in Philosophy*. Oxford: Oxford University Press, 2020.
Austen, Jane. *Pride and Prejudice*. New York: Norton, 2016.
Badowska, Eva. "On the Track of Things: Sensation and Modernity in Mary Elizabeth Braddon's *Lady Audley's Secret*." *Victorian Literature and Culture* 37, no. 1 (2009): 157–75.
Beatty, Paul. *The Sellout*. London: Oneworld Press, 2015.
Beer, Gillian. *Darwin's Plots: Evolutionary Narrative in Darwin, George Eliot, and Nineteenth-Century Fiction*. New York: Cambridge University Press, 2009.
Black, Scott. *Without the Novel: Romance and the History of Prose Fiction*. Charlottesville: University of Virginia Press, 2019.
Blackburn, Patrick, Maarten de Rijke, and Yde Venema. *Modal Logic*. New York: Cambridge University Press, 2001.
"Books of the Day." *Morning Post* [London], November 7, 1895, 6.
Braddon, Mary Elizabeth. *Lady Audley's Secret*. Orchard Park, NY: Broadview, 2003.
Brontë, Charlotte. *Jane Eyre*. New York: Penguin, 2006.

———. *Shirley*. London: Wordsworth Editions, 1998.
———. *Villette*. New York: Barnes & Noble, 2005.
Brooks, Peter. *Reading for the Plot*. Cambridge, MA: Harvard University Press, 1992.
———. *Realist Vision*. New Haven, CT: Yale University Press, 2005.
Buchanan, March. "Many Worlds: See Me Here, See Me There." *Nature* 448 (July 5, 2007): 15–17.
Bulwer-Lytton, Edward. *Paul Clifford*. Philadelphia: Lippincott, 1873.
Burney, Fanny. *Evelina*. New York: Norton, 1998.
Byrne, Ruth J. *The Rational Imagination: How People Create Alternatives to Reality*. Cambridge, MA: MIT University Press, 2005.
Carroll, David, ed. *George Eliot: The Critical Heritage*. New York: Routledge, 1971.
Carroll, Noel. "The Paradox of Suspense." In *Beyond Aesthetics: Philosophical Essays*, 54–69. New York: Cambridge University Press, 2001.
Chase, Richard. *The American Novel and Its Tradition*. Baltimore: Johns Hopkins University Press, 1980.
Claybaugh, Amanda. "*Jude the Obscure:* The Irrelevancy of Marriage Law." In *Subversion and Sympathy: Gender, Law and the British Novel*, edited by Martha Nussbaum and Allison L. LaCroix, 48–64. New York: Oxford University Press, 2013.
———. *The Novel of Purpose: Literature and Social Reform in the Anglo-American World*. Ithaca, NY: Cornell University Press, 2007.
Cohn, Elisha. "'No Insignificant Creature': Thomas Hardy's Ethical Turn." *Nineteenth-Century Literature* 64, no. 4 (2010): 494–520.
Collins, Wilkie. *The Woman in White*. New York: Penguin, 2004.
Cox, R. G. *Thomas Hardy: The Critical Heritage*. New York: Routledge, 1979.
Crank, James, ed. *New Approaches to "Gone with the Wind."* Baton Rouge: Louisiana State University Press, 2015.
Daly, Nicholas. *Modernism, Romance and the Fin de Siècle: Popular Fiction and British Culture, 1880–1914*. Cambridge: Cambridge University Press, 1999.
Dannenberg, Hilary. *Coincidence and Counterfactuality: Plotting Time and Space in Narrative Fiction*. Lincoln: University of Nebraska Press, 2008.
Dickens, Charles. *David Copperfield*. Oxford: Oxford UP, 1998.
———. *Great Expectations*. Oxford: Oxford UP, 1998.
———. *Hard Times*. Oxford: Oxford UP, 1998.
———. *Little Dorrit*. Oxford: Oxford UP, 1998.
———. *Master Humphrey's Clock*. Oxford: Oxford UP, 1998.

---. *The Pilgrim Edition of the Letters of Charles Dickens*. Vol. 2. Edited by Madeline House, Graham Storey, and Kathleen Tillotson. Oxford: Clarendon, 1969.

---. *A Tale of Two Cities*. Oxford: Oxford University Press, 1998.

Doležel, Lubomír. *Hetrocosmica: Fiction and Possible Worlds*. Baltimore: Johns Hopkins University Press, 1998.

Doniger, Wendy. *The Bedtrick: Tales of Sex and Masquerade*. Chicago: University of Chicago Press, 2000.

Dubey, Madhu. "Speculative Fictions of Slavery." *American Literature* 82, no. 4 (December 2010): 779–805.

Dunbar, Ann-Marie. "Making the Case: Detection and Confession in *Lady Audley's Secret* and *The Woman in White*." *Victorian Review* 40, no. 1 (2014): 97–116.

Duncan, Ian. *Modern Romance and Transformations of the Novel: The Gothic, Scott, Dickens*. New York: Cambridge University Press, 1992.

DuPlessis, Rachel. *Writing beyond the Ending: Narrative Strategies of Twentieth-Century Women Writers*. Bloomington: Indiana University Press, 1985.

Eaves, T. C. Duncan, and Ben Kimpel. *Samuel Richardson: A Biography*. Oxford: Oxford University Press, 1971.

Edel, Leon. *Henry James: A Life*. New York: HarperCollins, 1987.

Eigner, Edwin M. "Bulwer-Lytton and the Changed Ending of *Great Expectations*." *Nineteenth-Century Fiction* 25, no. 1 (1970): 104–8.

Eliot, George. *Adam Bede*. Peterborough, ON: Broadview, 2005.

---. *Daniel Deronda*. New York: Penguin, 1996.

---. *Middlemarch*. New York: Barnes & Noble, 2003.

---. *Romola*. New York: Penguin, 2010.

Estanove, Laurence. "'[A]s though / I Were not By': Marty South, Parenthetically." *Hardy Review* 15, no. 1 (2013): 78–95.

Ferguson, Niall, ed. *Virtual History: Alternatives and Counterfactuals*. New York: Penguin, 2011.

Fiedler, Leslie. *Love and Death in the American Novel*. London: Dalkey, 1998.

Fisher, Jason, and David Whitney. "Serial Dependence in Visual Perception." *Nature Neuroscience* 17 (2014): 738–43.

Fisher, Judith W. "'Don't Put Your Daughter on the Stage Lady B': Talking about Theatre in Jane Austen's *Mansfield Park*." *Persuasions: The Journal of Jane Austen Studies* 22 (2000): 70–86.

Forster, E. M. *Aspects of the Novel*. New York: Harcourt, 1955.

Forster, John. *Life of Charles Dickens*. 2 vols. Philadelphia: Lippincott, 1873.

Fowler, Virginia. "Milly Theale's Malady of Self." *Novel* 14, no. 1 (1980): 57–74.

Fraiman, Susan. *Unbecoming Women: British Women Writers and the Novel of Development.* New York: Columbia University Press, 1993.
Freedgood, Elaine. *World Enough: The Invention of Realism in the Victorian Novel.* Princeton, NJ: Princeton University Press, 2019.
Frege, Gottlob. "On Sense and Reference." Translated by Max Black. In *Translations from the Philosophical Writings of Gottlob Frege,* edited by Peter Geach and Max Black, 56–78. Lanham, MD: Rowman and Littlefield, 1980.
Fryckstedt, Monica Correa. *Geraldine Jewsbury's Athaneum Reviews: A Mirror of Mid-Victorian Attitudes to Fiction.* Uppsala, Sweden: S. Academiae Upsaliensis, 1986.
French, A. L. "A Note on Middlemarch." *Nineteenth-Century Fiction* 26, no. 3 (1971): 339–47.
Frye, Northrop. *Anatomy of Criticism.* Princeton, NJ: Princeton University Press, 1971.
Gallagher, Catherine. *The Industrial Reformation of English Fiction: Social Discourse and Narrative Form, 1832–1867.* Chicago: University of Chicago Press, 1985.
———. *Telling It Like It Wasn't: The Counterfactual Imagination in History and Fiction.* Chicago: University of Chicago Press, 2018.
Gaskell, Elizabeth. *The Life of Charlotte Brontë.* New York: Penguin, 1998.
———. *Mary Barton.* New York: Penguin, 2009.
Gatrell, Simon. "Wessex." In *The Cambridge Companion to Thomas Hardy,* edited by Dale Kramer, 19–37. Cambridge: Cambridge University Press, 1999.
Gilbert, Sandra, and Susan Gubar. *The Madwoman in the Attic: The Woman Writer and the Nineteenth-Century Literary Imagination.* New Haven, CT: Yale University Press, 1979.
Gill, Stephen. Review of *The Companion to "Great Expectations,"* edited by David Paroissien. *The Review of English Studies* 53 (August 2002), 456–57.
Girard, Rene. *Deceit, Desire, and the Novel: Self and Other in Literary Structure.* Translated by Yvonne Freccero. Baltimore: Johns Hopkins University Press, 1976.
Glatt, Carra. "When Found Make a Note Of: Tracing the Source of a Dickensian Legend." *Nineteenth-Century Studies* 28 (April 2018): 57–71.
Goodman, Paul. *The Structure of Literature.* Chicago: University of Chicago Press, 1954.
Greiner, Rae. *Sympathetic Realism in Nineteenth-Century British Fiction.* Baltimore: Johns Hopkins University Press, 2013.
Grener, Adam. *Improbability, Chance and the Nineteenth-Century Realist Novel.* Columbus: Ohio State University Press, 2020.

Griest, Guinevere. *Mudie's Circulating Library and the Victorian Novel.* Bloomington: Indiana University Press, 1970.
Hack, Daniel. *Reaping Something New: African American Transformations of Victorian Literature.* Princeton, NJ: Princeton University Press, 2017.
Hacking, Ian. *The Emergence of Probability.* New York: Cambridge University Press, 1975.
Haight, Gordon. "Dickens and Lewes on Spontaneous Combustion." *Nineteenth-Century Fiction* 10, no. 1 (1955): 53–63.
Hardy, Florence. *The Early Years of Thomas Hardy.* New York: Macmillan, 1932.
———. *The Later Years of Thomas Hardy.* New York: Macmillan, 1932.
Hardy, Thomas. *Jude the Obscure.* London: Macmillan, 1986.
———. *The Mayor of Casterbridge.* New York: Penguin, 2003.
———. *Tess of the D'Urbervilles.* New York: Penguin, 2003.
———. *The Woodlanders.* New York: Penguin, 1998.
Heinrichs, Rachel. "Critical Masculinities in *Lady Audley's Secret.*" *Victorian Review* 33, no. 1 (2007): 103–20.
Hintikka, Jaakko, and Merrill B. Hintikka. "Are There Nonexistent Objects? Why Not? But Where Are They?" In *The Logic of Epistemology and the Epistemology of Logic,* 37–44. Dordrecht, Netherlands: Kluwer Academic Press, 1989.
Hodgson, John A. "The Recoil of 'The Speckled Band': Detective Story and Detective Discourse." *Poetics Today* 13, no. 2 (1992): 309–24.
Holmes, Rupert. "The Writing on the Wall." *The Mystery of Edwin Drood Original Broadway Cast Recording.* London: Polydor Records, 1986.
House, Humphrey. *The Dickens World.* New York: Oxford University Press, 1960.
Ingham, Patricia. Introduction to *The Woodlanders,* xvi–xxxiv. New York: Penguin, 1998.
Jackson, Jeffrey E. "Elizabeth Gaskell and the Dangerous Edge of Things: Epigraphs in *North and South* and Victorian Publishing Practices." *Pacific Coast Philology* 40, no. 2 (2005): 56–72.
Jaffe, Audrey. *The Victorian Novel Dreams of the Real.* Oxford: Oxford University Press, 2019.
James, Henry. *The Ambassadors.* New York: Penguin, 2003.
———. *The Art of the Novel: Critical Prefaces.* Chicago: University of Chicago Press, 2011.
———. *The Wings of the Dove.* New York: Random House, 1993.
James, William. *The Varieties of Religious Experience: A Study in Human Nature.* Mineola, NY: Dover, 2018.

Jameson, Fredric. "The Politics of Utopia." *New Left Review* 25 (2004): 35–54.

Johnson, James Weldon. Preface to *The Book of American Negro Poetry*, 9–48. New York: Harcourt, 1931.

Jordan, John O. "Partings Welded Together: Self-Fashioning in *Great Expectations* and *Jane Eyre*." *Dickens Quarterly* 13 (March 1996): 19–33.

Joseph, Gerhard. "Who Cares Who Killed Edwin Drood? Or, On the Whole, I'd Rather Be in Philadelphia." *Nineteenth-Century Literature* 51 (September 1996): 161–75.

Kahneman, Daniel, Paul Slovic, and Amos Tversky, eds. *Judgment under Uncertainty: Heuristics and Biases*. New York: Cambridge University Press, 1982.

Keen, Suzanne. "Empathetic Hardy: Bounded, Ambassadorial, and Broadcast Strategies of Narrative Empathy." *Poetics Today* 32, no. 2 (2011): 349–89.

———. *Empathy and the Novel*. New York: Oxford University Press, 2007.

Kent, Christopher. "Probability, Reality and Sensation in the Novels of Wilkie Collins." *Dickens Studies Annual* 20 (1991): 259–80.

Kenton, Edna. "Henry James to the Ruminant Reader: The Turn of the Screw." *The Arts* 6 (1923): 245–55.

Kerfoot, J. B. "*The Ambassadors*. A Question. With Apologies to Henry James." *Life*, January 7, 1904, 22.

———. "The Latest Books." *Life*, December 11, 1903, 604.

Knoepflmacher, U. C. "The Counterworld of Victorian Fiction and *The Woman in White*," in *The Worlds of Victorian Fiction*, edited by Jerome H. Buckley, 351–70. Cambridge, MA: Harvard University Press, 1975.

Koch, Stephen. "Transcendence in *The Wings of the Dove*." *Modern Fiction Studies* 12, no. 1 (1966): 93–102.

Kramer, Dale. *Thomas Hardy: The Forms of Tragedy*. Detroit: Wayne State University Press, 1975.

Kramer, Stanley, dir. *Guess Who's Coming to Dinner*. Los Angeles; Columbia Pictures, 1967. 108 min.

Kripke, Saul. *Naming and Necessity*. Boston: Wiley-Blackwell, 1991.

Kucich, John. *Repression in Victorian Fiction: Charlotte Brontë, George Eliot, and Charles Dickens*. Berkeley: University of California Press, 1987.

Kushnier, Jennifer S. "Educating Boys to Be Queer: Braddon's *Lady Audley's Secret*." *Victorian Literature and Culture* 30, no. 1 (2002): 61–75.

Lang, Andrew. *The Puzzle of Dickens's Last Plot*. London: Chapman and Hall, 1905.

Langbauer, Laurie. "Dickens's Streetwalkers: Women and the Form of Romance." *English Literary History* 53 (1986): 411–31.

Leavis, F. R. *The Great Tradition: George Eliot, Henry James, Joseph Conrad.* Harmondsworth: Penguin, 1986.
Leavis, F. R., and Q. D. Leavis. *Dickens the Novelist.* London: Faber & Faber, 2008.
Levine, Caroline. *The Serious Pleasures of Suspense: Victorian Realism and Narrative Doubt.* Charlottesville: University of Virginia Press, 2003.
Levine, George. *Darwin and the Novelists: Patterns of Science in Victorian Fiction.* Chicago: University of Chicago Press, 1988.
———. *The Realistic Imagination: English Fiction from "Frankenstein" to "Lady Chatterley."* Chicago: University of Chicago Press, 1981.
Lévi-Strauss, Claude. *Myth and Meaning.* London: Routledge, 2001.
Lewes, George Henry. "The Principles of Success in Literature." *The Fortnightly* I (1865): 185–96.
Lewis, David. *On the Plurality of Worlds.* Malden, MA: Blackwell, 1986.
———. "Truth in Fiction." *American Philosophical Quarterly* 15, no. 1 (1978): 37–46.
Lind, Sidney E. "*The Turn of the Screw*: The Torment of Critics." *Centennial Review* 14, no. 2 (1970): 225–40.
Lodge, David. "Ambiguously Ever After: Problematic Endings in English Fiction." In *Working with Structuralism: Essays and Reviews on Nineteenth- and Twentieth-Century Literature,* 143–55. New York: Routledge, 1986.
———. "A Question of Judgment: The Theatricals at *Mansfield Park.*" *Nineteenth-Century Fiction* 17, no. 3 (1962): 275–82.
Lukács, Georg. *The Theory of the Novel.* Translated by Anna Bostock. Cambridge, MA: MIT Press, 1971.
Marcus, Steven. *Dickens from "Pickwick" to "Dombey."* New York: Norton, 1985.
Matthiessen, F. O. *Henry James: The Major Phase.* New York: Oxford University Press, 1944.
McAleavey, Maia. *The Bigamy Plot: Sensation and Convention in the Victorian Novel.* New York: Cambridge University Press, 2015.
McCarthy, Mary. *Ideas and the Novel.* New York: Harcourt Brace Jovanovich, 1980.
McKeon, Michael. *The Origins of the English Novel: 1600–1740.* Baltimore: Johns Hopkins University Press, 2003.
Meckier, Jerome. "Charles Dickens's *Great Expectations*: A Defense of the Second Ending." *Studies in the Novel* 25, no. 1 (Spring 1993): 28–58.
———. "Suspense in *The Old Curiosity Shop*: Dickens's Contrapuntal Artistry." *Journal of Narrative Technique* 2, no. 3 (1972): 199–207.

Meinong, Alexius. "On the Theory of Objects." In *Realism and the Background of Phenomenology*, edited by Roderick Chisolm, 76–117. Glencoe, IL: Free Press, 1960.

Mercer, Caroline, and Sarah Wangensteen. "'Consumption, Heart-Disease, or Whatever': Chlorosis, a Heroine's Illness in *The Wings of the Dove*." *Journal of the History of Medicine and Allied Sciences* 40, no. 3 (1985): 259–85.

Miller, Andrew J. "Lives Unled in Realist Fiction." *Representations* 98 (Spring 2007): 118–34.

———. *On Not Being Someone Else: Tales of Our Unled Lives*. Cambridge, MA: Harvard University Press, 2020.

Miller, D. A. "*Cage aux folles*: Sensation and Gender in Wilkie Collins's *The Woman in White*." *Representations* 14 (1986): 107–36.

———. *Jane Austen, or the Secret of Style*. Princeton, NJ: Princeton University Press, 2003.

———. *Narrative and Its Discontents: Problems of Closure in the Traditional Novel*. Princeton, NJ: Princeton University Press, 1989.

Miller, Henry Knight. *Henry Fielding's "Tom Jones" and the Romance Tradition*. Victoria, BC: University of Victoria, 1976.

Millhauser, Milton. "*Great Expectations*—The Three Endings." *Dickens Studies Annual* 2 (1972): 267–77.

Moretti, Franco. *The Way of the World: The Bildungsroman in European Culture*. London: Verso, 1987.

Moss, David. *Thomas Attwood: The Biography of a Radical*. Montreal: Queen's University Press, 1990.

Mulock, Dinah. "Review, *Macmillan's Magazine*, April 1861." In *George Eliot: The Critical Heritage*, edited by David Carroll, 154–61. New York: Routledge, 2009.

Nemesvari, Richard. "Robert Audley's Secret: Male Homosocial Desire and 'Going Straight' in *Lady Audley's Secret*." In *Straight with a Twist: Queer Theory and the Subject of Heterosexuality*, edited by Calvin Thomas, 102–21. Urbana: University of Illinois Press, 2000.

Newlin, George. *Understanding "Great Expectations."* Westport, CT: Greenwood Press, 2000.

Newsom, Robert. *A Likely Story: Probability and Play in Fiction*. New Brunswick, NJ: Rutgers University Press, 1988.

Oatley, Keith. "Fiction: Simulation of Social Worlds." *Trends in Cognitive Sciences* 20, no. 8 (2016): 618–28.

Ohi, Kevin. *Henry James and the Queerness of Style*. Minneapolis: University of Minnesota Press, 2011.

Orwell, George. "Charles Dickens." In *George Orwell: An Age Like This, 1920–1940.* New York: Harcourt Brace, 1968.
Parsons, Terence. *Nonexistent Objects.* New Haven, CT: Yale University Press, 1980.
Pavel, Thomas. *Fictional Worlds.* Cambridge, MA: Harvard University Press, 1986.
———. "'Possible Worlds' in Literary Semantics." *Journal of Aesthetics and Art Criticism* 34, no. 2 (1975):165–76.
Poole, Robert. "'A Poor Man I Know'—Samuel Bamford and the Making of *Mary Barton.*" *Gaskell Journal* 22 (2008): 96–115.
Portales, Marco. "Strether and Women." *Modern Language Studies* 11 (1981): 17–23.
Prince, Gerald. "The Disnarrated." *Style* 22, no. 1 (1988): 1–8.
———. "On Narrative Studies and Narrative Genres." *Poetics Today* 11, no. 2 (1990): 271–82.
Propp, Vladimir. *Morphology of the Folktale.* Translated by Laurence Scott. Austin: University of Texas Press, 1968.
Proudfoot, Diane. "Possible Worlds Semantics and Fiction." *Journal of Philosophic Logic* 35, no. 1 (2006): 9–40.
Pykett, Lyn. *The Sensation Novel: From "The Woman in White" to "The Moonstone."* Liverpool: University of Liverpool Press, 1994.
Rayner, K., Sarah White, and S. P. Liversedge. "Raeding ords with Jubmled Lettres: There Is a Cost." *Psychological Science* 17, no. 3 (2006): 192–93.
Recchio, Thomas. "Melodrama and the Production of Affective Knowledge in *Mary Barton.*" *Studies in the Novel* 43, no. 3 (2011): 289–305.
Redfield, Marc. *Phantom Formations: Aesthetic Ideology and the Bildungsroman.* Ithaca, NY: Cornell University Press, 1996.
"Review of *Jane Eyre: An Autobiography,* by Currer Bell." *Littell's Living Age* 17, no. 213 (June 1848): 481–87.
Rivkin, Julie. *False Positions: The Representational Logics of Henry James's Fiction.* Stanford, CA: Stanford University Press, 1996.
Roese, Neal J., and James M. Olsen. *What Might Have Been: The Social Psychology of Counterfactual Thinking.* Mahwah, NJ: Lawrence Erlbaum, 1995.
Ronen, Ruth. *Possible Worlds of Literary Theory.* New York: Cambridge University Press, 1994.
Rosenberg, Edgar. "Putting an End to *Great Expectations.*" In *Great Expectations,* edited by Edgar Rosenberg, 491–527. New York: Norton, 1999.
Rosenthal, Jesse. *Good Form: The Ethical Experience of the Victorian Novel.* Princeton, NJ: Princeton University Press, 2017.

Ruskin, John. "Extract from *Fiction, Fair and Foul*." In *George Eliot: The Critical Heritage*, edited by David Carroll, 166–67. New York: Routledge, 2009.

Russell, Bertrand. "On Denoting." *Mind*, n.s., 14, no. 56 (1905): 479–93.

Ryan, Marie-Laure. *Narrative as Virtual Reality: Immersion and Interactivity in Literature and Electronic Media*. Baltimore: Johns Hopkins University Press, 2001.

———. *Possible Worlds, Artificial Intelligence, and Narrative Theory*. Bloomington: Indiana University Press, 1991.

———. "Possible Worlds and Accessibility Relationships: A Semantic Typology of Fiction." *Poetics Today* 12, no. 3 (1991): 553–76.

Said, Edward. *Culture and Imperialism*. New York: Random House, 1994.

Saunders, Simon, Jonathan Barrett, Adrian Kent, and David Wallace, eds. *Many Worlds? Everett, Quantum Theory, and Reality*. Oxford: Oxford University Press, 2012.

Schaffer, Talia. *Romance's Rival: Familiar Marriage in Victorian Fiction*. Oxford: Oxford University Press, 2016.

Sedgwick, Eve Kosofsky. *The Epistemology of the Closet*. Berkeley: University of California Press, 1990.

Shaw, George Bernard. Preface to *Great Expectations*. Edinburgh: R & R Clark, 1937.

Shaw, Harry E. *Narrating Reality: Austen, Scott, Eliot*. Ithaca, NY: Cornell University Press, 1999.

Sheridan, Richard Brinsely. Richard Brinsley Sheridan to Thomas Grenville, October 30, 1772. In *The Letters of Richard Brinsley Sheridan*, edited by Cecil Price, vol. 1. Oxford: Oxford University Press, 1966.

Shields, Carol. *Jane Austen: A Life*. New York: Penguin, 2005.

Shklovsky, Viktor. *Theory of Prose*. Translated by Benjamin Sher. Normal, IL: Dalkey, 1990.

Showalter, Elaine. *The Female Malady: Woman, Madness, and English Culture, 1830–1980*. New York: Penguin, 1987.

———. *Literature of Their Own: British Women Novelists from Brontë to Lessig*. Princeton, NJ: Princeton University Press, 1977.

Spacks, Patricia Meyer. *Novel Beginnings: Experiments in Eighteenth-Century English Fiction*. New Haven, CT: Yale University Press, 2006.

Spencer, Edmund. *The Faerie Queene*. New York: Penguin, 1979.

Steele, Claude. *Whistling Vivaldi and Other Clues to How Stereotypes Affect Us*. New York: Norton, 2010.

Strawson, P. F. "On Referring." *Mind* 59 (1950): 320–44.

Sylvan, Richard. *Exploring Meinong's Jungle and Beyond: An Investigation of Noneism and the Theory of Items.* Canberra: Research School of Social Sciences, Australian National University, 1980.
Tamir, Diana I., Andrew B. Bricker, David Dodell-Feder, and Jason P. Mitchell. "Reading Fiction and Reading Minds: The Role of Simulation in the Default Network." *Social Cognitive and Affective Neuroscience* 11, no. 2 (2016): 215–24.
Thackeray, William. *Vanity Fair.* New York: Penguin, 2001.
Tillotson, Geoffrey. "The George Eliot Letters." In *Mid-Victorian Studies,* edited by Geoffrey Tillotson and Kathleen Tillotson, 65–71. New York: Bloomsbury, 2013.
Tintner, Adeline R., and Henry D. Janowitz. "Inoperable Cancer: An Alternative Diagnosis for Milly Theale's Illness." *Journal of the History of Medicine and Allied Sciences* 42, no. 1 (1987): 73–76.
Tomalin, Claire. *Jane Austen: A Life.* New York: Vintage, 1999.
Tondre, Michael. *The Physics of Possibility: Victorian Fiction, Science, and Gender.* Charlottesville: University of Virginia Press, 2018.
Trilling, Lionel. "Mansfield Park." In *The Opposing Self: Nine Essays in Criticism by Lionel Trilling,* 206–30. New York: Viking, 1969.
Veeder, William. "Strether and the Transcendence of Language." *Modern Philology* 69 (1971): 116–32.
Wallace, David Foster. *Infinite Jest.* Boston: Little, Brown, 1996.
Walpole, Horace. "The Castle of Otranto." *The Castle of Otranto and the Mysterious Mother.* Orchard Park, NY: Broadview, 2003.
Warhol, Robin. "Engaging Strategies: Earnestness and Realism." *Gendered Interventions: Narrative Discourse in the Victorian Novel,* 47–71. Columbus: Ohio State University Press, 1989.
———. "'What Might Have Been Is Not What Is': Dickens's Narrative Refusals." In *Counterfactual Thinking / Counterfactual Writing,* edited by Dorthee Blake, Michael Butter, and Tillman Köppe, 227–29. Boston: Walter de Gruyter, 2011.
Watt, Ian. *The Rise of the Novel: Studies in Defoe, Richardson, and Fielding.* Berkeley: University of California Press, 2001.
Weltman, Sharon Aronofsky. *Victorians on Broadway: Literature, Adaptation and the Modern American Musical.* Charlottesville: University of Virginia Press, 2020.
Williams, Raymond. *Culture and Society.* New York: Anchor, 1959.
Wilson, Edmund. "The Ambiguity of Henry James." *Hound and Horn* 7 (1934): 385–406.

———. "Dickens: The Two Scrooges." In *The Wound and the Bow: Seven Studies in Literature*, 3–85. Cambridge, MA: Houghton-Mifflin, 1941.

Woloch, Alex. *The One vs. the Many: Minor Characters and the Space of the Protagonist in the Novel*. Princeton, NJ: Princeton University Press, 2003.

Wyke, Terry. "Authenticating the Text: A Footnote in *Mary Barton*." *Bulletin of the John Rylands Library, Manchester* 80, no. 1 (1998): 103–23.

Yevish, Irving A. "The Attack on *Jude the Obscure*: A Reappraisal Some Seventy Years After." *Journal of General Education* 18, no. 4 (1967): 239–48.

INDEX

African American writers, 182; dialect poetry of, 183
Alger, Horatio, 138
allegory: aestheticized vagaries of, 35; minor character as, 155; moral clarity of, 6, 16; sacrifice of romantic, 61; stable and predictable world of the, 8, 58
"All-Kinds-of-Fur" (fairy tale), 87–88
Ambassadors, The (James): parody of, 110; preface to, 125; proxy narrative of, 122–35; question of the denouement of, 110; representation in, 194n7; social language of, 133. *See also* James, Henry
ambiguity, 64, 69; interpretation of, 128–29
American Dream, 138
American Renaissance, 5, 39
Amis, Kingsley: "What Became of Jane Austen?," 191n4
Anderson, Amanda, 165
Arabian Nights, The (compilation of folk tales), 190n15
Athenaeum, The (literary magazine), 189n5
Attwood, Thomas, 163–65, 195n9
Austen, Jane, 22, 192n6; *Emma*, 15; *Mansfield Park*, 82–84, 86, 91, 192n6; *Pride and Prejudice*, 12, 16, 82–83, 86, 188n13; *Sense and Sensibility*, 22–23
Australia, 59

Badowska, Eva, 95
Bamford, Samuel, 195n11
Beatty, Paul: *The Sellout*, 32, 175–77, 180–85
Beckett, Samuel, 177
Beer, Gillian, 18, 144
Bellamy, Edward, 161
Bible, 170. *See also* Christian parable
bildungsroman, 6, 15, 42, 54–56, 86, 184; hero of the, 96. *See also* novel
Black, Scott: *Without the Novel*, 189n2
Blackmore, Richard Doddridge: *Lorna Doone*, 158
Blackwood, John, 95, 193n12
Blackwood's (magazine), 140
Braddon, Maria Elizabeth: *Lady Audley's Secret*, 31, 77–78, 80, 86–96, 135. *See also Lady Audley's Secret* (Braddon)
Brontë, Charlotte, 42; *Jane Eyre*, 6–8, 15, 20, 23, 27–30; *Shirley*, 157; *Villette*, 23–30. *See also Jane Eyre* (Brontë); *Villette* (Brontë)
Brontë, Emily, 6, 42; *Wuthering Heights*, 43
Brontë, Patrick, 29
Brooks, Peter: *Reading for the Plot*, 65, 87–88, 193n2; *Realist Vision*, 47–48
Brydon, Spencer: *The Jolly Corner*, 125

Bulwer-Lytton, Edward, 50, 62, 190n17; *Paul Clifford*, 68–69, 96
Burney, Frances, 41–42; *Evelina*, 42

Calvino, Italo: *Invisible Cities*, 180
Canada, 161, 165, 173–74
Chase, Richard, 39, 129
Chaucer, Geoffrey, 168, 171, 174
Christian parable, 161, 164, 170–71. *See also* Bible
Claybaugh, Amanda, 139
Cohn, Elisha, 144
Collins, Wilkie, 18, 87, 193n15; *The Moonstone*, 41; *The Woman in White*, 31, 80, 97–109
comic opera, 96
Comte, Augustus, 144
Conan-Doyle, Arthur: "The Speckled Band," 138
Conrad, Joseph, 40
conversion narrative, 6–7, 19
counterfactual history, 11
counterfactual thinking: and literary realism, 12; nineteenth-century, 190n19; psychology of, 9
Cumberbatch, Benedict, 192n5

Dannenberg, Hilary, 11–12, 37, 48, 65, 69, 84, 190n19, 191n21
Dante, 162
Darwinism, 18, 144
Defoe, Daniel, 5
Dickens, Charles, 30, 46, 106, 185; ambivalent realism of, 46–49, 54–61, 74; *Bleak House*, 18; *David Copperfield*, 43, 50–51, 54–58, 62–63, 69; death of, 74–75; *Dombey and Son*, 51; genres of, 46–49; *Great Expectations*, 48, 50, 58, 61–69, 72–75; *Hard Times*, 5, 47, 50, 69–70, 140, 157; *Little Dorrit*, 70–74; *Master Humphrey's Clock* (periodical), 51; *The Mystery of Edwin Drood*, 75–76; *Nicholas Nickleby*, 47–48, 54, 59; *The Old Curiosity Shop*, 46–47, 49, 51–61, 65–68, 75, 78; *Our Mutual Friend*, 48; *The Pickwick Papers*, 51–52; romantic possibility for, 56–58, 61; *A Tale of Two Cities*, 50, 58, 70; triumphant resurrection of, 184; unexpected novels of, 50–54. *See also Great Expectations* (Dickens); *Old Curiosity Shop, The* (Dickens)
didactic novel, 19. *See also* novel
divine forgiveness, 157–58
divorce, 194n4
Dixie, Florence: *Gloriana*, 159
Douglass, Frederick, 185
Dubey, Madhu: *Speculative Fictions of Slavery*, 182
Dunbar, Ann-Marie, 105
Duncan, Ian, 53
DuPlessis, Rachel, 69; *Writing beyond the Ending*, 191n21

Eigner, Edwin, 190n17
Eliot, George (Mary Anne Evans), 4–6, 13, 21, 42, 142, 156, 187n1; *Adam Bede*, 10–11; *Daniel Deronda*, 17, 21, 23, 85; identity of, 193n12; *Middlemarch*, 2–3, 7, 20–23, 43, 94, 144, 159, 176; *The Mill on the Floss*, 94–95, 193n12. *See also Middlemarch* (Eliot)
empathy, 45; dream of, 137; of Gaskell, 163–64, 173–74; of Hardy, 144; moment of, 64
erotic, the, 101–3; legitimization in domestic fiction of the, 107. *See also* sexuality
Europe, 130–31
Everett, Hugh, 187n5

fantasy, 37; absurdist, 185. *See also* novel
farce, 153, 156

Faulkner, William, 177; *Absalom, Absalom!*, 113, 193n2
femininity: archetypes of, 101; demonic, 94; malignant, 92; succubus, 90–91. See also sexuality; women
feminism, 159. See also women
ficelle, 111, 124, 130, 134; definition of, 193n1
fiction: detective, 89; domestic, 107; endless possibilities of, 67; underplots of realist, 78; unnatural conventions of realist, 68; utopian, 157–65. See also Gothic fiction; novel; short story
Fiedler, Leslie, 112, 129
Fielding, Henry, 5, 13, 38, 42, 47; *Tom Jones*, 54, 189n3
Forster, E. M., 85
Forster, John, 51–52, 61–63, 68, 74–75
Fowler, Virginia C., 115
Fowles, John: *The French Lieutenant's Woman*, 69
Fraiman, Susan, 69; *Unbecoming Women*, 187n4, 188n13, 191n21
Freedgood, Elaine, 36
Frege, Gottlob, 187n6
French, A. L.: "A Note on Middlemarch," 192n10
friendship, 127, 129; platonic, 114, 124–25, 133
From Mansfield with Love (web series), 83
Fryckstedt, Monica Correa, 189n5
Frye, Northrop: *Anatomy of Criticism*, 189n4

Gallagher, Catherine, 195n12; *The Industrial Reformation of English Fiction*, 195n7; *Telling It Like It Wasn't*, 11
García Márquez, Gabriel, 49
Gaskell, Elizabeth, 31, 195n11; deep imaginative sympathy of, 161, 167–69; ethnographic tendencies in the narration of, 166; faith in the power of empathy of, 163–64, 173–74; *The Life of Charlotte Brontë*, 29; *Mary Barton*, 137, 140, 157–74; moralism of, 170–72; *North and South*, 16, 157, 161–62, 173; social vision of, 162. See also *Mary Barton* (Gaskell)
Gatrell, Simon, 141, 154
Gilbert, Sandra: *The Madwoman in the Attic*, 188n15
Gilman, Charlotte Perkins, 161
Girard, René, 95
Gone with the Wind (film), 192n7
Goodman, Paul: *The Structure of Literature*, 1
Gothic fiction: array of suggestive meanings drawn from, 99; eighteenth-century, 80, 100, 106; erotic energy of, 107–8; as horror, 135; as melodrama, 19, 48, 100; psychologically evocative landscapes of, 108; psychosexual terror of the, 88; and realism, 100; as romance, 7; and Victorian domestic fiction, 100–101. See also fiction; novel; sensation novel
Great Expectations (Dickens): closing of certain possibilities of, 66–74; ending of, 50, 61–63, 66, 72, 190n16, 190n20; systematic suppression of the most fantastic and anti-realistic elements of, 20. See also Dickens, Charles
Greimas, Algirdas Julien, 85
Grener, Adam, 18–19, 188n10
Grenier, Rae, 35
Gubar, Susan: *The Madwoman in the Attic*, 188n15
Guess Who's Coming to Dinner (film), 138–39

Hack, Daniel: *Reaping Something New*, 176
Hacking, Ian: *The Emergence of Probability*, 188n10
Haggard, H. Rider, 40

Hardy, Thomas, 22, 31, 48; apparent determinism of the novels of, 142–43, 147; editions of the early novels of, 141–42; *Jude the Obscure*, 142–43, 146–47, 154–56, 194n2, 195n4; *The Mayor of Casterbridge*, 145, 194n3; melodramatic plots of, 147, 150–51, 154–55; pessimism of, 140–44, 147, 155; "The Pine Planters," 154; poetry of, 141, 154, 156; protagonists of, 145, 148, 154–55; reparative social alternatives in the novels of, 142, 144; *The Return of the Native*, 143; social critiques of, 144, 147; *Tess of the D'Urbervilles*, 2, 140–42; *The Woodlanders*, 140, 148–56, 158. See also *Tess of the D'Urbervilles* (Hardy); *Woodlanders, The* (Hardy)
Harper's Weekly (magazine), 194n2
Hawthorne, Nathaniel, 111; *Blithedale Romance*, 95
Haywood, Eliza, 41
Hemingway, Ernest, 177
Herodotus, 22
Holmes, Rupert: *Drood* (musical), 75–76
House, Humphrey: *The Dickens World*, 189n10
Howells, William Dean, 194n2

identity: instability of human, 99, 108; marginal class allegiances that inform Jane Eyre's early, 187n4; suppression of racial, 183; unwillingness to reveal one's own, 28
imagery, 63
Ingham, Patricia, 152
interracial marriage, 139
irony, 119, 178, 180; of Austen, 191n4; dramatic, 76

Jaffe, Audrey, 37
James, Henry, 3, 80, 109–36; *The Ambassadors*, 31, 110, 114, 122–36; *The American*, 111; *The Bostonians*, 111, 114; *The Portrait of a Lady*, 124; *The Princess Casamassima*, 111–12; as protomodernist, 113; as realist author, 121; *The Spoils of Poynton*, 111; *The Turn of the Screw*, 114; *Washington Square*, 112; *What Maisie Knew*, 112; *The Wings of the Dove*, 114–22. See also *Ambassadors, The* (James); *Wings of the Dove, The* (James)
James, William: *The Varieties of Religious Experience*, 194n5
Jameson, Fredric, 158, 172
Jane Eyre (Brontë): competitor plots in, 6–8; elimination of the most radical possibilities in, 6, 20, 29–30; narratability of, 15; readings of, 188n15; social rise as betrayal of identity of marginal class allegiances early in, 187n4. See also Brontë, Charlotte
Jewsbury, Geraldine, 189n5
Jim Crow, 184
Johnson, James Weldon: *Book of American Negro Poetry* (preface), 183
Johnson, Samuel, 187n2
Jordan, John O., 64
Joseph, Gerhard: "Who Cares Who Killed Edwin Drood?," 191n23
journalism, nineteenth-century, 18
Joyce, James, 156, 177; *Ulysses*, 113
Judaism, 20
Judgment under Uncertainty (Kahneman, Slovic, and Tversky), 9

Kafka, Franz, 185
Kahneman, Daniel, 14
Keen, Suzanne, 144
Kenton, Edna, 194n3
Kerfoot, J. B., 110
King, Martin Luther, Jr., 181
Knoepflmacher, U. C., 103
Koch, Stephen: "Transcendence in *The Wings of the Dove*," 118

Kramer, Dale, 151
Kripke, Saul, 9
Kucich, John: *Repression in Victorian Fiction*, 190n14
Kushnier, Jennifer: "Educating Boys to Be Queer," 88, 93

Lady Audley's Secret (Braddon): Gothic as the dominant mode of, 91–92, 96–97; potential queerness in, 192n8; radical disconnect between narrator and plot in, 93; as a realist novel, 96; "same-but-different" plot of, 87; the secret of, 97. *See also* Braddon, Maria Elizabeth
Langbauer, Laurie, 190n15
language: discursive forms of, 105, 122; inevitable failure for James of, 122; realist, 108; referential signs of, 105; social, 133
Lawrence, D. H.: *Lady Chatterley's Lover*, 189n1
Leavis, F. R.: *Dickens the Novelist*, 47, 53, 189n10; *The Great Tradition*, 47
Levine, Caroline, 35
Levine, George, 37, 144; *The Realistic Imagination*, 189n1
Levi-Strauss, Claude, 85–86
Lewes, George Henry, 44
Lewis, David, 10
Life (magazine), 110
Lind, Sidney: "*The Turn of the Screw*," 194n3
Little Rascals, The (television series), 175, 177, 181–82
Lizzie Bennet Diaries, The (web series), 83–84
Lodge, David: "Ambiguously Ever After," 190n20
London, 1, 58, 116, 133, 162, 168, 175
Los Angeles, 175, 184
Lovely Lady trope, 92, 94

Loving v. Virginia, 194n1
Lukács, Georg, 4, 43, 45; definition of the "novel of romantic disillusionment" of, 55

Macmillan's Magazine, 193n13
Macready, William, 52
madness, 78
Malcolm X, 181
Manchester, 166, 171–72
Mandeville, Bernard, 168
Mann, Thomas: *Buddenbrooks*, 115
Marcus, Stephen: *Dickens from "Pickwick" to "Dombey,"* 189n11
Marxist criticism, 160
Mary Barton (Gaskell): confident endorsement of the power of traditional plot to bring about social change in, 157; dream of empathy in the vision of, 137; footnotes of, 166–68, 171, 195n11; formal oddities of, 157; hypothetical realism of, 159, 164, 171–72, 174; murder in, 160, 162, 165, 171–73; sensational scenario in, 173. *See also* Gaskell, Elizabeth
materialist commodity culture, 53
Matrimonial Causes Act (1857), 194n4
Matthiessen, F. O., 123
McCarthy, Mary: *Ideas and the Novel*, 111
McKeon, Michael: *The Origins of the English Novel*, 189n2
meaning: endless deferral of, 180; gap between content and, 31; James's characters as obsessive interpreters of ambiguities and makers of, 128–29; James's novels at the level of narrative, 193n2; postmodern denial of fixed, 24; as subtext added to a surface understanding, 31; unwritten plots as covert agents of narrative, 33. *See also* narrative
Meckier, Jerome, 56, 63–64, 190n18

melodrama, 147, 150–53, 156, 195n12; murder plot as, 157, 171–72; romantic, 161. *See also* plot
Melville, Herman: *Moby-Dick*, 40
metafiction, 178
metaphor, 117–18, 122, 192n10; and metonymy, 132
"Me Too" era, 82
Middle Ages, 37
Middlemarch (Eliot): compromised ending of, 21; generous dispersals of consciousness among the characters of, 144–45; as pinnacle of Victorian realism, 20. *See also* Eliot, George (Mary Anne Evans)
Miller, Andrew, 11, 23; "Lives Unled in Realist Fiction," 23, 50; *On Not Being Someone Else*, 23
Miller, D. A.: "*Cage aux folles*," 193n16; *Jane Austen, or the Secret of Style*, 188n13; *Narrative and Its Discontents*, 15, 27, 62
Miller, Henry Knight: *Henry Fielding's "Tom Jones" and the Romance Tradition*, 189n3
Milton, John: *Paradise Lost*, 63
mimesis, 39
modal logic, 9–11, 187n5; language of, 158–59. *See also* possible-world semantics
modernism: experiments of, 178; and postmodernism, 178; post-realist, 40; sensibilities of, 113, 121
Monod, Sylvère, 190n17
moral fable, 8, 48
morality: false, 134; laissez-faire, 133; private code of, 134; puritanical, 133; rigid New England, 123
More, Thomas: *Utopia*, 158
Moretti, Franco, 4
Morning Post (newspaper), 140
Morris, William, 40
Mulock, Dinah, 193n13
myth, 85

Nabokov, Vladimir: *Pale Fire*, 180
narrative: active possibilities in realist novels of, 13–23; closure of, 66–74; comprehensive theory of the meaning of, 85; constraint of possibilities of, 50; destiny of, 27; detective, 105; first-person, 27–28; Gothic, 106; limits of conventional, 147–48; narrative rightness and moral rightness, 39; phantom, 96; plotless wanderer in the discourse of, 156; proxy, 30–31, 77–136, 164, 174, 192n9; realist, 31–32, 66, 138, 148, 174, 182; traditional, 181–82; unwritten, 50. *See also* meaning; narrative dissonance; narrative probability; plot; reading
narrative dissonance, 82. *See also* narrative
narrative probability, 14–15. *See also* narrative
Nemesvari, Richard: "Robert Audley's Secret," 88
New England, 130; moralism of, 111
Newsom, Robert, 15
novel: alternative possibilities in the Dickens, 50, 66–67, 71; American, 129; classical utopian, 159; cultural capital of the, 19; discursive logic of a particular, 29; domestic, 144, 176; eighteenth-century, 38–43; English, 129, 176; European, 129; exhaustion of the narrativity of the traditional, 155; extension of the possibilities of the, 174; genres of the, 19; home epic, 26; industrial, 157, 161, 195n7; of manners, 15; melancholy, 29; modernist, 113–14, 190n20; moral stance of the, 67–68; multi-plot, 25–26; narrative world of a, 86; Newgate, 96; nineteenth-century, 5, 15, 20, 157, 184, 191n21; non-reformist, 139; picaresque, 36, 42, 54–55, 58, 96; protorealist, 36; of purpose, 139–40; queer readings of

the, 88; reformist, 31, 139, 144, 148; and the romance, 37–43; sensation, 31; sentimental, 41–42; sexual mores of the nineteenth-century British, 82; social alternatives as fundamental to the, 140; socially conscious, 138; standard account of the origins of the English, 189n2; twentieth-century, 193n2; unexpected, 50–54; Victorian, 113, 144; world of the, 71. *See also* bildungsroman; didactic novel; fantasy; fiction; Gothic fiction; picaresque romance; plot; postmodern novel; realist novel; romance; science fiction; sensation novel

Obama, Barack, 139, 177
Ohi, Kevin: *Henry James and the Queerness of Style*, 114
Old Curiosity Shop, The (Dickens): ambivalent realism of, 46–49, 54–61; proxy narrative of, 135; radical changes in the development of, 51; suspension of the minds of readers between two narrative alternatives in, 47. *See also* Dickens, Charles
Oliphant, Margaret, 140
Olsen, James M.: *What Might Have Been*, 9
ontological hierarchy, 12
Orwell, George, 193n14

Paris, 1, 110, 122
parody, 178
pastoralism, 96
Pavel, Thomas, 10
picaresque romance, 6, 19, 54–55, 58, 60. *See also* novel; romance
Plato, 33
plot: actual, 22, 31, 45, 71, 79, 106–9, 172; of allegorical determinism, 143; bigamy, 188n11; coincidence, 12; conventional, 20, 145, 147–48, 156, 177; counterfactual, 11–13, 65; detective, 86, 89, 91; determinism of romantic, 145; dominant, 65, 68, 180; eighteenth-century, 44; expansion of possibilities of the, 1–2, 7–8, 20; Gothic, 27, 31, 45, 80, 97, 105–8; grimly realist, 24; hypothetically realist, 32; inheritance, 106, 108; labyrinthine, 179; logic of the realist, 142; marriage, 6, 16–19, 22, 25–31, 45, 62, 72, 84–91, 97, 101, 107–9, 112, 129–35, 152–56, 188nn13–15; melodramatic, 147, 150–53; murder, 160, 173; nineteenth-century, 44; phantom, 95, 102, 107, 128; realist, 32–33, 37, 43–46, 49, 68, 80, 88, 105, 143–44, 147, 165, 177–79, 185; romance, 20, 37, 45–46, 148, 160–61, 164–65, 177; sentimental love, 7; silly revenge, 153; story and, 84–89; traditional, 146, 148, 178, 180–81; unwritten, 3–33, 37, 45, 49, 65–71, 78–80, 89, 94–99, 106–12, 121, 125–27, 136–37, 140–46, 155–56, 172–74, 177, 180, 186; utopian, 165; written, 7. *See also* melodrama; narrative; novel; realist novel; shadow-plot
Poitier, Sidney, 138
Poole, Robert: "A Poor Man I Know," 195n11
pornography, 87
Portales, Marco: *Strether and Women*, 194n6
positivism, 144
possible-world semantics, 10. *See also* modal logic
postmodernism: figure of, 183; modernism and, 178; radical instability of many postmodern texts, 190n19; unfeeling excesses of, 185. *See also* postmodern novel
postmodern novel, 66, 69, 175; realist underplots in the, 178–79. *See also* novel; postmodernism
poverty. *See* urban poverty

Prince, Gerald, 81, 189n8, 191n2
Propp, Vladimir, 85–86
prostitution, 101
Proust, Marcel, 156
Psalms, 118, 157, 180
psycholinguistics, 81
psychology: erotically charged, 101–3; of madness, 91–92, 104

racism, 177, 181, 192n7
Radcliffe, Ann, 27, 100
rap music, 185
Ravel, Maurice: *Boléro*, 181, 185
reading: collaboration in the construction of alternative narrative possibilities in, 137; for the plot, 193n2; postmodern, 180; proxy, 84, 91, 114–15, 121; of Victorian realism, 165. *See also* narrative
realism: accounts of, 44; conventional definitions of mimetic, 40; domestic, 100; eighteenth-century, 5, 38–41, 44; embrace of certain broad principles of, 139; emerging forms of, 32; English domestic, 188n15; expanding the scope of the narratable beyond the bounds of conventional, 156–57; Gothic fiction and, 100; gritty urban, 16; happy endings in, 62; hybrid genres of, 20, 54; hybridity of most works of Victorian, 79; hypothetical, 31, 137–74; methodologies of conventional, 106; mimetic, 13, 39, 141, 189n4; models of, 36; nineteenth-century, 40–44, 137; novelistic, 65; Richardsonian, 38, 43; rigid causality of realist texts, 190n19; and romance, 178; sensational, 80; solidifying the boundaries of, 8; suspicion of Hardy of the conventional order of, 144; tropes of romance in the language of, 93; urban, 195n12; utopian, 157–65; Victorian, 5, 12–13, 17, 21–22, 35–76, 112, 165. *See also* realist novel; social realism

realist novel, 3–4, 7, 35, 40, 67, 174; character system identified by Woloch in the, 147; conventions of the, 30; counterfactuals in the nineteenth-century, 12, 24; hybridity of a, 96; narrative probability in the, 15, 158; and novel of reform, 139; possibilities of the, 33, 117, 138; romantic plot possibilities of the Victorian, 44–45; transcendence of purely empirical understandings of the world in the, 19; of a transformed future, 140. *See also* novel; plot; realism; Victorian novel
Recchio, Thomas, 172
relativism, 125
religious sensibility, 138
representation: burden of, 67; constraint of, 115; realist emphasis on faithful, 139; relationships as, 130, 132; representational aesthetic, 134; of a scene, 125; self-effacing union of, 134
Rice, Condoleezza, 183, 185
Richardson, Samuel, 5, 13, 22, 38, 41–42; *Clarissa*, 38; *Pamela*, 42
Rivkin, Julie, 125, 130, 194n7
Roese, Neal J.: *What Might Have Been*, 9
romance: aestheticized vagaries of, 35; conventionalized world of the, 44; demotion of, 43–46; eighteenth-century, 40; Gothic, 89; historical, 70; imperial, 40; late nineteenth-century, 40, 189n6; the novel and the, 37–43; realism and, 178; sentimental, 108; suspension of disbelief required in, 158; three main types of, 39; tropes of, 30; Victorian, 40, 101; world of, 33. *See also* novel; picaresque romance
romanticism, 22–23; cloying improbabilities of, 185
Rosenberg, Edgar, 190n18
Rosenthal, Jesse: *Good Form*, 17–18, 21, 43
Ruskin, John: *Fiction, Fair and Foul*, 193n13

Russell, Bertrand, 187n6
Russian formalism, 85
Ryan, Marie-Laure, 10

Said, Edward, 40
satire, 178; high-concept, 180
Schaffer, Talia: *Romance's Rival*, 188n14
Scheherazade, 60–61
science fiction, 37. *See also* novel
Scott, Sir Walter, 36, 189n1; *Heart of Midlothian*, 160, 195n8
Second World War, 1
Sedgwick, Eve, 95; *Epistemology of the Closet*, 114
Selby, Thomas, 140–41
sensation novel, 77–109, 114; affective and instinctual logic of the, 106; conspicuous investment in the material and psychological conditions of modernity of the, 95; implausibility of a Victorian, 87; melodrama of the, 108; rational explanations for apparently supernatural events in the, 100; relationship to realism of the, 80; "sensation" awakened by the, 193n16. *See also* Gothic fiction; novel
serial dependence, 191n3
sexuality: anxiety of gender and, 88, 91; bigamous, 193n15; of dreams, 90; emasculated, 91; errant, 92; gender politics and, 192n8; premarital, 83. *See also* erotic, the; femininity
shadow-plot, 30–32, 61, 78, 96; dominant plot and, 65, 68; romantic, 45–46, 48, 56, 58, 61. *See also* plot
Shakespeare, William, 138; Bohemia of, 174; comedies of, 153
Shaw, Harry, 35, 189n1
Shelley, Mary: *Frankenstein*, 36, 189n1
Sheridan, Richard, 38
Shklovsky, Viktor, 85
short story, 53–54. *See also* fiction

Showalter, Elaine: *Literature of Their Own*, 192n8
Silverman, Sarah, 176
Slovic, Paul, 14
Smollett, Tobias, 47; *The Expedition of Humphry Clinker*, 60; *Roderick Random*, 16–17, 54, 60
social change: commitment of Victorian novelists to, 45, 139; description of the desperate conditions of the working poor for the sake of, 157; Gaskell's belief in, 173. *See also* social reform
socialism, 159
social realism, 32, 157, 159–61; world of conventional, 161. *See also* realism; social change
social reform, 159, 161–65; political specifics of, 161–63; urban, 96, 162. *See also* social change; urban poverty
Sophocles, 162
Spacks, Patricia Meyer, 187n2; *Novel Beginnings*, 38–39, 41
Spencer, Herbert, 144, 168, 174
Spenser, Edmund: *The Faerie Queene*, 92, 96, 104
spiritual autobiography, 6
Steele, Claude: *Whistling Vivaldi*, 181–82
Stein, Gertrude, 177
Stendhal (Henri Beyle): *The Red and the Black*, 55–56
Stevenson, Robert Louis, 40; *Jekyll and Hyde*, 40
Stoker, Bram, 43; *Dracula*, 1, 43
supernatural, the, 20; intimations of, 6

Tennant, David, 192n5
Tess of the D'Urbervilles (Hardy): immorality of, 140; parables of suffering in, 142; pessimism of, 140–41. *See also* Hardy, Thomas
Thackeray, William Makepeace, 42–43, 92–93; *Vanity Fair*, 6, 103

Thomas, Clarence, 175, 183
time: chronological, 81; narrative, 81, 85
Todorov, Tzvetan, 85
Tolstoy, Leo, 185
Tomashevsky, Boris, 85
Tondre, Michael, 18–19, 188n10
tragedy, 13; childhood, 25, 59, 61; everyday, 172; Greek, 142; quality of authenticity that transforms melodrama of Hardy into, 155
Trollope, Anthony: Barsetshire novels of, 36; inheritance plots of, 106
Tubman, Harriet, 180
Tversky, Amos, 14
Twain, Mark: *The Adventures of Huckleberry Finn*, 129–30

urban poverty, 53, 55, 160–64, 167. *See also* social reform
urban reform. *See* social reform
utopia, 157–65; feminist, 159; literary, 158–59; political, 158–59; visions of, 164, 172

Veeder, William: "Strether and the Transcendence of Language," 123
Victorian era: aesthetic theory and criticism of the, 18; censorship of the, 94–95; changing nature of the possible and the realistic a subject of deep interest to authors in the, 139; cultural and aesthetic values of the, 188n11; Darwinism in the, 18; illegitimacy in the, 97; literary realism of the, 35; "probabilistic revolution" in the social and biological sciences of the, 18–19; Queen Victoria of the, 111. *See also* Victorian novel
Victorian novel: concealment of sexual organs in the, 92; conclusions of the, 21; heroine of the, 101; hybridity of the, 17; immersive, 175; labyrinthine plots of the, 179; as "loose baggy monsters," 111; narrative construction of the, 3; plots of the, 6–8, 43–46, 157, 177; realism of the, 43–44, 177; series form of the, 16; tension between romantic and realist modes in the, 45; tropes of romance and the, 44; unwritten plots of the, 7–8, 13, 19, 33, 108–9. *See also* realist novel; Victorian era
Villette (Brontë): evidence for the author's choice of one plot over another in, 29; marriage not satisfactory outcome in, 79; plot possibilities of, 26–28; proxy narrative of, 135; readings of, 188n15. *See also* Brontë, Charlotte
Vivaldi, Antonio, 182–83

Wallace, David Foster: *Infinite Jest*, 32, 178–80, 182
Walpole, Horace: *The Castle of Otranto*, 100
Warhol, Robyn, 11, 165; "What Might Have Been Is Not What Is," 190n12
Watt, Ian, 4–5, 35, 39, 189n3
white minstrel tradition, 183
Williams, Raymond, 160–61
Wilson, Edmund, 191n22; "The Ambiguity of Henry James," 194n3
Wings of the Dove, The (James): prevailing critical reading of, 115; romantic possibilities in, 119; social language of, 133; spiritualized possibilities in, 117. *See also* James, Henry
Woloch, Alex: *The One vs. the Many*, 48, 146–47, 195n5
women: chlorosis as a popular diagnosis for "hysterical," 194n4; eighteenth-century female writers, 191n21; insanity of, 192n9; nineteenth-century female writers, 191n21; romantic fulfillment of, 21; as secular saints, 21;

sexual power of, 127, 149–50; suffrage of, 159; twentieth-century female writers, 191n21. *See also* femininity; feminism

Woodlanders, The (Hardy): absurdity of the plot of, 153; brutal commerce of, 154; erotic arithmetic of, 149; potential viability of a realist and social vision in, 148; radical egalitarian vision in, 148; unwritten plots of, 156. *See also* Hardy, Thomas

Woolf, Virginia, 156, 177; *To the Lighthouse*, 113

Wycliffe, John, 168

Wyke, Terry, 166, 195n11

Wyler, William: *The Heiress*, 112

YouTube, 83

Recent books in the
VICTORIAN LITERATURE AND CULTURE SERIES

Victorian Metafiction
Tabitha Sparks

Strangers in the Archive: Literary Evidence and London's East End
Heidi Kaufman

Evangelical Gothic: The English Novel and the Religious War on Virtue from Wesley to "Dracula"
Christopher Herbert

Reading with the Senses in Victorian Literature and Science
David Sweeney Coombs

Parting Words: Victorian Poetry and Public Address
Justin A. Sider

The Physics of Possibility: Victorian Fiction, Science, and Gender
Michael Tondre

Willful Submission: Sado-Erotics and Heavenly Marriage in Victorian Poetry
Amanda Paxton

Pirating Fictions: Ownership and Creativity in Nineteenth-Century Popular Culture
Monica F. Cohen

Mathilde Blind: Late-Victorian Culture and the Woman of Letters
James Diedrick

Poetry and the Thought of Song in Nineteenth-Century Britain
Elizabeth K. Helsinger

The Antagonist Principle: John Henry Newman and the Paradox of Personality
Lawrence Poston

Personal Business: Character and Commerce in Victorian Literature and Culture
Aeron Hunt

Second Person Singular: Late Victorian Women Poets and the Bonds of Verse
Emily Harrington

The Ghost behind the Masks: The Victorian Poets and Shakespeare
W. David Shaw

Victorian Poets and the Changing Bible
Charles LaPorte

Liberal Epic: The Victorian Practice of History from Gibbon to Churchill
Edward Adams

Supposing "Bleak House"
John O. Jordan

Feeling for the Poor: Bourgeois Compassion, Social Action, and the Victorian Novel
Carolyn Betensky

The Science of Religion in Britain, 1860–1915
Marjorie Wheeler-Barclay

Reading for the Law: British Literary History and Gender Advocacy
Christine L. Krueger

The Dynamics of Genre: Journalism and the Practice of Literature in Mid-Victorian Britain
Dallas Liddle

The Fowl and the Pussycat: Love Letters of Michael Field, 1876–1909
Edited by Sharon Bickle

Victorian Prism: Refractions of the Crystal Palace
Edited by James Buzard, Joseph W. Childers, and Eileen Gillooly

Nostalgia in Transition, 1780–1917
Linda M. Austin

The English Cult of Literature: Devoted Readers, 1774–1880
William R. McKelvy

Artist of Wonderland: The Life, Political Cartoons, and Illustrations of Tenniel
Frankie Morris

www.ingramcontent.com/pod-product-compliance
Lightning Source LLC
Chambersburg PA
CBHW021705230426
43668CB00008B/729